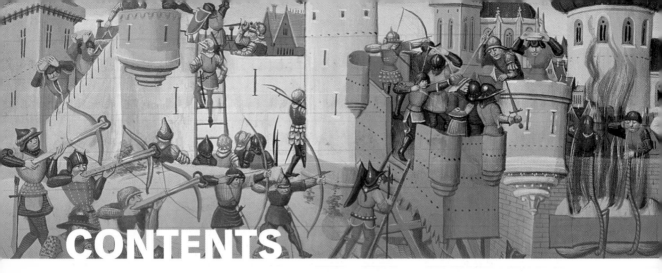

CONTENTS

INTRODUCTION

War has been a perpetual human activity since the beginning of history and it is sobering to contemplate that at no point has the world ever been wholly at peace. All wars change history and this selection of 25 conflicts ranging from the fifth century BC to the present day reflects this fact.

The earliest case considered, the Great Peloponnesian War, is important because it marked the demise of Athens, the most influential of the city states in ancient Greece. Alexander the Great's conquests brought a short-lived empire, but they are significant for being the first time Europeans embraced Asia. The final war of the ancient world is the civil war that transformed Rome from a republic into an empire.

Moving into Europe's Dark Ages, a major phenomenon of the time was the dramatic rise in the Middle East of a new religion, Islam. Within a short time it had swept across North Africa, engulfed Spain and crossed the Pyrenees into France. Charles Martel's stand against the Moors marks the high waterline of Islam in Europe, although Christianity was to clash with it again during the Middle Ages. The Crusades were a major influence on European history from the end of the 11th until the 14th century. I have focused on the Seventh Crusade in particular, since it was following this that the Crusaders realized their chances of regaining Jerusalem were slim.

Turning to China, the 14th century witnessed its liberation from Mongol influence, the end of the Mongol empire, and the beginning of the Ming dynasty, which united the country as never before. The fall of Constantinople marked the end of the Byzantine empire and the peak of the Ottoman empire. The 16th century ushered in an age of European exploration and overseas imperial expansion, particularly by Spain and Portugal. Most notable was the conquest of Mexico by Hernan Cortes. The century also saw the establishment of the Mughal empire, which would have a lasting influence on the Indian subcontinent, and clan warfare in Japan that eventually led to a united country, but one that was to isolate itself for the next 250 years.

The most significant conflict of the 17th century was the Thirty Years War, which proved to be one of the grimmest experiences that Europe had known, drawing in most of the continental powers of the day. The result was the decline of the Holy Roman Empire, with Germany, though still a collection of states, beginning to assume a distinct identity. Just over a century later the Seven Years War took place in Europe, confirming Prussia and Britain as military and colonial powers respectively. Yet, less than 15 years later, Britain's American colonies were in revolt and their success in gaining their independence established the infant United States of America. The end of this century saw Europe in turmoil once again because of another revolution, in France. Out of the subsequent chaos rose Napoleon Buonaparte, who came to dominate Europe as no one had before. While he was ultimately defeated, he left a deep imprint on the continent. The Napoleonic Wars left Europe exhausted, especially Spain, which had long been in decline. Two men, Simon Bolivar and José San Martin, took advantage of this to liberate and redraw the map of South America. Forty years later came the American Civil War, out of which grew the modern USA. The Franco-Prussian War, which finally unified Germany, followed.

One of the earliest conflicts of the 20th century was that between Russia and Japan over Manchuria. It signified Japan's transformation into a modern industrial state and the beginning of tsarist Russia's decline. The war of 1914–18 is most remembered for the slaughter on the Western Front, but it catalysed the Russian Revolution and ended the German, Ottoman and Austro-Hungarian empires. The ensuing peace treaties laid the seeds for the Second World War, which was even more global in nature than the First. It was also noteworthy in that civilians had never before been so much in the firing line. This was largely due to air bombing, the starkest demonstration of this being the two atomic bombs that ended the war against Japan. Yet, the Second World War left the world even more unsettled than it had been at its outbreak.

The Chinese Civil War that followed represented unfinished business for both sides of the conflict, but Mao Zedong's victory would eventually enable China to become a leading global power. The communist victory also became a facet of the Cold War that cast a shadow over the world for the 45 years following 1945. Although it was centred on a divided Germany, the Cold War was expressed in many forms throughout the world. Overarching the rivalry between capitalism and communism was the nuclear arms race, but in the end the economic impact of this rivalry hastened the collapse of the USSR. The long agony in Indo-China was another of its facets and one example of the West's attempts to prevent the spread of communism, a vain one in this case. It marked the decline of the French empire and scarred America for a generation. Also under tension in the immediate post-war years was the Middle East, with the creation of Israel immediately provoking conflict between the Arabs and Jews. It is Israel's devastating victory over its Arab neighbours in 1967 that has had the longest lasting effect in that, to Arab fury, it continues to retain territory captured from Syria and Jordan at that time.

The failure to resolve the conflict between Israel and the Palestinians is one of the factors underlying my final chapter, the ongoing War on Terror, as it is popularly known. What its ultimate effect on history will be is uncertain at the time of writing, but it is likely to be as significant as the other world-changing conflicts detailed in this book, featuring the ever-present echoes of religious and ideological confrontation, the struggle for power, and the role of human pride.

CHARLES MESSENGER

THE **GREAT PELOPONNESIAN** WAR

431–404 BC

'**I AM MORE AFRAID** OF OUR MISTAKES THAN OUR ENEMIES' DESIGNS.'

Pericles, in a speech to the Athenians, 432 BC

Ancient Greece was characterized by its city states. These had been created as independent communities built around towns that jealously guarded the rural areas surrounding them: because of the mountainous nature of much of the terrain, agricultural land was a precious commodity.

In time some of these states became more dominant than others, and by the sixth century BC the foremost were Athens, Corinth, Sparta and Thebes. Sparta and Thebes were dominated by landed aristocracies, the former becoming a militaristic state, while Athens developed into a democracy, whereby all male citizens had a voice in the running of the state through their membership of an assembly. Athens and Corinth created fleets and became maritime powers. Rivalry among the states was inevitable, with that between Athens and Sparta being at the forefront. The other states formed alliances with one or the other, depending on the perceived advantages that they would gain.

Alliances of the city states

At the beginning of the fifth century BC the city states of mainland Greece came together. The reason for this was the growth of the Persian empire, which had swallowed up Greek settlements on the Ionian coast, which today is Turkey's Aegean coast. The Greek city states supported their compatriots when they rose in revolt against the Persians in 499 BC. Ten years later, after the great Persian king Darius I crushed the revolt, he resolved to punish the mainland Greeks and sent a force by sea to invade. This was defeated at the Battle of Marathon in 490 BC. Ten years after this, Darius's successor, Xerxes, invaded again. The Spartans under Leonidas held the Persians for a time at the pass at Thermopylae, but could not prevent them from advancing on Athens. The Athenians evacuated their city. The Persians set it on fire, but the Athenians gained their revenge by defeating the Persian fleet at Salamis. A year later, in 479 BC, the Greeks won a major victory on land at Plataea. They then proceeded to drive the Persians out of the Aegean Sea.

Victory over the Persians resulted in Athens becoming dominant and her formation of an alliance called the Delian League. This consisted of all the island states and those in Asia Minor, together with many on the Greek mainland. Many were virtually colonies paying an annual tribute to Athens. The one notable exception was Sparta, which entered into a period of isolation. This period became known as the Golden Age of Athens. During this time most of Athens' famous buildings, like the Parthenon, were built. The city became a centre of culture. Literature, philosophy and drama flourished. Indeed, some of the most famous Greek personalities emerged at this time – the philosophers Plato and Socrates, the playwright Aristophanes and the historian Thucydides, to name

PREVIOUS PAGE *These two Greek hoplites, Chairedemos and Lykeas, were killed during the Great Peloponnesian War. The Greek round shield was worn on the left arm, leaving the extreme right flank of a phalanx open to attack.*

but a few. War with the Persians continued and the other states accepted Athenian leadership. It became noticeable, however, that Athens was becoming increasingly imperialist in her outlook, especially after 466 BC, when the Persian threat was finally removed. Some states tried to leave the Delian League, but Athens forced them to remain in it. Sparta, which had continued to remain on the sidelines, grew especially resentful at the authoritarianism of Athens, which did nothing to reduce the rising tension.

First Peloponnesian War

Sparta's opportunity came when Athens went to war with Corinth, her long-time mercantile rival, in 460 BC. Even though the Athenians destroyed the Corinthian fleet and captured the city of Corinth after besieging it, Sparta decided to enter what became known as the First Peloponnesian War and, joining with Thebes and other states in the Peloponnesian League, defeated an Athenian army at Tanagra in 457 BC. Thereafter Sparta largely left the war to her allies and the Athenians enjoyed a number of successes, both on land and at sea. But the strain of the conflict on Athenian resources became ever more marked. Finally, in 446 BC the Spartans became active once more and, with their allies, drove the Athenians from their conquests on the mainland. Facing the threat of revolts within its overseas empire, Athens was forced to make peace. Athens and Sparta recognized their respective leaderships of the Delian and Peloponnesian leagues and agreed that the two alliances would not interfere with each other's internal affairs.

The Athenian leader Pericles realized that Athens did not have the wherewithal both to dominate the mainland with a large army and to ensure the security of her widespread mercantile trade with a large navy. He decided that Athens should concentrate on the latter and adopt a defensive posture at home. To reinforce this he organized the construction of what became the Long Walls. These ran for some six miles on either side of the route that connected Athens to her port of Piraeus, through which the lifeblood of Athenian trade flowed.

The Thirty Years Peace, as it was called, was soon under threat. Friction continued among individual members of the

timeline

499–466 BC
Graeco-Persian Wars.

460–446 BC
First Peloponnesian War.

432 BC
Athens prohibits
Megaran trade.

431 BC
Peloponnesian invasion
of Attica starts Great
Peloponnesian War.

430 BC
Outbreak of plague in
Athens kills a quarter
of the population.

429–427 BC
Peloponnesians besiege
Plataea.

425 BC
Athenians defeat Sparta
at the Battle of Pylos.

421 BC
Truce agreed.

418 BC
Alcibiades leads
invasion of Arcadia.

415 BC
Expedition to Sicily;
defection of Alcibiades
to Sparta.

414 BC
Coup in Athens.

407 BC
Alcibiades returns
to Athens.

405 BC
Spartan blockade
of Piraeus begins.

404 BC
Athens surrenders.

two leagues and in 435 BC Corinth, a member of the Peloponnesian League, went to war with Corcyra (present day Corfu), of the Delian League. The latter asked for Athenian help and she deployed her fleet. It was under strict instructions not actively to engage that of Corinth, which was poised to capture Corcyra. Its mere presence was, however, enough to dissuade the Corinthians and Corcyra survived intact. The focus now switched to Potidaea, a vassal state of Athens that was situated at the base of today's Kassandra isthmus in northeastern Greece. The Athenians were concerned that Corinth was exercising undue influence over the city – it had originally been a Corinthian colony – and feared a revolt. They demanded that it tear down part of its walls and send hostages to Athens, as well as stopping the annual visit of Corinthian magistrates. Potidaea sent envoys to Athens to try to defuse the situation, but they also sent others to Corinth and Sparta to seek their support. Nothing came of the negotiations in Athens and an Athenian fleet, with troops on board, set sail and put Potidaea under siege. Going against the terms of the Thirty Years Peace treaty, Corinth infiltrated men to help the Potidaeans. The siege itself lasted for two years. The Athenians surrounding Potidaea had their numbers weakened by plague and were unable to prevail. Eventually an agreement was made on the ground, whereby the Potidaeans were allowed safe passage from the city and were resettled. Once again, Sparta's ally Corinth had been thwarted.

Great Peloponnesian War

Athens now turned on another Spartan ally. This was Megara, which still exists today and lies just over 25 miles west of Athens. Again it was originally a Corinthian colony and, like Athens, relied on mercantile trade. In 432 BC the Athenians issued a decree prohibiting Megara from trading with the Athenian empire. Coming so soon after the Corcyra and Potidaea crises, it provoked the Spartans, who again had been unwilling to become involved, to call a conference of the Peloponnesian League. Athens sent representatives to it and much time was taken up by argument with Corinth. But the Corinthians also turned on Sparta, condemning her inactivity and warning that she was in danger of finding herself without allies. The Spartan assembly took note of this and voted in favour of a declaration that Athens had broken the Thirty Years Peace. Hostilities therefore resumed in 431 BC. This marked the beginning of what became known as the Great Peloponnesian War.

The two sides adopted very different strategies. The Athenian empire was largely built around the islands of the Aegean and its security was dependent on naval power. Hence, Pericles resolved to remain on the defensive on land. In contrast to this, the Peloponnesian League members, with the notable exception of Corinth, were essentially land-based and reliant on their armies. That of Sparta was the most formidable, largely thanks to the toughness of its warriors, whose military training began as young boys.

The Spartan strategy was therefore to invade Attica in the hope of bringing Athens to her knees. But her army could not remain away from home for long. Sparta was very dependent on her *helots*, an underclass of serfs who tended the fields while the warriors trained, but these were always threatening revolt and the army was needed to keep them under control.

The Spartan invasion of Attica enabled them quickly to occupy the farmlands around Athens, whose inhabitants took refuge within the Long Walls. Within Athens herself, however, plague broke out in 430 BC. A quarter of the population perished, including Pericles himself. This loss of manpower would in time make itself felt. As it was, there was some consolation in that the Spartans, fearful of succumbing to the plague, hastily withdrew from Attica. Meanwhile, at sea the Athenian fleet had taken to the offensive, ravaging the Peloponnesian coast and then defeating two Peloponnesian fleets and establishing a blockade of the Gulf of Corinth. Athens' enemies now turned their attention to one of her most loyal allies, Plataea. A combined Spartan–Theban force laid siege to the city in 429 BC. It took two years to reduce it, with the defenders being massacred and Plataea razed to the ground. The Athenians, on the other hand, were faced with revolts by Corcyra and the island of Lesbos. Both were put down and it is significant that a Spartan attempt to help the rebels on Lesbos came to naught when

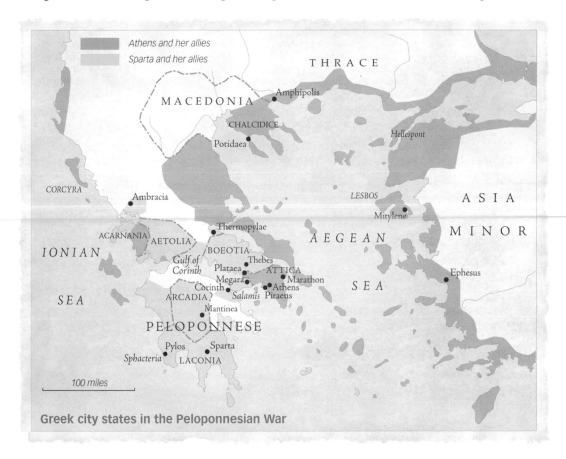

Greek city states in the Peloponnesian War

an Athenian fleet appeared and caused the troops which had been sent to be hastily withdrawn. Sparta and her allies also resumed their annual invasions of Attica, but these gained little tangible result.

In 426 BC the Athenians changed their strategy. Pericles' successor, Cleon, was very much more hawkish in his approach, as was his leading general, Demosthenes. They were also perhaps encouraged by the fact that, because of two earthquakes, the annual assault on Attica had not taken place. Hence, rather than remain on the defensive on the mainland, they decided to strike at Sparta's allies Boeotia and Thebes, with a view to knocking them out of the war. They launched an invasion from two directions. Demosthenes set out with a fleet and landed in Aetolia, aiming to attack Boeotia from the rear. The local tribesmen proved to be too strong in numbers and he was forced to withdraw. The second army, under Nicias, invaded Boeotia from the east, but withdrew after one inconclusive victory. The Spartans now sent a force to Aetolia. Demosthenes, who had remained behind after his army had withdrawn, since he feared censure by his fellow countrymen, had organized another army from Acarnania, which bordered Aetolia to the west. He based himself on Naupactus, another ally of Athens, and succeeded in defeating the Spartans and their Ambracian allies from north of Acarnania. In a secret deal Demosthenes allowed the Spartans to escape, but massacred the Ambracians with them and defeated a further Ambracian army the following day. The year thus ended on a high note for Athens.

The phalanx

THIS WAS THE BASIC UNIT of the armies of ancient Greece. It consisted of a block of well-trained heavy infantrymen or *hoplites* armed with spears, swords and shields. It was usually 8–16 ranks deep and was capable of limited manoeuvres. Controlled from the rear, the front ranks advanced with their spears levelled, while those in the rear tended to rest theirs on the shoulders of the men in front so as to provide some protection against arrows. Once the phalanx closed with the enemy it became a question of literally pushing forward until the opposing phalanx broke. Only then would the hoplites draw their swords. The phalanx was very vulnerable on broken ground, however, since formation keeping was difficult and gaps would inevitably appear in it.

The following year began with the usual pattern of a Spartan invasion of Attica and the Athenian fleet cruising around the Peloponnese. Then a Peloponnesian fleet invaded Corcyra before the Athenian ships could arrive there. Instead, and on the initiative of Demosthenes, who was with the fleet, they landed at Pylos on the east coast of the Peloponnese. His aim was to build a fort and use it as a base from which to carry out raiding operations designed to stir up the helots. When the Spartan king Agis heard of this he hastily withdrew from Attica and Corcyra and resolved to destroy the fort. By this time the Athenian fleet had withdrawn, leaving Demosthenes on his own. To prevent the Athenian fleet from coming to the rescue, the Spartans used their own ships to block the harbour at Pylos and landed troops on the nearby island of Sphacteria. While Demosthenes beat off attacks on the fort, the Athenian fleet returned and drove the Spartan ships ashore, isolating the force on Sphacteria. Sparta called for a truce and agreed to hand over all her ships in Laconia in return for her island garrison, but Cleon wanted more. He demanded the return of territories that Athens had handed back at the end of the First Peloponnesian War. The Spartans baulked at this and the war continued.

Peace and renewed conflict

The Athenians duly overran Sphacteria and kept the surviving Spartans as hostages. In 424 BC they tried once again to overrun Boeotia but were defeated by the Theban general Pagondas, his Athenian opposite number being killed. The leading Spartan general Brasidas now set out on a long march to Thrace to interdict the Athenian supply route to the Black Sea. Defeating two Athenian armies en route, Brasidas succeeded in capturing the city of Amphipolis. This was important to Athens, since its nearby silver mines were financing the war. Thucydides, the Athenian historian and soldier, arrived with his fleet too late to prevent the city's fall and was sent into exile for 20 years as a punishment. Brasidas's success forced Athens to seek a truce, which was agreed by Sparta but ignored by her general, who continued to overrun Athenian territory in Chalcidice and Thrace. Consequently, in 422 BC Cleon and Nicias arrived in the region, forcing Brasidas back to Amphipolis. There Brasidas launched a surprise attack and decisively defeated the Athenians, although he himself and Cleon were killed. Another truce was arranged and led to the optimistically named Fifty Years Peace of 421 BC. Both sides agreed to hand back the territory they had captured and Athens returned the Sphacteria hostages to Sparta.

Sparta's allies were dissatisfied with the peace terms, however. Led by Argos, which had largely stayed out of the war thus far, a breakaway coalition was formed with the other Peloponnesian states of Mantinea and Elis. Spartan efforts to dissolve the alliance failed. Emboldened by this, the Argives and their allies began to carry out raids into Sparta. The Athenians, angered that Sparta had not returned Amphipolis to them, joined the alliance and in 418 BC a rising young Athenian general called Alcibiades persuaded the allies to attack into Arcadia with a view to cutting Sparta off from her allies. King Agis of Sparta met the coalition's forces at Mantinea and decisively defeated them in what was the largest battle of the whole war, with some 10,000 men engaged on each side. This victory restored Sparta's position at the head of the Peloponnesian League and comparative peace returned.

In 415 BC events took a different turn. News came to Athens that one of her allies in far-off Sicily was under threat from Syracuse, whose people had blood ties with Sparta. Alcibiades persuaded his fellow Athenians that this presented the ideal opportunity to conquer the whole of the island, from which Athens imported much of her grain, and hence significantly enlarge the Athenian empire. Accordingly, an expedition set sail under Alcibiades, Nicias and Lamachus. Before it reached Sicily, Alcibiades was recalled to Athens to face charges of religious sacrilege, probably trumped up by his political enemies. Instead he fled to Sparta. Nicias and Lamachus laid siege to Syracuse, building walls to surround it on its landward side. Alcibiades advised the Spartans to send one of their best generals to help the Syracusans and he was able to prevent the Athenians from completing their walls. Then, in 413 BC, the Athenian fleet suffered a serious defeat at the hands of a Corinthian and Syracusan fleet in the narrow waters off Syracuse. Athens sent out reinforcements under Demosthenes. On arrival he attempted a night attack against Syracuse, but this failed. Demosthenes therefore recommended withdrawal, to which Nicias reluctantly agreed, but the night before it was due to take place Nicias was spooked by an eclipse of the moon. He declared that no withdrawal could take place for one month. This proved fatal. The Syracusan fleet destroyed that of the Athenians and forced Demosthenes and Nicias to withdraw inland. Harried mercilessly by the Syracusan cavalry, the Athenians were eventually forced to surrender, with both their commanders having been killed.

Decline of Athens

The Sicilian expedition was disastrous for Athens, but at home the situation was equally grim. Sparta declared war once more in 414 BC and fomented revolt among the Athenian tributary allies. Syracuse sent her fleet to help the Spartans and, in return for Spartan recognition of their sovereignty over Greek possessions in Asia Minor, the Persians agreed to supply money and ships. It seemed that Athens was about to perish and, indeed, there was a coup in the city. A group known as the Four Hundred seized power and began to negotiate with Sparta. But the Athenians had maintained a reserve of money and some 100 ships, which were now put into service, and, using the island of Samos as a base, began to oppose Peloponnesian naval operations in the Aegean. The men of this fleet objected to what they perceived as the undemocratic stance of the new regime in Athens and carried on fighting. Alcibiades, even though he was officially branded a traitor, still had support among Athenians, and returned to the fold, taking charge of the Samos fleet. At the same time the oligarchs in Athens were overthrown and democracy restored. All this served to reinvigorate the Athenians, and they won a series of naval victories during the period 411–408 BC. At one point the Spartans even offered to make peace, but this was rejected by Cleophon, the new Athenian leader.

The Persians had been very slow to provide the promised money and ships, and it was not until 408 BC that they began to cooperate closely with Sparta. The result of this was a new Spartan fleet. Commanded by Lysander, it first clashed with Alcibiades in 406 BC and won a partial victory at Ephesus. This resulted in Alcibiades being removed from command. The Spartans went on to blockade the Athenian fleet in the harbour of Mitylene on the island of Lesbos. The Athenians managed to organize another fleet and this gained such a victory over the Spartans that they again offered to make peace. Once again Cleophon rejected their overtures. It was a decision that he would rue. Lysander, who under Spartan law had been forced to give up command of the Spartan fleet after one year, was reinstated in 405 BC and the focus of attention switched to the Hellespont, the channel that led from the Aegean Sea towards the Black Sea and was a crucial Athenian trade route. Lysander sailed for here and the Athenian fleet attempted, without success, to bring him to battle. Instead he waited until the Athenians had relaxed their guard, then attacked their ships by night, when most of the crews were on shore. The fleet was entirely destroyed and Athenian naval dominance was at an end. Lysander was now able to impose a tight blockade on Piraeus and, after a six-month siege, Athens was starved into submission in April 404 BC. Its walls were destroyed and all its overseas possessions were lost.

The Great Peloponnesian War marked the end of Athens as a significant power, although the influence of her art and culture would remain. Economically the war affected the whole of Greece, with poverty becoming widespread. No longer would the city states of the region be able to combine effectively to deal with a common threat, as they had done against the Persians. Indeed, Greece's political influence over the outside world was in decline, and it would soon find itself under the sway of first Macedonia, then Rome.

✦ ✦ ✦

'**A TOMB NOW SUFFICES HIM** FOR WHOM THE WHOLE WORLD WAS NOT ENOUGH.' Alexander the Great's epitaph

ALEXANDER'S CONQUESTS
336–323 BC

The remarkable achievements of Alexander the Great during his comparatively brief life have remained a source of fascination down the centuries. He left a unique imprint on the ancient world, vestiges of which still survive today. He is also generally considered to be one of history's great captains of war.

Alexander came from Macedon, a region roughly equal to the modern Greek province of Macedonia and the former Yugoslav republic of the same name, but in those days located between Epirus and Thrace. It was not until the first quarter of the fourth century BC that Macedon was united as a single state under King Amyntas III, Alexander's grandfather. Macedon was, however, under continuous threat from the Illyrians in the northwest, the Thracians from the east and the Greeks to the south. On Amyntas's death in 369 BC his elder sons struggled in vain to protect the country from virtual disintegration. In 359 BC, after the death of Perdiccas III in battle against the Illyrians, the youngest of Amyntas's three sons, Philip, ascended the throne. He had spent time as a hostage of the Thebans and learned much from them about warfare. He used this knowledge to reform his own army, especially by introducing the phalanx. His first task was to secure his throne in the face of pretenders supported by Greek city states. He succeeded in this through a mixture of force and diplomacy and then drove the Illyrians out from the north of the country. Through a succession of marriages he secured Macedon's borders, but then adopted an ever more aggressive policy. He began to seize Athenian possessions in Thrace and by the end of 352 BC had secured Thessaly in northern Greece. Thereafter he overran the Greek settlements in Chalcidice, which lay southeast of Macedon.

Philip's most significant coup came in 346 BC. Ten years before, the Phocians had sacked Delphi during one of the numerous squabbles between the Greek city states. The Delphic or Great Amphictyonic League, which was responsible for looking after the temples of Apollo at Delphi and Demeter at Anthela, and to which most of the city states belonged, declared war on Phocis. Philip actively supported the League and at the conclusion of the conflict Macedon was made a member, taking the place of the now expelled Phocis. This gave Macedon an influence over Greek affairs and particularly alarmed Athens, which regarded the Macedonians as barbarians. Stirred by the speeches of the famous orator Demosthenes, and joined by Thebes, Athens declared war on Macedon. Philip met their combined forces at Chaeronea in 338 BC and decisively defeated them, his young son Alexander distinguishing himself in command of the Macedonian cavalry. This left Philip master of Greece and he formed the Hellenic League to unite the region. This comprised all of the states except Sparta, which chose to remain outside it. Philip's ambitions were not at an end, however. He now turned his

OPPOSITE *King Darius of Persia prepares to flee the Battle of Issus. The Persians had an organized regular army, augmented in wartime by levies and Greek mercenaries, but it lacked the discipline of Alexander the Great's troops.*

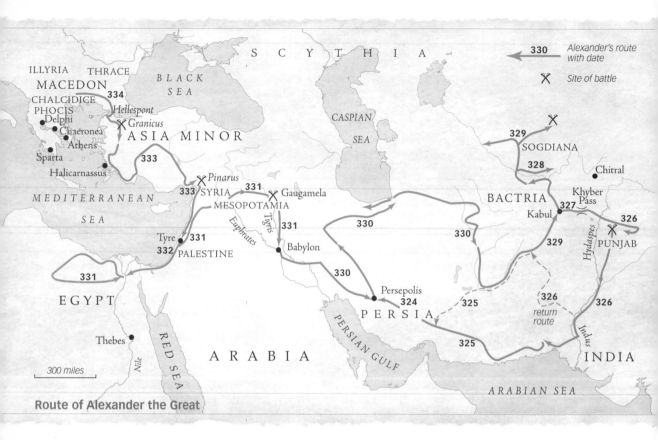

Route of Alexander the Great

eyes on Persia and in 336 BC sent two of his generals across the Hellespont with 10,000 men to prepare the way. Meanwhile, Philip oversaw the marriage of his daughter, but in the midst of the celebrations he was fatally stabbed by a Macedonian nobleman, probably on the instructions of Philip's former wife and mother to Alexander, who now succeeded him.

Alexander quells the Greeks

Alexander III ascended the throne of Macedon at the age of 20. He had already proved himself as a soldier and inherited a powerful army. His father's death brought about immediate crises, however. The Illyrians, Thracians and Greeks attempted to overthrow the shackles of Macedonian rule. Alexander reacted quickly, taking his army into Greece and restoring his rule there prior to marching north again to deal with the Thracians and Illyrians in turn. The following year, 335 BC, rumours spread in Greece that Alexander was dead. Thebes, the most powerful city state of the time, decided to revolt once more and tried to persuade the other states to join in. A furious Alexander immediately marched south, arriving at the walls of Thebes after just two weeks on the road. He gave the Greeks the opportunity to change their minds. The Thebans continued to oppose him, while the other states sat on the fence, preferring to await the outcome before making up their minds. The Macedonians successfully stormed Thebes, massacring many of its inhabitants and selling others into slavery. As a further lesson to Greece as a whole, the city, apart from its temples, was destroyed. Any thoughts of revolt among the other city states were quickly dispelled by this.

With Macedon's neighbours once more subdued, Alexander now turned his attention to the project that his father had been preparing, the invasion of Persia. Leaving one of his most experienced generals backed by a force of some 10,000 men to rule at home in his absence, Alexander crossed the Hellespont in spring 334 BC. His army consisted of 25,000 Macedonians, 7500 Greeks and 7000 Thracians and Illyrians. The Persians met him at a ford on the river Granicus near the site of ancient Troy. The Persian force was of the same size as Alexander's army, but half of it was made up of Greeks. They had joined their old enemy after Philip's defeat of them at Chaeronea four years before, such was their loathing of Macedon. Alexander appears not to have hesitated and assaulted across the river. The Persians soon broke, but their Greek allies stood and fought and were annihilated. Alexander then moved south 'liberating' Greek cities under Persian control. In some cases their Greek inhabitants resisted him, but never for long.

Persian conquests

While encouraged by these early successes, Alexander was very conscious of the Persian fleet's existence and, indeed, its domination of the eastern Mediterranean. There was the ever-present danger that it could cut his communications to his homeland across the Hellespont. Lacking a fleet himself, Alexander decided that the only way to destroy Persia's naval power was to capture the entire eastern Mediterranean coast in order to deny the Persian ships anchorage. This was to preoccupy his forces for the next two years. He began by conquering the coastal regions of Asia Minor, including the main naval base at Halicarnassus, albeit after a hard siege. Then, as Alexander continued to move south, a Persian army of some 100,000 men with King Darius III at its head arrived at his rear, thereby cutting his communications. Alexander retraced his footsteps and met Darius at Issus on the river Pinarus in October 333 BC. Although greatly outnumbered, Alexander attacked. He drove back the Persian covering force and then crossed the river himself to push the Persian centre back with his infantry, while his cavalry destroyed the Persian left wing. The Persian cavalry crossed the river to attack Alexander's right wing, but was repulsed. The Persian centre now began to give way and panic set in. Darius fled, leaving his family in Macedonian hands. Half his army perished in this second of Alexander's great victories.

Alexander's next objective was the main Persian naval base at Tyre. Most of the city was actually situated on an island just off the coast and in January 332 BC the Macedonians began to construct a wooden causeway to reach it. The inhabitants did their best to interrupt its construction, often using fireships. Progress was therefore slow and Alexander decided to gather captured ships from elsewhere and form his own fleet. This took on the Tyrian navy and succeeded in bottling it up in its harbour. After eight months, a breach was finally made in Tyre's walls and the port city fell. As a warning to others Alexander virtually razed Tyre to the ground and sold its people into slavery.

King Darius was now desperate and made peace overtures to Alexander, offering him all the Persian lands west of the Euphrates, a vast sum of money, and any of his daughters' hands in marriage. Alexander responded that he wanted the whole of the empire and that he could marry Darius's captive daughter any time he liked. The war thus went on, with the Macedonians occupying the remainder of Syria and Palestine. Only at Gaza was Alexander forced to adopt siege tactics. It fell after two months and, like Tyre, was sacked. At the end of 332 BC Alexander moved into Egypt and occupied it, founding the city that is today called Alexandria, the first of a number of cities that he established with his name. Yet, back in Greece there had been a revolt against Macedonian rule. It was led by Sparta, with many of the southern states joining in. Alexander's regent, Antipater, decisively defeated the rebels and then sent Alexander a sizeable reinforcement of men, which joined him in Egypt. He would not remain there for long.

Battle of Gaugamela

Word came to Alexander that Darius was assembling another army in Mesopotamia. Consequently, in April 331 BC, he left Egypt, marched to Tyre and then turned eastwards across the rivers Euphrates and Tigris. He eventually came across the Persians on the plain of Gaugamela (otherwise known as Arbela), near present-day Irbil in Iraq. Some ancient historians claim that the Persian army was one million men strong. This is clearly an exaggeration, but it was certainly very much larger – perhaps as much as ten times – than Alexander's force of 47,000. The Macedonians had first located the Persians at night, spotting their camp fires, and Alexander's generals urged him to launch an immediate surprise attack. He declined, declaring that a victory on level terms by day was more likely to dissuade Darius from continuing to resist him.

The following day, 1 October 331 BC, the two armies were deployed. That of the Persians was a polyglot organization made of up several races, and it was drawn up in two lines. Their cavalry was on the wings and chariots and elephants were deployed in front. Alexander's army had a much more formalized organization, thanks to the reforms of his father. His infantry consisted of three different types. Within the phalanx were found the *pezetaeroi* (foot companions), armed with a spear some 13 feet long, sword, shield and body armour, and the more lightly equipped *hypaspistai* (shield-bearers). They had a shorter pike and were more manoeuvrable. There were also the *peltasts*, who were true light infantry and whose task was to protect the flanks and rear of the phalanx, as well as cover its advance. The infantry were organized in units, the lowest consisting of a file of 16 men. Four of these files made up a *tetrarchy*, which equated to a modern day platoon, and four *tetrarchies* a *syntagma*. Finally, there was the *taxis*, which was a territorially recruited regiment of 1500 men. As for cavalry, Alexander possessed two types: the Companions (see Box) and his mercenary Thessalian cavalry. They were generally armed with a lance, though they had a sword as well, since the former weapon was often used like a javelin.

Alexander usually deployed his army with the cavalry on the wings and this was what he did at Gaugamela. He advanced obliquely towards the Persian left wing. Concerned that it was about to be outflanked, this wing then attacked, leaving a gap between it and the Persian centre. Seeing this, Alexander personally led the Companions and a phalanx into it, throwing the Persian centre, where Darius was positioned, into confusion. Overcome by terror the Persian king fled the field for a second time. Meanwhile the Persian right attempted to envelop the Macedonian left, but this stood firm and eventually, after Alexander had come to the rescue, these Persians also joined the panic-stricken retreat. In the hope of catching Darius, Alexander immediately set off in pursuit, but halted after some 35 miles, his men now exhausted. He then marched on Babylon, entering it without a fight. He continued southeastwards, overrunning other cities and plundering much treasure, until he arrived at the ancient Persian capital of Persepolis, which he destroyed.

Alexander was still determined to track Darius down and eventually caught up with him the following summer as he made his way into Bactria, a region which today encompasses the northernmost part of Afghanistan and the southern parts of the states to its north. But Alexander failed to take Darius alive, since he was murdered by Bessus, the satrap or ruler of Bactria, who proclaimed himself the Persian king of kings. This was totally unacceptable to the Macedonian king and, after giving Darius a royal funeral, he set out for Bactria to track Bessus down. But there was some discord within the ranks. To secure his rapidly expanding empire Alexander appointed many Persians as provincial governors, enlisted Persians into his army, and encouraged his soldiers to marry Persian women. He himself also adopted Persian dress for ceremonial occasions.

Alexander's Companions

THE COMPANIONS WERE, in essence, Alexander's household troops and were originally recruited from the Macedonian aristocracy. They were mounted, acted as both his bodyguards and a shock force designed to seal victory on the battlefield, and were led by Alexander himself. Their strength was some 1800 men organized in eight squadrons or *ilae*. Each Companion was responsible for providing his own arms and equipment. When deployed for battle they normally took up position on the right of the infantry phalanx, while the Thessalian cavalry were on the left.

Very proud of their own Macedonian culture, some of his subordinates resented their king's policy and in 330 BC rumours of a plot against him began to circulate. Alexander acted swiftly. He tortured and executed the supposed ringleader, Philotas, the commander of his cavalry, and Philotas's father, the veteran and much respected general Parmenio. Several others suffered a similar fate. He then demanded that his subjects prostrate themselves in his presence. His men baulked at this, since this was something they only did when worshipping their gods, and Alexander was forced to back down.

It took two years to secure Bactria, including capturing Bessus, in what was a largely guerrilla campaign. Alexander then moved north across the river Oxus and into the easternmost part of the former Persian empire, Sogdiana. There his army had several fierce clashes with the wild Scythians, with whom Alexander, after defeating them, formed an alliance. He then built a line of forts to protect his northern frontier. But Sogdiana, led by its king, now rose in revolt. It was only after a tough campaign that Alexander was able to crush the resistance. The king was killed by his own people and to ensure Sogdiana's future loyalty Alexander married the daughter of one of its chieftains and made him governor.

Indian campaign

With the northern part of his empire now reasonably secure Alexander turned his attention to the southeastern flank, which bordered India. As it happened, he received a request for help from the king of Taxila who was at war with the most powerful rulers in the Punjab, King Porus. Thus, in spring 327 BC, Alexander set out for India. Arriving at Kabul, in present-day Afghanistan, he split his army into two, with one part arriving in India from the Khyber Pass while he led the other through Chitral. After subduing several tribes, the Macedonians eventually faced Porus across the river Hydaspes (now the Jhelum) in March 326 BC. The river was in full flood at the time and unfordable. Alexander therefore marched his army up and down the river, making a series of feints to lull his opponent into a false sense of security. With waters subsiding, he eventually spotted a crossing place some 16 miles upstream from his camp. After preparing boats, Alexander took advantage of a storm to take part of his army to the crossing point. It began to land on the far bank at dawn and Alexander sent the cavalry element to get to the rear of Porus's camp while his infantry took up position by the river. Porus attacked with his elephants, but the Macedonian light infantry discomforted them and they stampeded through their own lines. Alexander's cavalry then attacked the Indians in the rear. The Indians resisted fiercely but eventually gave way. Porus himself was wounded and captured, but Alexander restored him to his throne as a way of gaining his loyalty.

Alexander now wanted to move on to the river Ganges, which he decided should be the eastern boundary of his empire. His men, however, had had enough. They had marched some 17,000 miles in the previous eight years and now wanted to go home.

Alexander acceded to their wishes and began the return journey. After further fighting the army reached the mouth of the Indus, where Alexander constructed a fleet. He sent this up to the Persian Gulf, while part of his army returned to Persepolis via what is now Afghanistan. Alexander took the remainder on a hard march through the Persian deserts, making contact with his fleet en route. By spring 323 BC he was back in Babylon, planning further expeditions and working hard to meld the Macedonians, Persians and other races of his newly created empire into one nation. But at the beginning of that June he fell ill with malaria and died in the royal palace in Babylon on the 13th of the month, one month short of his 33rd birthday.

Alexander left no named successor and after his death squabbling among his generals resulted in his empire being split into four main parts: Egypt under the Ptolemies, Asia under the Seleucids, Macedonia under the Antigonids and India under Chandragupta. Yet, in his 12 years' reign he had not only redrawn the map of the ancient world, but also brought West and East into contact as never before. Indeed, it can be said that his empire was the foundation of what in time, under the Roman empire, would become a world trade system.

✦ ✦ ✦

ROMAN CIVIL WAR

33–30 BC

By the beginning of the first century BC the dominant power in the Mediterranean region was Rome. Her growing empire now encompassed the whole of the north Mediterranean coast, including Greece, and a sizeable portion of Asia Minor. Half of Spain was also under her thrall and the defeat of Carthage had given her a foothold in North Africa. At home, however, schisms were beginning to appear: those virtues that had until then given the Republic its strength were becoming tarnished and the century would quickly degenerate into a series of power struggles.

The Roman system of government was based on the annual election of magistrates. Two of these were elected consuls in whom overall executive power, including military, was invested. The consuls were controlled by the Senate, which was primarily responsible for foreign policy and for overseeing the conduct of campaigns. The good of Rome was the principle that underlay government, but self-interest was now making itself felt. As the empire grew and trade expanded, so the opportunities for corruption increased. Rapidly rising numbers of slaves led to unemployment and land became increasingly restricted to the possession of the few.

Growth of military power

In 107 BC there was a major reform of the army. Traditionally it had relied on a militia system whereby citizen-farmers were called up for service annually or in times of emergency. But as the empire grew, so did the military commitments, and the soldiers found that they remained away from home for considerably longer than hitherto and hence were unable to maintain their farms and other civil pursuits. Morale fell and, after a number of defeats in battle, Consul Gaius Marius began to recruit volunteers to be regular soldiers. The Roman army therefore became a professional organization. Yet, although this made it more efficient, its soldiers began to pledge their allegiance and loyalty to their commanders rather than to the state. This was soon to manifest itself in the first of the civil wars that would dog the first century BC.

Although a good soldier, Marius abhorred the Roman nobility and throughout the six times that he was consul did his best to reduce the powers of the Senate in favour of the Assembly, which contained representatives of the lower orders and was largely responsible for law-making. He was unable to control the Roman mob, though, and in 100 BC he was forced to retire in disgrace. There followed more than a decade of problems for Rome. First, her Italian allies rose in revolt since they were being denied full Roman citizenship. They fought Rome for two years before their wish was granted. Then there was trouble in

OPPOSITE *The naval Battle of Actium, which sealed Mark Antony's and Cleopatra's fate. The galleys relied on their oars when in battle. The tactic was to ram opposing vessels and, if necessary, board them.*

Asia Minor, where the Greek cities were discontented with Roman rule. The Senate elected the conservative Lucius Cornelius Sulla as consul, but the leaders of the people demanded that Marius be re-elected. Sulla reacted by occupying Rome with his troops and forcing through a law by which no measure could be voted on by the Assembly without the Senate's approval. He then left for Asia Minor. Marius, who had been in Africa, now returned with his own troops, massacred his opponents in the Senate and appointed himself and one of his generals consul. Soon afterwards he died. The revolt spread to the Greek mainland, but Sulla crushed this and in 83 BC returned to Italy. He inflicted two defeats on the Marian forces, entered Rome and made himself dictator, purging Marius's supporters and ensuring the primacy of the Senate. After three years in office, he allowed free elections and retired in 79 BC. Marian resistance continued, however, in the Iberian peninsula, where his supporters declared an independent state. This was eventually eradicated by Gnaeus Pompeius Magnus, better known as Pompey, in 72 BC.

First triumvirate: Pompey, Crassus and Caesar

Pompey was the up-and-coming man. In 67 BC he was appointed to command the Roman forces in the East. They were engaged in a war with King Mithridates of Pontus in Asia Minor. Although his predecessor had won significant victories, it was Pompey who brought about the king's final defeat. He was then given command of the whole of the Mediterranean by the Senate in order to rid it of pirates, which were proving a major problem. Not only did he achieve this, but he also swept eastwards as far as the Caspian Sea and then south to annexe both Syria and Palestine. He returned to Rome in triumph in 61 BC. By this time another star was rising. This was Julius Caesar, a politician lately turned soldier, whose first significant achievement was to bring the remainder of present-day Spain and Portugal under Roman control.

Caesar returned to Rome in 60 BC expecting a triumph to be held, but it was denied him. He then allied himself to Pompey and Marcus Licinius Crassus, a rich banker who had played a lead role in putting down the slave revolt led by Spartacus a decade before. This triumvirate now split up the empire among them. Pompey went off to look after Spain, Crassus sailed to Syria and Caesar went north to begin his campaign against the Gauls in present-day France and the Low Countries. The rivalry among the three men was intense, but in 53 BC Crassus was killed in a battle against the Parthians. Caesar, meanwhile, had succeeded in bringing Gaul under control and had also gained the subservience of a number of German tribes, as well as carrying out expeditions to Britain. Jealous of Caesar's success, Pompey returned to Rome, which was in a state of anarchy, in 52 BC. He had himself elected as sole consul and became a virtual dictator. Caesar was concerned both at his rival seizing power and for his own safety. Indeed, with Gaul now secured, Pompey and the Senate insisted that he give up his command and return to Rome or be branded a traitor. With the legions in Gaul and northern Italy at his back, Caesar marched on Rome. Although he had the support of the Senate, Pompey realized that he did not have sufficient forces loyal to him in Italy and withdrew to Greece, enabling Caesar to enter Rome unopposed at the beginning of 49 BC.

There followed five years of civil war. Apart from those in Gaul and Italy, the legions were initially loyal to Pompey. He also had the fleet. Caesar, who had himself appointed dictator, began by overcoming Pompey's forces in Spain and then those in North Africa. At the beginning of 48 BC Caesar managed to avoid Pompey's ships and land in Greece. After a number of inconclusive actions the armies of the two met at Pharsalus in August. The battle resulted in a decisive victory for Caesar, with Pompey fleeing to Egypt. Caesar followed him there and learned that he had been murdered by compatriots. These persuaded Ptolemy XII and his sister Cleopatra, the Egyptian rulers, to resist Caesar. They made life difficult for Caesar for a time before he defeated them in February 47 BC. This gave Caesar control over Egypt and he allowed Cleopatra, with whom he had become enraptured, to retain the throne, together with a younger brother. Further campaigns in Africa and Spain followed before Caesar finally brought the civil war to an end with the defeat of Pompey's elder son at Munda in 45 BC.

Julius Caesar now returned to Rome as her undisputed ruler. But some now became concerned at his despotism. They included former supporters of Pompey and even some of Caesar's own followers. In March 44 BC he was assassinated on the steps of the Senate. Power was left in the hands of Mark Antony, Caesar's fellow consul. Yet instead of bringing them to book, Mark Antony allowed the leading conspirators to take up governorships abroad. It was now that Caesar's young nephew, Gaius Julius Caesar Octavius – usually known as Octavian – came to prominence. He asserted that he was Caesar's natural political successor, but Mark Antony refused to accept this. Octavian therefore began to gather a force from Caesar's veterans. At the end of 44 BC he moved north into Gaul and temporarily allied himself to Decimus Brutus, governor of the province and one of the conspirators against his uncle. Mark Antony ordered Brutus to leave Gaul, but he refused, allowing himself to be besieged. Back in Rome the two newly elected consuls set out with armies to join Octavian. They eventually defeated Antony, but at the cost of their own lives. Octavian forbade any pursuit of his adversary because he was playing a deep game. He wanted to reach an accommodation with Antony before turning on those who had murdered his uncle, notably Brutus and Gaius Cassius Longinus, then governor of Syria. Once they had been despatched he intended to remove Mark Antony to achieve total power for himself. While Antony moved into southern France and joined up with Aemilius Lepidus, another of the Julius Caesar faithful, Octavian marched with his legions to Rome to cement his power base. He demanded to be made consul in place of those killed by Mark Antony's forces and the Senate was forced to agree. Finally, in November 43 bc, he met Mark Antony and Lepidus to form the second triumvirate. This was to rule the empire and hunt down Caesar's assassins.

Second triumvirate: Octavian, Mark Antony and Lepidus

Brutus himself went off to Macedonia and met with Cassius, who came up from Syria. Then, in September 42 bc, Antony and Octavian took their own army to Greece. They met Brutus and Cassius at Philippi on 3 October. The battle was a draw, but fearing that he was about to be defeated, Cassius committed suicide. Three weeks later a second battle took place on the same site. This time Mark Antony routed Brutus, who also committed suicide. The triumvirate now agreed to govern the empire with Octavian and Lepidus in the west and Mark Antony in the east. Resistance to Octavian continued during the next few years, however. First, Mark Antony's brother, who had been made consul, clashed with him, but was quickly defeated. This prompted Mark Antony to ally himself briefly to Pompey's younger son, who had succeeded in gaining Sardinia, Sicily and the Peloponnese for himself. Mark Antony then returned to Octavian's side. In return, Octavian helped him in an invasion of Parthia (present-day northern Iran), which had been raiding Syria. The triumvirate also reaffirmed their governance of the empire. Mark Antony would remain with the East, Lepidus would now only have Africa, while Octavian took Dalmatia, Italy, Sardinia, Spain and Gaul. Mark Antony also married Octavian's sister to cement their alliance.

Mark Antony set off for Parthia in June 36 bc. He reached Armenia, but was bested by the Parthians at the Battle of Phraaspa, though he succeeded in extricating his army. In that same year the younger Pompey was finally overcome when Marcus Agrippa decisively defeated his fleet off the north coast of Sicily. Sextus Pompey fled, but was later caught and executed without trial by one of Mark Antony's lieutenants. It was at this time also that Lepidus made his bid for power. Under the guise of helping Octavian in his campaign against Pompey, he brought an army to Sicily with a view to securing the island for himself. His troops mutinied, however, and went over to Octavian, who held Lepidus under house arrest in Rome until his death over 20 years later. With just

Octavian and Mark Antony left in the arena, the final act of the long series of civil wars that had plagued Rome was about to be played out.

The Final War of the Republic

Like Julius Caesar before him, Mark Antony had become smitten by Cleopatra and had begun an affair with her in 42 BC when he returned to the Middle East after Philippi. She bore him twins and the affair continued even after his marriage to Octavia, with Cleopatra giving birth to a third child in 36 BC. Not until three years later did Mark Antony finally divorce his wife and marry the Egyptian queen. Octavian had all along been waiting for the opportunity to unseat his rival and the personal insult to his family that the divorce represented provided the trigger. He was also angered that Antony had named Cleopatra's illegitimate son by Julius Caesar as his true heir instead of Octavian. But rather than attack his rival direct, which the Roman people would probably not have supported, he launched a bitter propaganda campaign against Cleopatra, accusing her of wanting to take over the Roman empire and of putting Mark Antony under a spell. This struck a chord with Romans and early the following year the Senate declared war on her, stripping Antony of his official triumvirate title at the same time.

Mark Antony and Cleopatra spent the winter of 33–32 BC at Ephesus in Asia Minor and assembled a large army and fleet there to deter Octavian from invading. They were perhaps encouraged by the fact that both the consuls of the time and a third of the Senate joined them. During the following winter both their army and ships were based around Cape Actium on Greece's west coast. Greece, however, could not produce enough supplies to maintain their 85,000 soldiers and 250,000 sailors so they had to have a long supply line back to Egypt and Asia Minor. Early in 31 BC Octavian crossed to Greece with an army of similar size to that of Antony and Cleopatra, while Agrippa's fleet (400 ships compared to the other side's 480) began to harry Antony and Cleopatra's supply lines off western Greece. By June Agrippa had managed to break the Antonine supply lines through the seizure of islands and other key points along the coast. Octavian had meanwhile taken his army to a point five miles north of Actium.

The Roman legion

THE *LEGION* WAS TO THE ROMANS what the phalanx was to the Greeks. Under the Marian reforms it was the *cohort* of some 500 men that was the basic building block, although for administrative purposes this was made up of five *centuries*, each commanded by a *centurion*. Ten cohorts comprised a legion and they usually adopted a chequerboard formation in battle. This made the legion much more flexible than the phalanx, and its troops were trained in a variety of manoeuvres. Each legion had its standard, the equivalent of today's colours in the British and other armies, and its soldiers were all made Roman citizens on enlistment. Marius's introduction of regular soldiers meant that the legions tended to be permanently based around the Roman empire. Thus, the 9th and 20th Legions became a permanent fixture in Britain during the years of Roman occupation.

Antony and Cleopatra were now facing a multitude of problems. Not only were they in very real danger of running out of supplies, but sickness, especially malaria, was also rife. Furthermore, the close proximity of Octavian was resulting in an increasing number of desertions. They therefore could not wait on events and had to take action. Antony decided to sever Octavian's water supply, the river Luro, which lay to the north of his camp. Accordingly, he sent out a force of mainly cavalry and landed at the mouth of the river. As it advanced inland Octavian sent out his cavalry to attack it. A significant number of Antony's troops immediately deserted and he was forced to withdraw the remainder. The future looked grave and Antony's army commander Canidius advised him to abandon his fleet, since the ships were becoming shorthanded, and to withdraw the army to Macedonia. It appears that it was Cleopatra who rejected this advice. She was convinced that the issue could only be decided at sea. Antony ordered those ships for whom crews could no longer be provided to be burnt. He planned to sally out into the Ionian Sea, where Octavian's fleet would be waiting and to use the wind, which tended to shift from the west to the northwest at midday, to outflank Octavian's northern wing and drive his fleet away from his camp. But he also had to be prepared for defeat, so ensured that his ships had their sails on board, which was not standard practice in naval battles at the time.

Thanks to a deserter, Octavian was aware of Antony's plan. Accordingly, he deployed his fleet, three squadrons in line, and waited. On 2 September Antony duly came out, also with three squadrons in line, but with a reserve of 60 ships under Cleopatra at the rear. Both of the northern squadrons tried to outflank each other, with Antony's heavier ships initially gaining the upper hand. But Antony's centre and southern squadrons suddenly turned about and made for harbour. Cleopatra's reserve prevented some ships from doing this, but they immediately raised their oars in surrender. Cleopatra's squadron then hoisted sail and made for the open sea, leaving Antony, who was commanding the northern squadron, still bitterly grappling with his opponents. Seeing that she had left, Antony then gathered what ships he could and set off back to Egypt after her. Some 300 of their ships were left in Octavian's hands. Even worse, when Canidius tried to withdraw the army, it mutinied.

The Battle of Actium marked the end of Mark Antony's dreams of greatness. He returned to Egypt broken in spirit, while Cleopatra was filled with fanciful dreams of founding a new empire. It was inevitable that Octavian would land in Egypt. He did so in July 30 BC. Mark Antony summoned up one final spark of energy to delay his advance into Alexandria. Hearing a rumour that Cleopatra had committed suicide, he then fell on his sword. She herself surrendered, but learning that Octavian intended to take her back to Rome in triumph she, too, committed suicide.

Octavian now stood alone, the master of Rome and her empire. The internal power struggles of the previous 70 years were finally at an end, but so was the republic of Rome. When he returned to Rome in triumph in 29 BC Octavian was granted the title *imperator* or emperor. Yet, like his uncle, who had been granted the same title, Octavian retained at least the facade of republican democracy. Two years later, probably at the prompting of Octavian's scheming wife, Livia, the Senate granted him the name Augustus. This made him a demigod and it was in this style that Rome and her empire would be ruled for the next four centuries.

✦ ✦ ✦

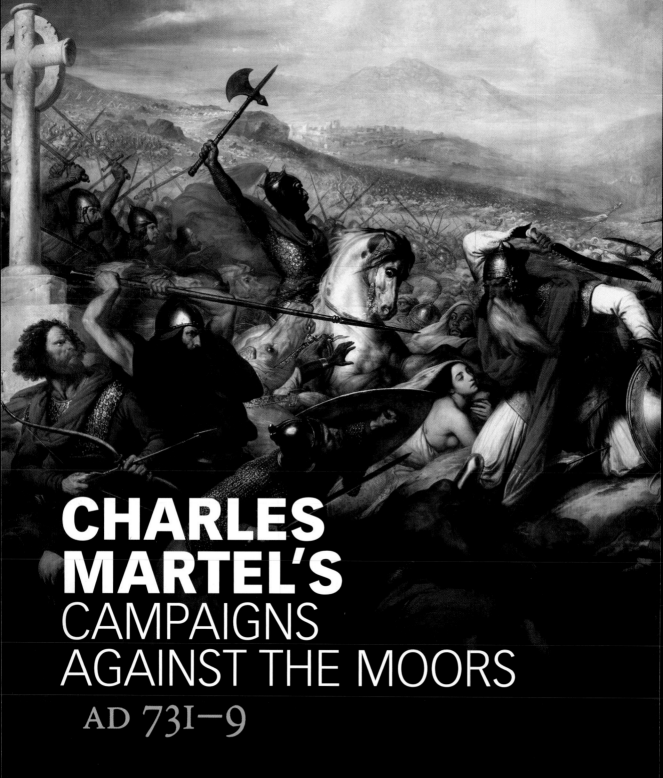

CHARLES MARTEL'S
CAMPAIGNS
AGAINST THE MOORS
AD 731–9

'**THE MEN OF THE NORTH** STOOD AS MOTIONLESS
AS A WALL; THEY WERE LIKE A BELT OF ICE FROZEN
TOGETHER, AND NOT TO BE DISSOLVED, AS THEY
SLEW THE ARABS WITH THE SWORD.' Isidorus Pacensis, eighth-century
chronicler, describing the Battle of Tours

The period in Europe between the final fall of Rome in the fifth century and the eleventh century AD has often been referred to as the Dark Ages. Indeed, the Roman empire began to disintegrate after the death of Emperor Constantine the Great in 337. The cause was a series of invasions, which would continue for the next few centuries.

Initially, these were by peoples from the north and east – Goths, Vandals, Huns and others. The collective term 'Barbarian' best described them as they overran western and southern Europe. Only the eastern Roman empire managed to remain intact and became the Byzantine empire. By the seventh century Byzantium encompassed North Africa, Palestine, Syria, Asia Minor, Greece, the Adriatic coast and parts of Italy. Western Europe, on the other hand, was divided into three Barbarian kingdoms: most of Italy was under the Lombards, the Visigoths held most of Spain, and the Franks reigned over France, the Low Countries and western Germany.

Development of the Frankish kingdoms

The Franks themselves were made up of a number of tribes that originally came from east of the river Rhine. Many had served in the Roman army and were granted land in France and western Germany at the end of their service. They became united under Clovis in the late fifth century. Significantly, he converted to Christianity, but on his death in 511 his kingdom was divided among his four sons and only came together thereafter for brief periods. In time the Frankish lands became three separate kingdoms: Neustria, covering northwestern France; Austrasia, the Low Countries and the Rhineland; and Burgundy, central and southern France. These fought amongst each other and also with neighbouring states, all of which served to weaken Frankish power as a whole. Many of the rulers of the Frankish kingdoms were mere boys when they came to the throne and had to rely on regents, who came to hold the reins of power. It was one of these, Pepin of Herstal, regent of Austrasia, who succeeded in reuniting the Franks after the defeat at the Battle of Tertry in 687 of a fellow regent who controlled the other two kingdoms at the time. When Pepin died in 714, he appointed his grandson in his place, but his illegitimate son Charles Martel objected and seized power for himself. It was he who would now have to deal with a new external threat to the Kingdom of the Franks.

Far away in Arabia in about 610, a former caravan conductor called Mohammed had declared himself the Prophet of God. Within a few years Islam, as the new religion was called, had swept through Arabia, uniting the Arabs as never before. On Mohammed's death in 632, Abu Bakr was appointed Caliph or successor to the Prophet. His first task

OPPOSITE *This painting of the Battle of Tours by Charles Steuben (1788–1856) is heavy with symbolism, especially in its inclusion of a stone Christian cross and a triumphant Charles Martel flourishing a battle-axe.*

was to deal with the Arab tribes that tried to break away from Islam's political embrace, but such was the momentum of the movement that it began to spread like wildfire through the Middle East and beyond. Syria and Palestine were rapidly wrested from the Byzantine empire, with Jerusalem falling in 638. Egypt came under the Muslim sway by 650 and the movement thereafter spread rapidly along the North African coast. Simultaneously, the Muslims moved north, overrunning Mesopotamia and then Iran. As early as 655 the Caliph of the day sent a naval expedition to capture Constantinople, capital of the Byzantine empire, but this was abandoned as a result of his death, even though he had defeated the Byzantine fleet. Throughout the next 50 years and more, the Muslims would make several more attempts to capture the city.

On the southern shore of the Mediterranean, the Islamic wave continued to advance across North Africa and reached the Atlantic coast early in the eighth century. They had initially been resisted by the indigenous Berbers or Moors, but the promise of booty brought them onto the Muslim side. The governor of the North African province of Ifrikquiya, Musa ibn Nusair, now turned his eyes across the Straits of Gibraltar to Spain, which was then dominated by the Visigoths. Partly to keep the Moors occupied and happy at the prospect of more booty, Musa sent 400 men across to Algeçiras on a reconnaissance mission. This proved successful and, encouraged by the fact that the Visigoth king Roderic was engaged in fighting the Franks in northern Spain, Musa launched an invasion the following year, 711. After besting the Visigoths twice in battle his forces occupied Toledo, Roderic's capital. By the end of 712 all of Spain, apart from the Atlantic coast in the far north, was in Musa's hands. A major reason for Spain succumbing so quickly was the Muslim two-handed approach to their conquered territories: they practised religious tolerance and allowed other faiths to continue to flourish, although a special tax was levied on their adherents. On the other hand, they were prepared to use terror against anyone resisting their rule.

It was inevitable that Moorish raiding parties would begin to cross into Frankish territory from Spain, but this developed into a full-scale invasion during the next few years. A major reason for this was that in 717 the Muslims had once again besieged Constantinople, but the following year decisive defeats both at sea and on land forced them to withdraw. They then came up with a new strategy. This was to move through France and Germany and take Constantinople from the rear, thereby making the Mediterranean a Muslim sea. Accordingly, in 719 the Moors occupied Narbonne, which lies on the Mediterranean close to the Spanish border. Two years later they laid siege to Toulouse. This was frustrated by Eudo of Aquitaine, a rival of Charles Martel, who defeated them outside its walls and forced them to withdraw. Undeterred by their reverse at Toulouse, the Moors continued to raid southern France and, indeed, in 725 invaded once more. They secured a sizeable belt of land north of the Pyrenees and also carried out a major raid up the Rhone valley. To safeguard Aquitaine, in 730 Eudo cemented an alliance with the Moorish potentate who now held the territory north of the Pyrenees, giving him his daughter in marriage.

Throughout these years Charles Martel had been largely absent. He had been busy in Germany extending the Frankish embrace to tribes as far east as the river Danube, as well as converting them to Christianity. He considered it more important to secure his eastern flank than to worry about the Moors, who were still well to the south of the Frankish heartland. He was aware that Eudo was aiming to make a clean break with Frankish influence and, indeed, usurp him, but believed that the Moorish threat was great enough to dissuade him from taking any positive steps in this direction.

Charles Martel confronts the Moors

In 731, with Germany now secure, Charles Martel set about dealing with his problems closer to home. He began by crossing the river Loire and threatening Eudo from the north to remind him of the consequences of attempting to compete with the Franks. This encouraged Abd ar-Rahman, the ruler of Spain, to deal with his subordinate Othman ben abi Neza, who had formed the alliance with Eudo. Rahman chased him into the mountains, where Othman threw himself off a precipice to avoid capture. His wife, who was renowned for her beauty, was sent to Damascus to join the Caliph's harem. Rahman now decided to invade Aquitaine. While booty was probably at the forefront of his mind it is likely that he also recognized the possibility of putting the original Muslim strategy of overrunning Germany and southeastern Europe into effect. It has been estimated that Rahman's army consisted of some 50,000 men, but it was probably smaller, since it is recorded as marching in a single column. It set out in 732 and advanced along the Bay of Biscay coast towards Bordeaux, but sent a detachment eastwards to Arles on the river Rhone, to keep the opposing forces dispersed and strike terror throughout Aquitaine.

Eudo met the Moors at Bordeaux and this time was decisively defeated. They sacked the city and continued northwards, pillaging as they went, and advancing in several columns to increase the scope for booty. Rahman now heard that the abbey at Tours, which stood on the north bank of the Loire, contained much treasure and headed for it. Meanwhile, a desperate Eudo had made his way to Paris and threw himself at the feet of Charles Martel, who agreed to help him provided that Eudo accepted Frankish rule over Aquitaine. Accordingly, in early October Charles Martel crossed the Loire and moved to confront the Moors.

The two armies were very different in make-up. The Moors were mainly mounted and armed with swords and lances, but had no armoured protection. They had mules with them, but these were primarily used for carrying booty and not supplies, since the Moors lived off the land. Their tactics consisted of simply charging at an enemy until he broke. Charles Martel's army consisted of two elements. The core of the army was made

up of professional soldiers, many of whom had been with him for some years. These men were paid, largely through Charles having seized land and property which he had previously given to the church. This had brought about threats of excommunication, but the church realized in the end that he was their best hope of overcoming the Islamic menace. The other element was the levies. These could only be called out between the crops being sown and their harvesting and hence could not operate far from home. They were very poorly trained and were mainly used to forage. The most significant difference between Charles Martel's army and that of the Moors was that his consisted solely of infantry. Indeed, it would appear that only the nobles had horses, but they used them only on the march. This meant that Charles Martel could not attack and would have to try to draw the Moors towards him, on ground of his choosing.

Martel selected a position barring the way to Tours that was wooded and on high terrain. By forcing the Moors to use the slope to attack him they would lose momentum and the trees would help to break up the attack, as well as making it difficult for the Moors to estimate his actual strength. He also formed his infantry up in a rectangular-shaped phalanx. When Rahman came across the Franks he was caught completely by surprise since he had had no warning of their approach. This was thanks to Charles Martel keeping well away from the roads during his march. Rather than attack immediately, Rahman drew in his outlying columns to increase the size of his army. For seven days the two armies faced one another, with only minor skirmishes taking place, but Rahman became increasingly desperate. Winter was coming on and he needed to reach Tours to obtain supplies, let alone the abbey's treasure. He therefore attacked. As Charles Martel hoped, Rahman's cavalry were unable to produce the shock action that had brought about their previous victories. They did, apparently, manage to break into the phalanx, but the Frankish veterans stood firm. It appears that Charles Martel now sent some of his levies to pillage the Moorish camp, or that rumours of this began to percolate through their ranks. In any event, part of Rahman's force withdrew to protect their booty. Seeing this, the remainder also began to pull back. Rahman himself was killed trying to rally them and any hopes of restoring order were dashed.

Lacking cavalry, Charles Martel did not pursue his foe. Indeed, he fully expected the Moors to attack again the next day and so remained in his original position. Once

ABOVE *The Moorish presence in Spain and France made a profound and lasting cultural impression. Moorish buildings like the mosque at Cordoba in southern Spain, for instance, strongly influenced the development of European architecture.*

daylight had come and the Moors did not reappear he sent reconnaissance parties to the Moorish camp. They discovered it abandoned. The Moorish force had literally fled back to Spain, carrying with them what booty they could. The Battle of Tours has ever since been regarded as a decisive victory in that it turned back the Islamic invasion of western Europe, as the Byzantine rebuff of the Muslims in front of Constantinople 15 years before had halted their onrush into eastern Europe. Yet, it did not mark the end of the Moorish attempts to occupy France.

Charles Martel and Eudo did manage to clear the Moors from France, apart from the province of Septimania, the Mediterranean coastal region running from the Spanish border almost to the east bank of the Rhone. Then, in 735, Eudo died. Charles Martel

The rise of feudalism

CRITICAL TO CHARLES MARTEL'S SUCCESS was retention of the loyalty of the Frankish nobles. He achieved this primarily by giving them land. This quickly developed into a system whereby the noble knelt in hornage before his king and was in return granted land by what was called *fief*. This meant that although in theory it still belonged to the monarch, the noble was free to do with it what he wished. In return, the noble was expected to demonstrate his loyalty through service to his master in time of war and to produce so many men to fight in it. In time, the nobility adopted the same system to ensure the loyalty of those under them. The military contribution was measured primarily in terms of the number of mounted knights that each vassal was expected to provide, but also armoured infantry (men-at-arms), bowmen and unarmoured militia, which were provided by the lowest levels of society in return for small strips of land.

hoped to annexe Aquitaine, but its nobility proclaimed Eudo's son duke, and Charles Martel was forced to recognize him. But any hopes that the new duke might have had of regaining independence from Charles Martel were quickly dashed by another Moorish invasion in that same year. He was forced, like his father during the previous invasion, to acknowledge Charles Martel as his overlord.

This time the Moors went eastwards after crossing into France. They seized Arles and then advanced north into Provence, capturing Avignon. They were helped in this by Maurontus, the ruler of Provence, who saw the Moors as a way of preventing Charles Martel from taking over his territory. This time the Moors were more cautious than in their previous invasion. Every city or town they captured was fortified and a garrison left to hold it. Charles Martel had meanwhile allied himself with the Lombards, who ruled northern Italy, to deal with this new threat. During 736 he recaptured Avignon and Nîmes. Then, after defeating a Moorish army outside its walls, Charles Martel destroyed Arles to prevent the Moors from reoccupying it. In the next three years he recovered almost all the territory that had been occupied by the Moors in France, with one of the reasons for his success being the introduction of Frankish cavalry, which gave his army a mobility that it had not previously enjoyed. Charles Martel's only frustration was that he was unable to take Narbonne. Although he decisively defeated the Moors outside the city, those inside were not prepared to surrender. Charles Martel was fearful of losing too many men in a direct assault on it and was unwilling to tie down troops in a protracted siege designed to starve the inhabitants out.

The reason for this reluctance was that the Frankish leader felt that he was nearing the end of his days and wanted above all to ensure the succession of his sons. Although he was still nominally regent or *major domo* of the Frankish kingdom, the throne had been vacant since the death of King Theuderic IV in 737 and the real power still lay with Charles Martel. A year before his death in 741 he divided the Frankish territory between his two elder sons. Carloman received Austrasia and Alemannia (present-day western Germany), with Bavaria as a vassal state, while Pepin the Younger was given Neustria and Burgundy, with Aquitaine as a vassal. The youngest son Grifo received nothing and on their father's death unsuccessfully fought his two older brothers for a share of the kingdom. Both Carloman and Pepin campaigned to ensure the security of the Frankish kingdom, but it was Pepin who finally cleared the Moors from France and regained Narbonne.

Legacy of Charles Martel: the Carolingian empire

In 747 Carloman decided to give up his public responsibilities and enter a monastery. This left Pepin in sole charge. Although he did proclaim himself Duke of the Franks in 737, Charles Martel had never cared for titles. His son thought differently and asked the pope whether a king should be he who merely inherited the title or the person who held real power in the state. Heavily reliant on Frankish support in maintaining the independence of the Holy See, the pope duly proclaimed Pepin King of the Franks and he was crowned as such in 751. It was the beginning of the Carolingian dynasty, which would rule France up until almost the end of the tenth century and would dominate western Europe, especially under Pepin's son Charles, better known as Charlemagne.

The primary impact of Charles Martel's campaigns was to halt and turn back the spread of Islam into western Europe. Simultaneously, he consolidated the hold of Christianity over the region. As for the Moors themselves, they retained their hold on the Iberian peninsula for centuries to come. Not until the early 13th century were they driven out of the central region, and it took almost another 300 years to clear them entirely from Spain. Their imprint remains to this day in elements of the Spanish language and architecture.

Charles Martel himself has other legacies. His introduction of heavy cavalry during his second campaign against the Moors gave rise to the heavily armoured knight, which would become one of the major features of medieval warfare. On the wider canvas of history, it was he who began to introduce feudalism (see Box), which characterized the Europe of the Middle Ages.

✦ ✦ ✦

THE
SEVENTH
CRUSADE
1248–54

'**THE TRIUMPHS OF THE CRUSADES** WERE TRIUMPHS OF FAITH. BUT FAITH WITHOUT WISDOM IS A DANGEROUS THING.' Steven Runciman, *A History of the Crusades*

One of the most extraordinary phenomena of the Middle Ages was the Crusades, the campaigns by Christian Europeans to liberate the Holy Land in the Middle East from the followers of Islam. They were to dominate events in both Europe and the eastern Mediterranean for more than 200 years, with many of the leading European monarchs of the day taking part.

The rise of Islam and the Muslim occupation of Palestine in the seventh century had not put an end to Christian pilgrimages to the Holy Land, a practice that had been started by the Roman emperor Constantine in the fourth century. Indeed, the Muslims were generally not hostile to the pilgrims and also held Jerusalem in reverence because the Prophet Mohammed had visited the city. The situation changed, however, during the 11th century. The cause of this was the Seljuks, a nomadic Sunni Muslim race from central Asia that had begun to sweep westwards. In 1071 they decisively defeated the forces of the Byzantine empire at Manzikert and annexed almost the whole of Asia Minor. They also overran Syria and Palestine. Renowned for their ruthlessness, the Seljuks now barred entry to Christian pilgrims and there were fears for the Holy Places.

At the time western Europe had begun to assume the political shape that it has today. In the aftermath of the Frankish empire France had become a recognizable state. England, recently overrun by the Normans, was the same. The Normans also held southern Italy and Sicily. The remainder of Italy, present-day Germany and Austria made up the Holy Roman Empire. Christianity was also spreading into eastern Europe. This was the Latin version, since that other bastion of religion, the Byzantine empire, practised its own form of Christianity and there was a schism between the two. Much of this spread of religion was the work of missionaries rather than military conquest, however. This was a result of a succession of popes preaching peace rather than war and was set against an atmosphere of increased piety, which had been initiated by the Benedictine abbey of Cluny in France in a bid to rid Christianity of the corruption that had dogged it. The church, however, did encourage violence in one particular area: the campaign to rid Spain of the Moors and restore it to Christianity.

Regaining the Holy Land

The trigger that set the Crusades in motion was provided by the Byzantine emperor Alexius I when he appealed to Pope Urban II for mercenaries to help him regain Asia Minor from the infidels. The pope was happy to accede to this request, but he was thinking on a wider canvas. For a start, this seemed an ideal opportunity to bring the Byzantine church back into the Roman fold. It would also have enabled Christianity to regain the Holy Land. Fired with this vision he began to preach a Holy Crusade in 1095,

OPPOSITE *Crusaders attacking a city in the Holy Land, using both crossbows and longbows. A siege tower offers a better chance of getting into the city than the scaling ladder in the background.*

promising a remission of their sins for all who took part. He caught the mood of the time. French nobles, in particular, flocked to his standard, as did the king of Norway. They and their followers made their way to Constantinople, but were preceded by an unarmed collection of pilgrims, who intended to make their way overland to the Holy Land. Most died of starvation or at the hands of the Seljuks. Alexius was suspicious of the Crusaders themselves when they arrived at his capital and kept them outside its walls. He was right in that it soon became clear that their aim of liberating the Holy Land differed from his of regaining Asia Minor, and it took almost a year to reach a compromise. Eventually, in spring 1097, both Crusaders and the Byzantine army set out across the Bosphorus. After scoring successes against the Seljuks in Asia Minor the Crusaders carried on towards Syria and Palestine on their own. By the end of 1099 they had captured Jerusalem, slaughtering most of its inhabitants, and established four independent states: Antioch, Edessa, Tripoli and Jerusalem. Thus ended the First Crusade, but with much of Syria and Palestine still held by the Muslims.

Relative peace followed for nearly 50 years, largely because the Muslims were divided. By 1130 a new Muslim leader had appeared: Zangi, the ruler of the Mosul region, was determined to make Syria his own, and at the end of 1144 succeeded in recapturing Edessa. This brought about the Second Crusade, which was led by Conrad III of Germany and Louis VII of France. They lost heavily in men en route, but met up with the resident Crusaders and attempted to capture Damascus. The Muslims then bribed the Syrian Crusaders to give up the siege and the two monarchs returned home having achieved nothing. There now appeared a man who succeeded in reuniting the Muslims. This was Saladin, a Kurd born on the Tigris who was fanatically anti-Christian. From his power base in Egypt he managed to unite the Muslims and in 1187 recaptured Jerusalem. The Christian response was the Third Crusade, which was led by Philip II of France, Richard I of England and the Emperor Frederick I. The last-named drowned, but Richard seized Cyprus from the Byzantines and this became an important Crusader base. He and Philip quarrelled incessantly, but succeeded in taking Acre and then, after Philip had returned home, Richard defeated Saladin at the Battle of Arsuf. The latter now adopted a 'scorched earth' policy as Richard advanced on Jerusalem. Realizing that he could not maintain his army in a siege of the city, Richard made a treaty with Saladin that allowed pilgrims to visit the Holy Land, and returned to Europe. The following year, 1193, Saladin died and the subsequent rifts in his empire allowed the Crusaders a brief respite.

The sack of Constantinople

Six years later, Pope Innocent III called for another effort to retake Jerusalem. It was agreed that the Crusaders would land in Egypt and the idea was that the Venetians should provide the necessary shipping and supplies. Protracted negotiations with the

Doge followed but the plans were then blown off course. To the fury of the pope the Crusaders agreed to help the Venetians regain the dependency of Zara on the Dalmatian coast, which they did in 1202. Encouraged by the deposed Byzantine ruler Isaac II and his son, the Holy Roman emperor Henry VI dreamed of bringing the Byzantine church back into the Roman fold. Accordingly, the majority of the Crusaders went on to Constantinople, which they captured and sacked in April 1204 – an event that ensured the permanent separation of the Roman Catholic and Orthodox churches. Thus, the Fourth Crusade did not go near the Holy Land. Its successor, which began in 1217, did land in Egypt and enjoyed early successes, including the capture of Damietta, near the mouth of the Nile. But the Crusaders' attempt to advance on Cairo at the height of the Egyptian summer was disastrous and they were forced to give up Damietta in return for a safe passage home.

The Sixth Crusade was more successful. This was even though its leader Emperor Frederick II had fallen out with the pope and been excommunicated, which meant that other Crusader contingents did not recognize him. He chose to negotiate with the Muslim leader Al-Kamil and remarkably managed to gain a ten-year lease on Jerusalem, with a land corridor to connect it to the coast, as well as Nazareth and Bethlehem. To celebrate this he had himself crowned King of Bethlehem in February 1229 and made his peace with the pope that August. While this left Frederick nominally in control of the Crusader states, the leaders within them were unwilling to recognize his authority and also quarrelled among themselves. In 1244 the Khwarezmians, who had been driven out of central Asia by the Mongols, recaptured Jerusalem. Allying themselves with Egypt, they also went on to take Ascalon.

Seventh Crusade: Louis IX and the rise of the Mamelukes

The reaction in Europe to the loss of Jerusalem did not reflect the same outrage of previous similar occasions. Most of the leading monarchs also had other matters on their minds. The Emperor Frederick had been excommunicated once more and Henry III of England was coping with unrest at home. Only Louis IX of France showed enthusiasm and in 1248 set sail

timeline

1071
Byzantine empire defeated at Manzikert, losing Asia Minor to Seljuks.

1095–9
First Crusade: Pope Urban II calls for Crusade to liberate the Holy Land.

1147–9
Second Crusade: Conrad III and Louis VII fail to take Jerusalem.

1187–92
Third Crusade: Richard I's treaty with Saladin allows pilgrims to Holy Land.

1202–4
Fourth Crusade: diverted to Constantinople.

1217–21
Fifth Crusade: limited success in Egypt.

1228–9
Sixth Crusade: Frederick II gains Jerusalem.

1248–54
Seventh Crusade: Louis IX fights the Mamelukes.

1270
Eighth Crusade: Louis IX's final push is diverted to Tunis.

1271–2
Ninth Crusade: Prince Edward obtains truce with the Mamelukes.

1302
Ruad falls to the Mamelukes.

from southern France with a force of 20,000 cavalry and 40,000 infantry to open the
Seventh Crusade. He spent the winter on Cyprus and then, as had happened during
the Fifth Crusade, he landed at the mouth of the Nile in June 1249 and seized Damietta.
This time he waited until November before beginning an advance on Cairo. During this
time he received reinforcements from Syria, but when Louis resumed his advance he
found his way blocked 30 miles from Cairo by a large army on the far bank of a canal.
It was the same place at which the Fifth Crusade had come to grief. The Crusaders
began to build a causeway across the canal, but were harassed by the Egyptians. Their
sultan died in the midst of this, but this was kept secret and one of his wives ruled in
his stead.

The stalemate was eventually broken in early February 1250. The Crusaders
discovered a ford some four miles from the causeway and crossed it. There was no
opposition and Louis's brother the count of Artois, who was commanding the cavalry
vanguard, wanted to press on immediately and attack the Egyptians, but the Templars
(see Box) who were with them urged him to await the arrival of the king with the main
body. The count refused to listen and they pressed on, driving the Muslims into the

village of Mansura. Once in its streets the knights were disadvantaged and were soon in trouble. The Muslims rallied and drove them back, killing Artois. Louis himself was put in danger when he came up with the remainder of the cavalry and the situation was only saved by the Crusader infantry, who managed to build a bridge from the end of the causeway. Thus, the Crusaders managed to hold on to their bridgehead on the south bank of the canal in spite of a fierce Egyptian counter-attack a few days later. They now moved to cut the Crusader communications with Damietta. Soon Louis's army was in danger of starvation and was also suffering from disease. He therefore began to withdraw towards Damietta, harried all the way by the Muslims. Louis now tried to negotiate, hoping to make a deal that would give him Jerusalem in return for Damietta. Realizing the plight that the Crusaders were in, the Muslims played for time, forcing them to continue the retreat. Finally, on 6 April, the Muslims attacked and literally broke Louis's army. He himself was captured and threatened with torture in an attempt to force him to surrender the Christian fortresses in Syria and Palestine. Eventually he agreed to surrender Damietta in return for his freedom and that of his followers. At that moment the Egyptian sultan, the last of the heirs of Saladin, was murdered by Mamelukes, who

were slave soldiers originating from central Asia. The new sultan was a Mameluke and he increased the size of the ransom. Louis was forced to agree to this and was released in the middle of May 1250. Significantly, the Muslim rulers of Aleppo and Damascus were furious that the Mamelukes had released Louis and in 1251 marched against Egypt, only to be utterly defeated.

The Mamelukes themselves were a formidable military force. Much of the reason for this was their thorough training. Each man was expected to become a master of the sword, lance and bow, both on horse and on foot. One of their most notable weapons was the mounted bowman. The cornerstone of the Crusader armies was the mounted knight, protected generally by mail armour, although the plated version was beginning to make an appearance. The knight's principal weapon was the lance, and since the introduction of the stirrup into Europe in the ninth century, he was now able to withstand the shock of it striking its target without falling off his horse. Another Crusader weapon was the crossbow, which had greater range and accuracy than the conventional bow. It had been outlawed by the Vatican in 1139 as being too barbarous to be used against Christians, but there was

LEFT *Louis IX of France (1214–70) led both the Seventh and Eighth Crusades. He came to the throne aged 12 and subsequently earned the respect of Europe for his sanctity, eventually being canonized as St Louis.*

no objection to it being used against infidels. Both sides were highly skilled at siege warfare and the Crusader castles, some of which can still be seen today, were spectacular examples of how sophisticated the art of fortification was becoming.

Instead of returning home like most of his surviving followers, Louis IX sailed to Acre. There he concentrated on improving the defences of the Crusader ports of Caesarea, Jaffa and Sidon. At the same time he tried to negotiate with a new force in Middle East affairs – the Mongols, who were rampaging westwards like wildfire. He hoped to enlist their support in regaining the Holy Land and perhaps convert them to Christianity. The Muslims were making similar overtures, but the Mongols were not interested in supporting either side and hence Louis's flirtation with them was a failure. Likewise, he also failed to persuade the pope and the Holy Roman emperor to sink their differences so that more material and spiritual support could be given to the liberation of Jerusalem. His one success before he sailed home in 1254 was to conclude a 15-year truce with the Mamelukes.

Louis IX's Seventh Crusade was thus a failure. Jerusalem remained in Muslim hands and hopes of recapturing it faded. Enthusiasm in Europe for crusading was on the wane and all that remained for the Crusaders was to try to hold on to the territory they still held in the Middle East. The other significance of the Seventh Crusade was the appearance of a new military power in the region – the Mamelukes. It was they whom the marauding Mongols now had to face in a battle for mastery of the region.

Aftermath of the Seventh Crusade

In 1258, four years after Louis IX had returned to France, the Mongols, with a grandson of Genghis Khan, Hulagu, at their head, overran northern Syria. They then paused because the death of the overall Mongol ruler required Hulagu to return home to take part in the election of a new overlord. He left a detachment to hold his gains and this allied itself to the ruler of one of the Crusader states, Bohemond VI of Antioch, while the other states remained aloof. The Mamelukes reacted to the Mongol incursion by gathering a large army. The two sides fought near Nazareth in 1260, with the Mamelukes emerging the victors. Soon after this the Mameluke sultan of Egypt was assassinated and his place was taken by Baibars al-Bunduqdari, who had already proved himself as a general. Baibars now turned on the Crusader settlements and besieged Acre without success in 1263. He did win a number of other victories over them and in May 1268 captured Antioch. It was this that prompted Louis IX to embark on another Crusade to help the remaining embattled Crusader states. He set out in 1270 but immediately diverted to Tunis, since he understood that the bey was prepared to convert to Christianity. This proved not to be so and Tunis was besieged. Soon afterwards the Crusaders were hit by an epidemic, which claimed Louis's life. That was effectively the end of the Eighth Crusade.

Military religious orders

ONE OF THE UNIQUE FEATURES of the Crusades was the creation of *military orders* of monks. The most well known at the time were the Knights Templar, who were established after the First Crusade to provide security for pilgrims. They soon developed into a significant military force, recognizable by the white surcoat with a red cross emblazoned on it that each member wore over his armour. The Order also had a powerful financial arm, which gained control of the European economies to such an extent that early in the 14th century the pope felt forced to disband it. The Knights Hospitaller were founded slightly earlier to take care of poor and sick pilgrims, but soon developed into a military order. After the ultimate defeat of the Crusaders, the Order moved to Rhodes and then to Malta. It persists in a number of guises today, notably in Britain as the St John Ambulance. Finally, there were the German Teutonic Knights, who took part in the First Crusade but thereafter devoted themselves to the spread of Christianity into eastern Europe and beyond. While these orders were in many ways the cornerstone of the Christian occupation of the Holy Land, their constant bickering with one another became a major weakness.

Arriving too late to take part in this Crusade was Prince Edward of England, who then sailed via Cyprus to Syria. On arrival he made overtures to the Mongols, who sent a contingent of troops to Syria in autumn 1271. This caused some panic among the local Muslims, but Baibars was quick to react and launched a counter-offensive. The Mongols hurriedly withdrew to east of the river Euphrates, but Edward was able to reach a ten-year truce with the Mamelukes. He then had to return to England because of the death of his father King Henry III and assumed the throne as Edward I.

The new English king maintained his contacts with the Mongols during the first few years of his reign and in time these did bear some fruit. In 1281 the Mongols once more swept into Syria and linked up with the Crusaders. Sultan Qala'un, who had succeeded Baibars on his death, fought them at Homs. There was no clear result, but it was enough to encourage the Mongols to withdraw once more. The Mamelukes then turned on the remaining Crusader strongholds. Tripoli fell in 1289 and Acre, so long the bastion of Christian hopes, two years later. The very last Christian foothold, the island of Ruad, just off the Syrian coast, was overcome by the Mamelukes in September 1302. Ironically, this was shortly after another Mongol invasion of Syria, which foundered because the anticipated Christian support did not materialize. The Mamelukes themselves remained the dominant power in the Middle East until the early 16th century when they were conquered by the Ottomans. As for the Crusaders, their title has had a recent revival, with the term often being used by Islamic fundamentalists to describe their enemies in the West today.

✦ ✦ ✦

THE
MING
OVERTHROW
OF MONGOL RULE
IN CHINA
1351–88

'**BUILD HIGH WALLS,** STOCK UP RATIONS, AND DON'T BE TOO QUICK TO CALL YOURSELF A KING.'

Advice given to Zhu Yuanzhang (later Emperor Hongwu) at the outset of his campaign to liberate China

Significant among the events of the Middle Ages

was the rise of the Mongols. During the first half of the 13th century, principally under Genghis Khan, they swept into northern China and Asia, and reached Moscow and the gates of Vienna in the west. Later in the century the Mongol incursions penetrated Syria and threatened Egypt. Under Kublai Khan they also overran the remainder of China, attempted two invasions of Japan, and reached into southeast Asia.

The Mongol conquests inevitably proved too large to control and they were in time forced to withdraw. In the case of China, the conflict to oust the Mongols resulted in the emergence of one of its greatest emperors and the beginning of a new dynasty. The struggle also encompassed civil war among rival warlords.

Song and Yuan dynasties

Prior to the Mongol conquest, China was ruled by the Song dynasty, but it was not a united country. The northern expanse of the country was ruled by the Northern Song, which was established by a general in AD 960. In time it fell victim to political corruption and was overthrown by the Jin dynasty in the first part of the 12th century. This had been founded in what is today northern Manchuria and its rulers were not strictly Chinese. The Southern Song ruled the rest of China and frequently clashed with the north, at one point even allying itself with the Mongols. Once he had subjugated southern China, Kublai Khan established the Yuan dynasty to rule over the entire country and made Dadu (present-day Beijing) its seat of government. His weakness, however, lay in indulging in further conquests, such as his two attempts to invade Japan, both of which foundered because of bad weather, rather than consolidating his hold on China. Allied to this was the class system that the Mongol emperors introduced. At the top of the pile were the Mongols themselves, followed by other immigrants, and then the northern Chinese. The southern Chinese were at the bottom. The Mongols also enjoyed an extravagant lifestyle and the Chinese paid for this through heavy taxation. China also suffered a series of natural disasters, including frequent flooding of the Yellow River. Furthermore, after the death of Kublai Khan in 1294 there were numerous squabbles over the Yuan succession and no emperor remained on the throne for long.

It is therefore not surprising that resentment grew, eventually manifesting itself in growing unrest from the late 1340s onwards. Resistance was originally fomented by the White Lotus Society, a secret messianic Buddhist organization. The real fuse was lit in 1351, however, when the Yuan rulers organized a force of 170,000 labourers to rechannel

OPPOSITE *A typical Mongol court, showing Mongol warriors with their high pointed helmets. Mobility was their great advantage. Each warrior might have up to seven sturdy ponies, enabling a Mongol army to cover 50 miles per day.*

the Yellow River as a means of preventing further flooding. The White Lotus was active in persuading some labourers to desert and join the Red Turbans. This was a wider group, which included the White Lotus, and was so called because its members wrapped red cloths around their heads. At the same time the authorities arrested the White Lotus leader. Fearing a crackdown on the movement, the Red Turbans openly revolted and immediately seized the city of Yingchou (present-day Fuyang) on the Huai River, which runs between the Yellow River and the Yangtze. Rebel leaders took over other cities and declared themselves independent rulers. Allied to this was rural unrest and an increase in banditry. Much of the rural agitation was directed against the landlord class. As a result, this was allowed by the Yuan government to raise forces to protect its interests. By 1354, these local militias had succeeded in pacifying significant areas of southern China. In the north one landlord figure in particular stood out: Chaghan Temur succeeded in halting the rebel advance in the Huai region and in time came to control much of northern China on behalf of the Yuan.

The success of the landlord militias caused the Red Turban leadership to rethink its strategy. They now began to woo the landlords and bring them over to their side, especially since the Yuan government had proven incapable of giving the landlords much material support. The Red Turbans once more began to gain territory, encouraging the landlords to take up administrative posts in the fiefdoms that they established in order to maintain their loyalty. Many, however, hoped for the installation of a new Chinese emperor who would reunite the country. For a time it looked as though the Song dynasty might make a reappearance. This was especially since the White Lotus leadership claimed to be members of it. In 1355 they established a new Song capital at Po-chou in eastern Hunan province and then used this to coordinate the operations of the various rebel groups. Initially they enjoyed some success and in 1358 were able to move to the former Northern Song capital of Bianjing (present-day Kaifeng). But now they clashed with Chaghan Temur, who captured Bianjing the following year, together with most of the trappings of Song rule. That ended the Song bid for power and the focus now turned on southern China, where other warlords were battling for supremacy and to which the Song emperor had fled.

Rise of Zhu Yuanzhang

One of the southern warlords was Guo Zixing (also spelt Kuo Tzu-hsing), who controlled present-day Anhui province in southeast China. In 1355 he appointed an unusual man as commander of his army. Twenty-eight-year-old Zhu Yuanzhang (also spelt Chu Yuan-chang) was a peasant, who had lost all his immediate family to famine and disease. He had become a trainee Buddhist monk, but had been forced to leave when his monastery ran out of food. He had become a travelling beggar and in 1352 had joined the Red Turbans. He quickly proved himself a natural soldier, hence his rapid promotion. He had also married Guo's foster-daughter. Within a year his master had

OPPOSITE *Emperor Hongwu, founder of the Ming dynasty, was a successful soldier and a very able administrator. He never forgot his peasant upbringing and instituted wide-ranging agricultural reforms to improve the lot of the peasant farmer.*

大明太祖高皇帝

died and Zhu took his place. By this time he was fired by the dream of not only ridding China of the Mongols, but also of uniting it as one country.

Zhu moved quickly. In 1356 he captured Nanking and made it his capital. He had already gathered around him a staff of hand-picked, intelligent advisers and within a short time his system of efficient government attracted many refugees from the more lawless regions and the population of the city swelled. At this time Zhu allowed himself to be seen as a servant of the Song dynasty, and its 'emperor' Han Lin-erh confirmed him as the ruler of the Nanking region. This was especially done to keep his generals loyal and to bring the northern landlords and their militias to his side. But he now had rival warlords, rather than the Mongols, in his sights. In particular, there was Chen Youliang, who had a much larger army and controlled the centre of the Yangtze valley.

In 1360 the two began to fight each other openly and the climax came three years later on Lake Poyang, China's largest freshwater lake, which lies to the northeast of Nanchang. Chen's forces were besieging Nanchang, today the capital of Jiangxi province. The city is situated on the river Gan jiang and Chen was besieging it from the water. Zhu set out from Nanking with what ships he could gather and reached Lake Poyang. The initial clash took place on 30 August 1363. After dropping off some of his troops to help the defenders of Nanchang, Zhu made a frontal assault on Chen's much larger fleet, using fireships and various explosive devices. He destroyed some 20 vessels, but his own flagship was set on fire and grounded on a sandbank. It was only rescued with difficulty. Zhu made further fireship attacks on the following day, again with some success. There was now a pause while both fleets made repairs. They clashed again on 2 September and Zhu enjoyed some further success, largely through boarding Chen's ships. News then came through that Zhu's troops had lifted the siege of Nanchang. He therefore withdrew

The Ming military system

EMPEROR HONGWU REFORMED CHINESE MILITARY ORGANIZATION in a way that prevented any general from becoming too powerful. The system was called *Weiso* (literally 'guard post'). Units called *Wei* were formed as a standing army. There were some 500 of these scattered along China's frontiers and at strategic points within the country. A Wei was 5600-men strong and broken down into five sub-units. Commanders were answerable direct to the central Ministry of War and not to the local civil administration. Hongwu also created the concept of the military family, which lived where the Wei was stationed and was expected to grow its own food, thereby making the Wei self-sufficient. In times of war, a mass mobilization took place and the Ministry of War appointed the generals to command the forces in the field. Once the conflict was over, the troops returned to their peacetime military districts and the generals relinquished their commands. In terms of weaponry, the Chinese had developed gunpowder weapons in the 13th century, but guns were regarded as just another missile-throwing weapon, along with crossbows and various types of large catapult and sling. Indeed, both infantry and cavalry relied more on discharging their weapons at a distance than hand-to-hand fighting, though the latter frequently did take place.

his fleet to the mouths of the Yangtze and Gan jiang rivers, but continued to watch and blockade Chen's fleet. Finally, on 4 October, he launched another fireship attack. During the course of the ensuing action Chen was killed by an arrow and his fleet surrendered.

The protracted Battle of Lake Poyang proved to be a major turning point in that it established Zhu as the strongest warlord. The Song emperor recognized this fact by promoting Zhu from duke to king, but a year later Han Lin-erh was drowned on his way to Nanking and the Song dynasty was finally at an end, with Zhu ordering all reference to it to be erased. One significant warlord still held out against him, however. This was Zhang Shicheng, a salt merchant, who had been ruling the area around Suzhou, west of Shanghai, as a self-proclaimed king for a decade. Zhu's forces defeated him in 1366. Thereafter he swept further north, the Mongols offering little resistance. In 1368 he secured the Yuan capital Dadu and renamed it Beiping, which meant 'the north is pacified'. Beiping was later renamed Beijing ('northern capital').

The Ming dynasty and the decline of Mongolia

In that same year Zhu proclaimed himself emperor of what he called the Ming ('brilliant') dynasty, giving himself the name Hongwu ('vast military power'), but maintained Nanking as his capital instead of moving to Beiping. Indeed, one of his first acts was to rebuild its city walls. Emperor Hongwu's own campaigning days were over, as he concentrated on reforming the country, but there was still plenty of work for his armies. Outlying Chinese provinces needed to be brought back into the fold. Thus, in 1369 General Xu Da secured the provinces of Shanxi and Shaanxi in the northwest. Sichuan, Shaanxi's southern neighbour, proved more obstinate and it took two years to liberate it. This left just Yunnan province in the far southwest yet to be reclaimed.

The Yuan dynasty was, however, still in place to a degree. In 1370 the reigning monarch, Toghun Temur, died. His place was taken by Crown Prince Ayushiridar, whose seat was at Karakorum, which had been built by Genghis Khan to be the capital of the Mongolian empire. Joining him there was a soldier of mixed Chinese-Mongol parentage, Koke Temur. A native of Henan province, he had fought alongside his uncle Chaghan Temur during his successful campaign against the Red Turbans. He had taken command of Chaghan's forces after his uncle's death in 1362 and had then sided with the crown prince during a factional dispute. Now he had to face invasion by a Ming army, with Xu Da again at its head. Bucking the trend of seemingly endless Ming victories, Koke inflicted a severe defeat on Xu Da. He could not, however, turn back the tide for good. Xu Da had his revenge and forced the Yuan army to retreat across the Gobi desert.

Yet Koke Temur still believed that Yuan sovereignty could be reimposed on China. He soon reappeared and advanced into northern China with the object of reclaiming it for the Mongols. He penetrated as far south as Shanxi province, but died in 1375, bringing the Mongol advance to an end. Ayushiridar followed him three years later and with his death the last hopes of regaining China were extinguished. Yunnan province was reincorporated in 1383 and then, in 1388, came the final denouement. Emperor Hongwu's forces advanced across the Gobi desert and invaded the Mongol heartland. They decisively defeated the Mongols on the Kerulen River and drove them out of their capital Karakorum. Many of the ruling family were captured and taken back to China. The Mongols then splintered into separate tribes, marking the end of their power.

Consolidation of Ming power

Hongwu himself spent his 30 years as emperor (he died in 1398) reorganizing the governance of China. Conscious that the delegation of power had weakened the Yuan dynasty's hold on China and furthered the prospects of a successful revolt, he believed in centralization. He created six ministries – personnel, revenue, religious rites, war, justice and works – which were answerable directly to himself. Each province was divided into counties, with a magistrate in charge of each. He created a secret police force to check on the loyalty of his subjects. All secret societies, a great tradition in Chinese life, were banned, including the White Lotus which had been such a driving force in overthrowing Mongol rule. He reinstituted civil service exams to ensure the quality of administration at all levels and was particularly concerned to eradicate corruption, with those found guilty paying for it with their lives. Yet, while Hongwu favoured Buddhism, he did allow other religions to be practised. When it came to the defence of China, he concluded that there was little threat from Korea since it remained a vassal state, as it had been under the Mongols. In the north the Mongol threat remained, though at a much lower level and it was more in terms of raids by individual tribes. To counter this, Hongwu initiated the building of a protective wall along the northern frontier. The Great Wall of China remains today an enduring monument to the Ming dynasty, a dynasty that would remain in place for some 300 years.

Given the humble background from which he came, Hongwu's achievements were impressive, to say the least, and make him one of China's greatest emperors. Not only did he reunite China, but he also oversaw the demise of Mongol domination outside their own territory.

CONSTANTINOPLE

1453

'CANNOT THERE BE FOUND A CHRISTIAN TO CUT OFF MY HEAD?'

Words attributed to the Byzantine emperor Constantine Palaeologus just before his death at the hands of the Turks

The Balkans have always been seen as a geostrategic fault line, with the European 'plate' on one side and the Asian on the other. In the Middle Ages, the bulwark, at least in Christian terms, against the Asian tide sweeping into Europe, had long been the Eastern empire centred on Constantinople.

The Byzantine empire had reached its peak in the 11th century, 700 years after its founding by Emperor Constantine the Great. Thereafter it had steadily lost territory in Asia Minor to the Seljuk Turks. After being overwhelmed by the Mongols in the middle of the 13th century the Seljuk empire had rapidly disintegrated. In its place arose a new force, the Ottomans, an Anatolian tribe that came to prominence at the beginning of the 14th century. Initially, under Osman I, the Ottoman Turks had begun to drive the Byzantines from their remaining possessions in Asia Minor.

Expansion of the Ottoman empire

In 1345 the Ottomans made their first foray into Europe and in less than a decade had established their first permanent foothold, on the Gallipoli peninsula in the Dardanelles. Thereafter they overran Thrace. By the end of the 14th century, Bulgaria and much of Albania and present-day Greece were in Turkish hands, and the remnants of the Byzantine empire were increasingly beleaguered. There was now a slight pause in the Ottoman pursuit of conquest, as a new threat had arisen from the east in the form of the Tartar Tamerlane. Persia, Mesopotamia and parts of southern Russia quickly fell into his hands and in 1402 he invaded Anatolia, defeating the Ottoman sultan before returning, as quickly as he had come, to his homeland of Samarkand. He left the Ottoman lands in a state of civil war as the three sons of the sultan he had defeated fought for the succession. Eventually, in 1413, Mehmed I appeared the winner and during the eight years of his reign he consolidated the Ottoman hold on Asia Minor. His one upset was a naval defeat off Gallipoli at the hands of the Venetians, who held territory on the coast of Albania and Epirus. His successor, Murad II, quickly gained revenge, forcing Venice to cede some of its Balkan possessions. He then invaded Hungary and Serbia, without success. Following this, the last of the Crusades came in 1443. Led by Poland and Hungary, the Crusaders attempted to drive the Turks back across the Bosphorus and bring relief to the Byzantines. They enjoyed some initial success, including forcing Murad's temporary abdication, but he decisively defeated them at Varna in 1444.

Mehmed II and Constantine Palaeologus

Murad died in 1451 and was succeeded by 19-year-old Mehmed II, who would become known as The Conqueror. By this time the Byzantine empire had been reduced to

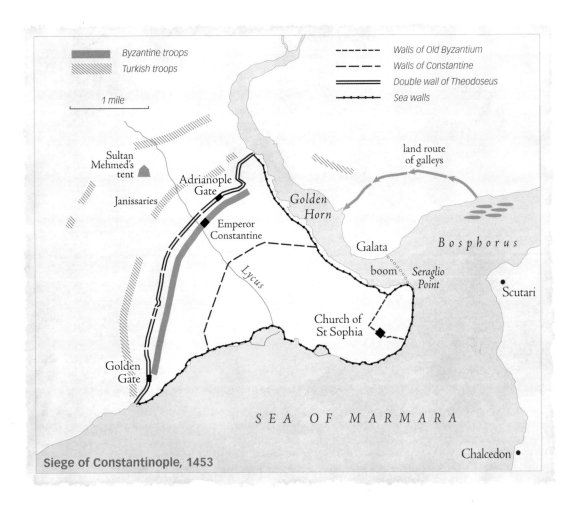

Siege of Constantinople, 1453

Constantinople itself. Successive emperors had pleaded to the West for help, but Rome would only countenance this if the Eastern Orthodox Church returned to the Roman Catholic fold, and this was anathema to the Orthodox members. The city was in a dilapidated state and much of the population had left. Yet, there was still a Byzantine emperor in the form of Constantine Palaeologus, who had come to the throne in 1448, and he still had an army, though it only totalled some 10,000 men, of whom 2000 were mercenaries from western Europe.

In Sultan Mehmed's eyes, Constantinople had too long been a thorn in the Ottoman side. Not only did it physically separate the Ottoman empire in Asia from its territory in Europe, but its emperor was also forever fomenting unrest in the latter. Besides which, Constantine was holding a pretender to the sultanate, which paid him an annual fee to ensure that this individual remained in custody. Constantine now demanded that the fee be doubled. This was the last straw, and Mehmed saw the capture of Constantinople as his first task.

It would not be the first time that the city was directly attacked. It had been sacked by the Crusaders in 1204 and occupied for almost 60 years. Civil war between claimants to the Byzantine throne in the mid-14th century had led to the usurper John VI seizing the city and the throne, and at the end of the century the Ottomans besieged Constantinople for eight years, but were forced to withdraw because of the threat from Tamerlane. Sultan Murad II had also briefly besieged it in 1422 because the Byzantines had backed a rival to the Ottoman throne. Mehmed therefore had plenty of precedents on which to draw. Rather than attempt a direct attack, he decided that the city must first be totally isolated. His first action was to renew the peace treaty with Hungary to prevent Constantinople receiving any help from the north. He then mounted a campaign designed to deter the independent emirate of Karaman, which was situated in the area of Asia Minor immediately north of the island of Cyprus, from causing trouble while his back was turned. He also wanted to ensure that Constantinople could receive no help from the sea. Mehmed did this by building a fortress at the narrowest point of the Bosphorus. This was opposite one that had been constructed by Sultan Bayezid during his siege of the city at the end of the previous century.

By spring 1453 Sultan Mehmed was ready to begin the siege. He had gathered an army of upwards of 80,000 men. The cream of these were the Janissaries, who had been established by Sultan Murad I in the second half of the 14th century. They were initially drawn from prisoners of war and slaves, and were unique at the time in that they received regular pay, as opposed to just drawing it in time of war, and wore a distinctive uniform. At this time they served as infantry and were equipped with firearms. Mehmed also had an impressive siege train (see Box) and had several ships built, including over 70 galleys.

Faced with all these preparations, Constantine sent envoys to several European countries asking for help, warning that if it was not forthcoming Constantinople would perish. The response was disappointing, but not unexpected given the Orthodox church's continuing refusal to acknowledge Rome. Indeed, the only significant contribution came not from a government, but from an individual: Giovanni Giustiniani Longo was a Genoese and an acknowledged expert in siege warfare, who brought 700 men to help. Constantine also had the Ottoman pretender Orhan and his followers. Even so, his total of 10,000 soldiers, with some 30,000 civilians to repair the city walls, paled into insignificance when compared to the massive Ottoman strength.

Constantinople besieged

On 2 April 1453 the Ottoman forces began to arrive outside the city walls. On that same day the Byzantines laid a chain boom across the Golden Horn, the estuary that flanked Constantinople in the north and contained its harbour. Three days later the sultan himself appeared and the siege began in earnest. Mehmed decided to make his main attack roughly in the centre of the walls on the landward side and began to deploy his artillery accordingly. Constantine noted this and deployed most of his garrison in this area. On 12 April the bombardment opened, although the Turkish heavier guns could only fire seven to eight rounds per day. Simultaneously the Turkish fleet, which was anchored in the approach to the Golden Horn, began to bombard the Byzantine ships in their harbour. Neither was particularly successful. The naval bombardment was ineffective because the ships' guns could not attain sufficient trajectory. Apparently it was the sultan himself who overcame this problem by designing a mortar whose shot could attack vessels from above. As for the land bombardment, damage to the walls was repaired as soon as it was inflicted.

After ten days a now impatient Mehmed ordered an assault, even though a proper breach had not been achieved. The Ottoman navy's attempt to break through the boom failed and the land assault never got beyond the ditch in front of the walls, such was the intensity of the Byzantine fire. The sultan was furious and was only dissuaded with difficulty from firing the corpses of his dead soldiers over the city walls with trebuchets. On 25 April a naval battle occurred that pitted sail against rowing power: three Genoese galleons with men and supplies for Constantinople had taken shelter off the island of Chios in March because of contrary winds. They had set sail again on 15 April and fallen in with a Byzantine grain ship. The four vessels had continued on their way. As they neared Constantinople, they were intercepted by 145 Turkish galleys. The result should have been a foregone conclusion, but a strong wind enabled the four ships to crash straight through the galleys. Then, just off Seraglio Point, the wind died. The galleys closed in once more and their crews tried to board. After two hours of desperate fighting the wind picked up again, the harbour boom was lowered and the four ships arrived safely in Constantinople harbour. It was a major boost to the morale of the defenders.

It became clear to Mehmed that he must gain control of the Golden Horn so as to force the Byzantine garrison to deploy additional troops to defend the sea wall. To do this

The Ottoman siege train

THIS WAS THE MOST POWERFUL of its day, the reason being its heavy guns. While it possessed more traditional weapons, especially the trebuchet, which was a giant mechanical sling, the train's newly acquired 70-odd bombards or cannon caused the most significant damage during the siege of Constantinople. The barrels were cast by a Hungarian called Orban. In 1452, he offered his services to Constantine first, but the emperor had lacked the funds. Orban then visited Sultan Mehmed at his European capital of Edirne, 140 miles west of Constantinople. Orban was confident that he could construct a weapon that would penetrate Constantinople's walls. The result was a 27-foot long bronze barrel, with a 30-inch diameter, which could fire a stone projectile weighing over half a tonne. He continued to forge barrels, though smaller than the original. The guns then had to be moved from Edirne to Constantinople, which took some six weeks. The ammunition was obtained from stone quarried on the Black Sea's north coast. On arrival the guns were organized in batteries of four guns each. Orban and his foundry workers provided the gun crews, although it is claimed that he himself was killed while operating the largest gun. The siege marked the first true concentration of artillery in history.

he decided to move some of his smaller ships across the strip of land that separates the Golden Horn from the Bosphorus. This was done by levelling the ground and laying a wooden trackway that was greased so that the vessels could be slid along it. It was a highly successful manoeuvre and took the Byzantines by surprise when the ships took to the water in the Golden Horn. An attempt to destroy them in a night attack failed and Mehmed then quickly erected a bridge of boats to unite his forces on either side of the Golden Horn.

Gloom now descended on the city of Constantinople. Hopes were pinned on the arrival of a Venetian fleet and on 5 May a small Byzantine vessel disguised as a Turkish ship slipped out by night in an attempt to locate it. Throughout this time the Turkish bombardment continued, but two further assaults on the city walls were repulsed with heavy casualties. Mehmed became concerned, since it was difficult to keep his large army supplied, and believed that unless Constantinople fell by the end of the month he would have to lift the siege. Rumours of the impending arrival of the Venetian fleet and of a Hungarian army from the north were also beginning to discomfort his soldiers. His next attempt employed a massive wooden tower, from which fire was poured on the defenders before they blew it up by rolling barrels of gunpowder into the ditch where it stood. The Turks then tried to mine under the walls, but the defenders countermined and either blew up the opposing miners or smoked them out. Mehmed now called a council of war and it was decided to make one final combined land and sea assault. He set the date as 29 May.

The Byzantine gloom deepened when the brigantine returned after seeing no sign of a Venetian fleet. A lunar eclipse, unseasonably cold weather, thunderstorms and fog added to the sense of impending catastrophe. During the two nights prior to the attack the Ottoman camps were illuminated by fires, giving the impression that the city was ringed by flames. On the night of 28–29 May, Emperor Constantine harangued his followers. All who could be spared then attended a final service in the church of St Sophia. The 4000 surviving members of the garrison then took up their posts.

Mehmed's plan was for the fleet to bombard the sea walls in order to prevent the defenders from reinforcing the land walls. He intended to attack the latter in three places, with the section of wall in the Lycus valley being the principal objective. Vast amounts of equipment had been gathered: scaling ladders, iron hooks to pull aside the barricades that the defenders had placed in breaches in the walls, and fascines to drop into the ditch. His troops were to attack in three waves, with the Janissaries providing the last. At about 1.30 a.m. on 29 May the comparative stillness was broken by a cacophony of trumpets, drums and shouts. The first wave, containing Mehmed's least-trained men, rushed the ditch, placed their scaling ladders against the walls and began to climb. Every form of projectile was fired at them, and Greek fire and boiling oil poured on them. Realizing that they were making little progress, Mehmed withdrew them and sent his second wave forward. This managed to make a lodgement but, after a desperate hand-to-hand struggle, was driven out again.

Dawn was now breaking and the Janissaries moved in to attack. At about this time the Genoese lost their leader Giovanni Giustiniani Longo. He was wounded and made his way to a ship in the harbour. His men thought he was dead and began to waver. At the same time a party of Janissaries found an undefended gate, which they used to take those defending the key sector in the Lycus valley in the flank. In this way the Turks were able to penetrate the city. A Turkish flag was hoisted near the Adrianople Gate and Constantine's troops began to withdraw. Seeing that his men were breaking, he himself charged into the fray and was struck down.

End of the Byzantine empire

Panic now spread throughout the city as the Turks swarmed about killing everyone they found and looting the palaces and churches. Mehmed himself entered the city at about midday and restored some order. Some 5000 people were massacred: considerably fewer, in fact, than when the Crusaders had sacked the city in 1204. Fifty thousand others were put into slavery. All of the Byzantine nobility that had not escaped were put to death on Mehmed's orders. The sultan made the city his capital, renaming it Istanbul. Thus, after 1100 years, the Byzantine empire had finally come to an end. Although the title of Byzantine emperor was now defunct, Constantine's nephew Andreas Palaeologus used it from 1465 until his death in 1503. Thereafter it vanished into history. The Orthodox brand of Christianity, which was the driving force behind the empire, did survive, however. Grand Duke Ivan III of Muscovy, who had married Andreas Palaeologus's sister, declared himself patron of the Eastern Orthodox Church. In time, after his grandson became Russia's first emperor, his church became known as the Russian Orthodox Church. As for the church based in Constantinople, it also survived. Sultan Mehmed did not ban Christianity, but allowed it to continue even though its adherents were now isolated from both the church in Rome and that in Moscow. It became the Greek Orthodox Church.

From the Ottoman point of view, the capture of Constantinople not only enabled Sultan Mehmed to consolidate his empire, but also to enlarge it. Although he initially suffered a setback when Janos Hunyadi of Hungary foiled his attempt to capture Belgrade and drove him out of Serbia and Bosnia, in 1461 he overran the remainder of Greece and drove the Genoese out of the Aegean. A lengthy war with the Venetians followed, in which the latter lost their remaining Balkan possessions on the Adriatic coast. Mehmed also eventually regained much of what had been lost to Hungary in the Balkans. Indeed, shortly after his death in 1481, the Ottoman hold on the Balkans was total, and during the next 200 years the empire grew, reaching almost to Vienna in the north, the Caspian Sea in the east, the coastal territories on either side of the Red Sea in the south, and almost the whole of the North African coast. Thereafter the Ottoman empire went into slow decline, but it was not finally dissolved until 1922.

SPANISH CONQUEST OF MEXICO

1519–39

"IT WILL GIVE ME GREAT PLEASURE TO FIGHT FOR MY GOD AGAINST YOUR GODS, WHO ARE A MERE NOTHING." Hernan Cortes to the Aztec priesthood, 1521

The early 16th century was a dramatic time in world history. It was when Europe, through its explorers, reached out to the New World. Led largely by the Portuguese and Spanish, European sailors had during the 15th century begun to investigate what lay beyond the horizons of Europe.

The Portuguese had begun to open up Africa's secrets and in 1498 Vasco da Gama reached India by sailing round the Cape of Good Hope. There was also a desire to find a route to the Far East by sailing westwards, and it was this that revealed the New World of the Americas. In 1497 the Italian John Cabot (Giovanni Caboto), who was sponsored by the English king Henry VII, reached North America, while at much the same time fellow Italian Christopher Columbus, under Spanish patronage, discovered South America. He had previously explored the West Indies and now made a landfall on the Venezuelan coast. Subsequently he explored the coast of Central America and learned of the existence of the Pacific Ocean.

The primary motive for these explorations was the opening up of new trading routes to China and the Far East, but the Spanish quickly discovered that Central and South America were themselves sources of treasure, especially gold and silver. While this was the rationale for their colonization of the islands of the Caribbean, the source of the treasure lay on the mainland. It therefore needed to be conquered. Allied to this was a religious element: the Roman Catholic Church gave its blessing to enable a continent's worth of heathens to be converted to Christianity.

Expedition to Mexico

The Spanish annexations in the Caribbean were to be the launch pad for the invasion of the mainland and it was this colonization that resulted in Hernan Cortes leading the expedition to Mexico. He arrived on Hispaniola from Spain at the age of 18 in 1503 and became a notary. In 1511 he took part in the conquest of Cuba and became the mayor of Santiago. Seven years later Diego Velazquez, the governor of Cuba, put Cortes in charge of an expedition to claim the Mexican hinterland for Spain. Two expeditions had already recently visited the country. The first, under Hernandez de Cordoba, had reached the Yucatan peninsula in 1517, but had been attacked in the night by the indigenous Mayans. Cordoba lost his life and only a remnant of the expedition returned to Cuba. The following year Velazquez sent out another expedition, this time under his nephew, with the task of visiting the Tabasco region, which stretches from west of Yucatan to the Caribbean coast. This, however, had not yet returned when Cortes set out.

Governor Velazquez's orders to Cortes were primarily concerned with establishing trade with the tribes, but he appears to have become suspicious that Cortes had a more

OPPOSITE *The final and decisive battle for Tenochtitlan as portrayed by an Aztec artist. It shows the advantages that the Conquistadors enjoyed over the Aztec warriors in terms of both personal protection and the possession of guns.*

ambitious agenda and attempted to prevent the expedition from taking place. Cortes ignored his superior's orders and set sail from Santiago in February 1519. His force consisted of 600 men, 17 horses and 12 cannon carried in 11 ships. The Mexico that he was approaching was made up of two significant groupings. The southern part of the country had traditionally been home to the Mayan civilization, traces of which can still be seen today, especially its pyramids. By the time the Spanish arrived Mayan power was in decline and had already broken up into a number of small independent city states.

Central Mexico was dominated by the Aztecs. They were not a single tribe, but an alliance of three city states – Tenochtitlan, Texcoco and Tlacopan – which were situated in the Valley of Mexico, the region around Mexico City today. Tenochtitlan was the leading city, while the empire stretched from coast to coast. Much of it contained other city states that paid tribute to the three core states. In 1519 the overall Aztec ruler was Moctezuma II (popularly but incorrectly known as Montezuma) who had ascended the throne in 1502.

Cortes encounters the Aztecs

Cortes made his first landfall at Cozumel, an island off the Caribbean side of the Yucatan peninsula. He spent some time trying to convert the natives to Christianity and also made contact with two survivors of a Spanish shipwreck of 1511. One, Geronimo de Aguilar, joined the expedition and, with his knowledge of local languages, proved very useful to Cortes. The other man had taken a Mayan wife and preferred to remain. Cortes then sailed round the Caribbean side of the peninsula and landed on the Tabasco coast. He fought a brief but successful battle against the local Mayans and acquired another valuable asset. This was an Aztec woman, known as La Malinche, who had been a slave of the Mayans and was to become Cortes's mistress, bearing him a child. With Aguilar translating Spanish into Mayan, and La Malinche Mayan into Nahault, the language of the Aztecs, Cortes could now speak to the Aztecs, who were to be his main obstacle.

The Spanish set sail once again. It was now July and Cortes set about preparations for an advance into the Aztec heartland. His policy was to try to bring the native states that he came across to his side, initially through negotiation. He was at first successful with the local Totonac people. They helped him build a settlement, which he called La Villa Rica de la Vera Cruz ('the rich town of the true cross'), today the major Mexican port of Veracruz. Cortes's men appointed him captain-general and as such he considered that he was no longer answerable to Velazquez but to King Charles of Spain, who had just been elected the Holy Roman emperor as Charles V. Cortes learned that Moctezuma's seat of power was at Tenochtitlan and decided that this must be his next objective.

Some of his men were still loyal to Velazquez and there were indications that they might mutiny and take ship back to Cuba. Cortes therefore took the drastic action of burning all his ships, apart from one which he would use to carry despatches and treasure back to the Spanish court. Then, in September 1519, he set off inland, leaving 100 of his men at Vera Cruz. Included in his force were some of the local natives whom he used to haul his guns. The province neighbouring Vera Cruz was, and still is, Tlaxcala. This was a loose confederation of a number of towns based around the city of Tlaxcala, which were under constant threat from the Aztecs. The Tlaxcalans were initially hostile, and after a number of skirmishes, the Spaniards found themselves surrounded on a hill. Their opponents then had second thoughts and decided that Cortes would be a useful ally against the Aztecs. They therefore welcomed him into Tlaxcala. Cortes respected their way of life and their temples, though he did put pressure on the Tlaxcalan leaders to convert to Christianity. Some at least appear to have done so, though they merely regarded the Christian god as an addition to their own deities.

Cortes soon met representatives from Moctezuma. It seems that they regarded him as an emissary of their serpent god Quetzalcoatl and they wanted him to move on to Cholula, a town south of Tlaxcala that was under Aztec influence. The Tlaxcalans, on the other hand, wanted him to visit a city allied to them. Cortes decided to make for Cholula, sending two of his officers on ahead to Tenochtitlan. He was accompanied by 3000 Tlaxcalan warriors. What happened when Cortes arrived in Cholula is a matter of debate: some accounts state that Moctezuma ordered the Cholulans to prevent the Spaniards from advancing further, so they hatched a plot to kill Cortes's men in their sleep. Others say that this was because a Tlaxcalan ambassador had been tortured by the Cholulans. Whatever the cause, Cortes turned on his new hosts, massacring many of their leaders. He then continued on his way to the Aztec capital.

On 9 November 1519 the Conquistadors ('conquerors'), as these Spanish soldier explorers came to be known, finally arrived at Tenochtitlan, then one of the largest cities

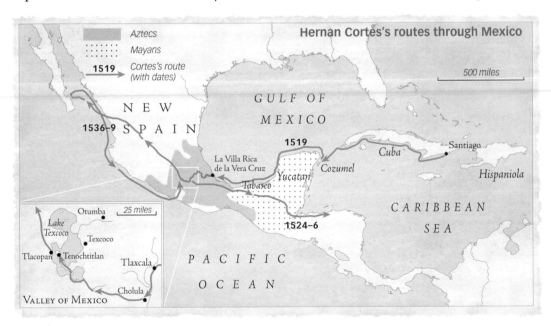

The Aztec warrior

THE AZTECS WERE A WARRIOR RACE. On the birth of a male child, its umbilical cord was buried with a shield and arrows so as to dedicate it to war. While some would go on to be priests, others would join a military school, where they learned the arts of war. However, if they were to be acknowledged as professional warriors, they had to prove themselves by killing enemies or capturing prisoners. The opportunities for this were numerous, since there was constant skirmishing among the Mexican city states. The Aztec warrior had a further motivation: his sun god Huitzilopochtli required a daily human sacrifice to placate him. Live prisoners were therefore a valuable commodity. The main Aztec weapons were the bow, javelin, sword and a wooden club with sharp cutting edges fashioned from volcanic rock, which was called a *macuahuitl*. The cream of the warriors wore entire jaguar skins and were known as the Jaguar Knights. A typical Aztec battle began with a barrage of arrows and javelins, followed by a charge and then hand-to-hand fighting. Following the warriors would be other soldiers equipped with rope to secure prisoners. Since, unlike the Conquistadors, they wore no armour and their only protection was a small round shield, the Aztec warrior was little match for 16th-century European weaponry, though his courage was never found wanting.

in the world and situated in the midst of a large lake. Moctezuma had heard of what happened at Cholula and gave Cortes and his men a warm welcome. He housed them all in one of the royal palaces and gave Cortes gifts of gold. In return, Cortes demanded that the Aztec ruler accept Emperor Charles V as his overlord, and provide more gold as proof. He also ordered the removal of some of the Aztec idols and that they should be replaced by Christian shrines. The Aztecs did as he wished, but it was not enough. To ensure that there was no revolt Cortes imprisoned Moctezuma in his own palace and demanded further large amounts of gold as a ransom. Cortes seemed to be in total control, but he now faced a major distraction.

Governor Velazquez was still determined to bring Cortes to book for ignoring his orders to cancel the expedition. He therefore sent out a force of more than 1000 men under Panfilo de Narvaez to land in Mexico and arrest Cortes. As soon as news reached the Conquistador in Tenochtitlan he set out with some 450 men to confront Narvaez, leaving the remainder under Pedro de Alvarado to hold the Aztec capital. Cortes defeated Narvaez and persuaded his surviving followers to join him. He then went back to Tenochtitlan to find a very different state of affairs to that which he had left. Fearing a revolt, Alvarado had massacred a number of Aztec nobles. This triggered an uprising and the Conquistadors found themselves besieged with Moctezuma in his palace. Cortes got the imprisoned ruler to speak to his people, but they merely threw stones at him, injuring him to such an extent that he later died from his wounds. There was now only one option in Cortes's view: he would have to evacuate the city.

On the night of 30 June 1520, Cortes carried out his break-out, using a portable bridge to get across gaps in the causeway on the lake. The Aztecs resisted bitterly and the Spanish casualties, and those of their allies, were heavy. Nevertheless, they succeeded and then made their way round Lake Zumpango towards the relative safety of Tlaxcala. The Aztecs fought them again at Otumba on 7 July, but were defeated. This enabled Cortes to reach Tlaxcala, where he licked his wounds and made preparations to regain the Aztec capital.

Destruction of the Aztec empire

Cortes decided that there were two essential requirements. He needed ships to get across the water surrounding Tenochtitlan, since trying to force the causeways would be likely to cause unacceptable casualties. He therefore set about constructing a dozen or so vessels. He also needed the active help of the Tlaxcalans. After some debate the latter agreed in return for not having to pay tribute to the Spanish, being given the city of Cholula, and being granted the right to construct a fortress in Tenochtitlan so that they could control the city. Cortes eventually set out once more in May 1521. Brushing aside opposition and capturing other Aztec cities, Cortes reached Tenochtitlan at the end of the month and besieged it. His vessels, each armed with a cannon, dominated the lake. The Aztecs were also suffering from smallpox, which the Conquistadors had brought with them and against which the natives had no immunity: a common fate for indigenous peoples who came into contact with early European explorers and colonists. Eventually, on 13 August, Cortes made his final assault from three directions. Cuauhtemoc, the last of the rulers, surrendered to him and the Aztec empire was at an end.

Tenochtitlan itself had been badly damaged during the siege. Cortes completed its destruction and then began to construct a new city over the ruins, which today is Mexico City. He was now the *de facto* ruler of Mexico, and was appointed governor and captain-general of 'New Spain of the Ocean Sea' by Emperor Charles V. But he did not have things all his own way, since the emperor insisted on sending out four officials to assist him. Indeed, there were suspicions back in Spain that Cortes was attempting to create an independent kingdom for himself. As a further restraint on him the Spanish crown sent a separate force to conquer northern Mexico. Cortes complained to Charles V and the force's commander was ordered not to interfere with him politically, which placed him under Cortes's control. In 1524 Cortes led an expedition southwards into present-day Honduras. He defeated another Conquistador, who, with the support of Cortes's old enemy Velazquez, had claimed the territory for himself. On his return he found that he had been suspended from office by a commissioner with special powers, who had been sent out from Spain. Eventually, in 1528, the new governor ordered Cortes out of the country, so he sailed back to Spain to plead with Charles V.

Mexican treasure and the wealth of Spain

Spanish law stipulated that a fifth of all treasure acquired in the New World had to be sent back to the monarch. This was transported in the so-called treasure fleets, which sailed twice a year. One of the charges levelled against Cortes was that he had retained more treasure than was permitted. He was able to convince the emperor that this was not so and that he had spent much of his own money on the rebuilding of Tenochtitlan. Charles V was impressed and made Cortes marquis of the Oaxaca valley, which confirmed him as possessor of the land that he had acquired in Mexico. The new marquis returned to Mexico in 1530, but he no longer had complete power. This was confirmed five years later with the appointment of a viceroy who had total political control of New Spain. Cortes was, however, allowed to remain military commander and this enabled him during 1536–9 to explore and annexe northwestern Mexico, including the peninsula known today as Baja California, for the Spanish crown. But he still had enemies and in 1541 felt forced to return to Spain to defend himself in the courts against accusations of abuse of power and debts. He decided to return to the New World in 1547, but died of pleurisy before he could leave Spain.

The region of Mexico that took longest to subdue was the Mayan territory in the south. Apart from the fierce resistance of the Mayans themselves, the region lacked the sources of treasure that the remainder of the country enjoyed. Consequently, the Spanish did not have the same motivation to control it. Indeed, it was not until the end of the 17th century that the last of the Mayan city states were finally subdued. Even so, well before this it was not just local treasure that was filling Spanish coffers, but also goods from the Far East, which Spanish ships were soon transporting to Mexico's Pacific coast. Allied to this was the conquest of the remainder of Central and South America.

In the 1520s the Spanish had begun to explore the northwest coast of South America and establish colonies. In 1531 Francisco Pizarro landed on the coast of Peru and quickly overcame the dominant people there, the Incas, capturing and then murdering their emperor. The Spanish also secured Chile. There was, however, considerable in-fighting among the Conquistadors and it was not until 1580 that royal authority over the region was properly established. Simultaneously with this Spanish activity the Portuguese were slowly absorbing Brazil. Later in the century the Spanish also began to settle Argentina and swallowed up the remainder of the continent, apart from the extreme northeast, where the Dutch and the French established their own small footholds.

The Spanish empire in the Americas would last for nigh on 300 years. It would leave an enduring legacy in the form of language, the Roman Catholic religion and architecture. But it also caused the sudden demise of ancient indigenous civilizations. For a time the empire – especially Mexico, the first of its major conquests and, on account of its natural resources, the jewel in the crown – would make Spain rich. Yet, the acquisition of this empire bred envy among other European nations and the resultant rivalry would prove a source of conflict throughout the coming centuries, beginning with attacks on the Spanish treasure fleet well before the 16th century had ended.

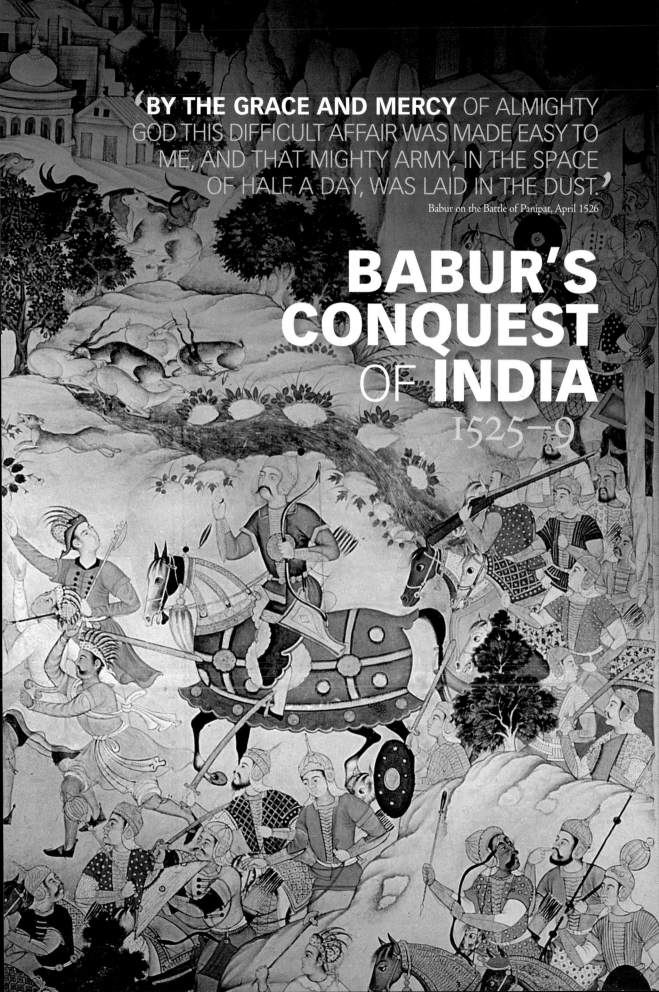

'**BY THE GRACE AND MERCY** OF ALMIGHTY GOD THIS DIFFICULT AFFAIR WAS MADE EASY TO ME, AND THAT MIGHTY ARMY, IN THE SPACE OF HALF A DAY, WAS LAID IN THE DUST.'

Babur on the Battle of Panipat, April 1526

BABUR'S CONQUEST OF INDIA
1525–9

India in the early 16th century was essentially two major regions divided by religion. The south of the country was the traditional home of the Dravidians, who were thought to be the original inhabitants of the subcontinent and whose languages were similar. The north, on the other hand, was originally the land of the Aryans. They had invaded from the north *c.*1500 BC.

In more recent times, from the 11th century AD onwards, northern India had been subjected to further invasion from the followers of Islam. This became the dominant religion in the north, as Hinduism was in the south. Yet, none of these invasions succeeded in uniting the subcontinent into one country.

The Delhi sultanate
The Delhi sultanate, which was established at the beginning of the 13th century, succeeded in exerting influence even over the south of India during the first half of the following century, but it did not last. By 1350 the south had broken away again. The Delhi regime still ruled over most of northern India, but this became splintered when the Mongol conqueror Tamerlane invaded in 1398. He took Delhi, virtually destroyed it, and, after leaving a trail of destruction, returned to Samarkand from whence he had come. He did leave a governor, but his control was at best tenuous, and the regime often found itself at war with neighbouring states that had broken away. During the second half of the 15th century the Delhi sultanate revived to an extent under the Lodhi dynasty, which was Afghan in origin. This was especially so under Sikander Lodhi, but a split occurred on his death in 1517. His elder son Ibrahim came into conflict with Afghan refugees, who had been driven south by the Mongol invasions and felt they were being treated as second-class citizens. It was in this context that Ibrahim's younger brother Jalal Khan tried to form a breakaway kingdom in the east. Ibrahim defeated and executed him. He then had to face a revolt by the Afghan Pashtuns in northern Punjab.

Babur plans a rebirth of Mongol power
To the north of the sultanate the king of Kabul had been watching events. Zahir-ud-Din Muhammad, or 'Babur', was a descendant of both Genghis Khan and Tamerlane. While the latter had created a significant empire based in Samarkand, it had steadily crumbled under his successors. When Babur succeeded as an 11-year-old boy in 1494, his kingdom consisted merely of the city of Fergana in present-day eastern Uzbekistan. His throne was under threat from his uncles from the outset, but he was determined to re-establish the Timurid empire of his ancestors. He began in 1497 by recapturing Samarkand, but then

PREVIOUS PAGE *A Moghul army pursuing a defeated enemy, with at least one man (right centre) carrying a firearm. Although Babur had the instincts of his Mongol ancestors, he inevitably faced superior numbers and knew the value of gunpowder weapons.*

lost both it and Fergana to the Uzbeks. Four years later he briefly held Samarkand again and set about building up a new army before crossing the mountains into present-day Afghanistan, capturing Kabul in 1504. This provided him with a new kingdom. He later formed an alliance with Ismail I, the ruler of Persia, which enabled him to seize Samarkand for the third time. In return, Babur adopted the dress and customs of a Shi'ite Muslim, Persia being the stronghold of this branch of Islam. Samarkand was, however, a Sunni base, and Babur's Shi'ite posture was strongly resented. Thus, he was unable to hold the city, which was regained by the Uzbeks. With Fergana also beyond his reach, Babur began to turn his eyes southwards to India.

Babur's reasoning was that since Tamerlane had overrun the Delhi sultanate and installed his own deputy to govern it, it was his duty to reclaim it for the Timurids. But, bearing in mind the reverses that he had suffered in the past, he needed to proceed with a certain amount of caution. He began by sending Ibrahim a message demanding that he recognize Babur's claim to the sultanate. Unsurprisingly this was not accepted. Then, fearing that the Uzbeks might strike from the west, he laid siege to the mighty fortress city of Kandahar, which was held by the Arghuns, another Mongol race. It took Babur three years to wear it down and it did not finally fall until 1522. Babur had already been carrying out raiding operations into northern India, but now he could prepare for a full-scale invasion.

He had already allied himself with the Janjua Rajputs from Kashmir, who had long rebelled against the rule of the Delhi sultanate, and helped them to defeat their enemies the Gakhars, who inhabited the region immediately north of Punjab. Admiring the martial qualities of the Rajputs, Babur appointed a number of them officers in his army. He then made an alliance with Daulat Khan Lodhi, the governor of Punjab, who proposed that Babur attack the city of Lahore. Daulat Khan arranged, however, for Babur to be confronted by an Afghan army. This was defeated and Babur entered Lahore and sacked it, leaving after four days. He learned of Daulat Khan's double dealing and imprisoned him and his uncle. He then returned to Kabul to deal with unrest there.

The Battle of Panipat and the end of the Delhi sultanate

Towards the end of 1525 Babur set out again. He had an army of 12,000 men, which was small compared with the forces that the Delhi sultanate could mass against him, but he possessed two valuable weapons. The first was his highly manoeuvrable mounted archers – the traditional Mongol weapon. More important, and unlike his enemies, he had gunpowder in the form of cannon and matchlock arquebuses. In 1514 Babur's ally Ismail I of Persia had been soundly defeated by the Ottomans at Chaldiran and the Turkish use of gunpowder weapons had made a deep impression on Babur. He had therefore introduced them in his army and arranged for a Turk called Ustad Ali to train his cannoneers and matchlockmen. This time there was no attempt to hold him up at

Lahore and so he bypassed the city and pressed on towards Delhi. His first clash with Ibrahim Lodhi's forces came at the end of February 1526. Babur's 17-year-old son Humayan, on his first campaign, was commanding the advanced guard and contacted the leading sultanate elements. It was a hard-fought skirmish, which Humayan won. Some 100 prisoners were captured and Babur had them shot to send out a message to his enemy.

Yet the two armies were not to have a major clash for almost two months. Babur eventually closed with Ibrahim's army at the village of Panipat, just over 50 miles north of Delhi, on 12 April. Knowing that he was heavily outnumbered (Ibrahim had some 100,000 men and 100 elephants), Babur decided to take up a defensive position and invite Ibrahim to attack him. He placed his cannon and matchlockmen in the centre and, as the Turks had done at Chaldiran, fortified their position with a line of wagons and breastworks. He also fortified his left and right flanks with ditches and walls of felled trees. He was careful, however, to leave gaps so that his cavalry could pass through when the opportunity arose. Ibrahim watched these preparations impassively, making no attempt at all to attack, even when he was constantly provoked by the frequent raids of Babur's cavalry.

Eventually Babur became impatient and on 20 April he mounted a night attack. It was not a success and was repulsed with some ease. This clearly encouraged Ibrahim and he decided to attack on the following day. Preceded by the elephants, his men advanced in close order towards the right wing of Babur's position. Babur now employed another Mongol tactic, sending out some of his cavalry to sweep round both flanks of Ibrahim's

Afghan army in order to attack it in the rear. The Afghan infantry came to a halt in front of the ditch and wooden wall and began to suffer dreadfully from shot and arrows. Babur sent more horsemen through the gaps in his line to deal with the elephants, which became maddened by arrow wounds. Babur now began to counter-attack with his left wing. The Afghans resisted for a time and even renewed their attacks, but there was no stopping Babur's troops. His flanking cavalry had by now got into the rear of Ibrahim's army, cutting off its line of retreat. Ibrahim himself perished and by midday there was no doubt that Babur had won a great victory and brought the Delhi sultanate to an end.

He immediately sent his son Humayan off to Agra, which had been the sultanate's capital since 1504, to secure its treasures. Babur himself made for Delhi, reaching it in three days. After celebrating there he joined Humayan in Agra. It was here that Humayan presented his father with a fabulous diamond which had been in the possession of the Rajahs of Gwalior. Known as the *Koh-i-Noor* or 'Mountain of Light' it is today the centrepiece of the crown of Queen Elizabeth of Great Britain.

Babur may have secured the sultanate, but to the southwest lay the lands of the Rajputs, a confederation of princely states headed by Rana Sanga of Mewar. True, he had allied himself with Babur to overthrow the sultanate, but his main ambition was to reclaim the territory to the north that the Rajputs had lost to the Muslims nearly three and a half centuries earlier. Rana Sanga was therefore determined to challenge Babur and was encouraged by reports that his troops were discontented, especially by the heat of the Indian summer, and wanted to return home. He therefore began to mass an army. For the first time Babur was opposed by a non-Muslim enemy (the Rajputs were Hindus). To ensure that his discontented troops would do his bidding, he therefore declared a *Jihad* or holy war.

Holy war against the Hindus

Babur now advanced to meet the Rajputs and did so at Khanua (also known as Khanwa), some 40 miles west of Agra in mid-March 1527. Once again Babur was outnumbered, but, as with the sultanate, his opponents did not possess gunpowder weapons. Yet, in the first clash Babur's advance guard was entirely destroyed. Rana Sanga failed, however, to follow up this initial success, largely because of bickering among his allies. This enabled Babur to do as he had done at Panipat. He hastily constructed defences, with gaps in them for his cavalry and artillery. On 17 March Rana Sanga eventually attacked. His 500 elephants could not stand the artillery fire and stampeded. The fire also caused heavy casualties among the massed Rajput ranks. Others were caused by flank attacks from Babur's cavalry. Rana Sanga also added to the many wounds that he had already received in battle, being struck by an arrow. Yet, the Rajputs continued to display their customary martial ardour and the fighting raged for several hours with the issue still in doubt. Finally, sensing that the battle was about to be lost, one of Rana Sanga's most trusted generals took his men over to Babur's side. This proved to be the turning point and Rana Sanga was forced to withdraw. He himself died of his wounds soon afterwards, although many suspected that he had been poisoned. Babur, however, did not follow up his victory by advancing on Mewar but instead returned to Agra, giving himself the title of *Ghazi* ('holy warrior'), as the great Tamerlane had done during his Indian campaign.

Expansion of the Mughal empire

Babur now began a short period of consolidation of his growing empire. He ennobled a number of people, some of whom had been former enemies, to govern the provinces and granted them permission to raise their own armies, thus saving himself the cost of doing so. He also promised them as yet unconquered land. He set out on an ambitious building programme, constructing palaces whose architecture combined the traditional indigenous form with those used by the Turks and Persians. Noteworthy were his gardens, each containing shaded areas to protect from the fierce Indian sun. But his campaigning days were not yet over.

Ibrahim Lodhi's brother was still alive and had been mobilizing the Afghan nobility in northeastern India. On 6 May 1529 Babur's forces met the Afghans on the river Gogra (or Ghaghra) near Patna and defeated them. The third of his great victories gained Babur Bengal and Bihar. He was now master of northern India and the age of the Mughal empire had begun.

Babur himself died in 1530 at the age of 48. He was not only a great warrior, but also a man of letters, who wrote his own autobiography and several poems. Indeed, he was very enlightened for his time. He was succeeded by his son Humayan, whose reign was an uneven one. He seized Gujerat and then lost it. But in 1537 the governor of Bihar, an Afghan-Turk called Sher Khan revolted, defeated Humayan in battle and forced him to flee to Persia. Sher Khan ruled northern India for six years as Sher Shah, but was killed during a siege in 1545. The region then suffered a decade of anarchy, which eventually enabled Humayan to regain his throne, only to die in 1556. His eldest son, 14-year-old Akbar, succeeded, but only after fighting another battle at Panipat against a Hindu rival. He proved to be as enlightened as his grandfather, especially in the religious tolerance that he exercised.

Thus the Mughal empire was restored and began to expand. It reached the height of its power during the reign of Aurangzeb (1658–1707), when it encompassed Afghanistan and almost the whole of the Indian subcontinent, apart from its southern-most tip. But Aurangzeb also sowed the seeds of its decline. Unlike his predecessors, he was a religious zealot, instituting a tax on non-Muslims and allowing tax collectors to become a landed aristocracy. The resultant resentment caused a weakening of the bonds that bound the empire together and led to the rise of the Hindu Marathas. By the 1750s

War elephants

THE USE OF THE ELEPHANT as a weapon of war on the Indian subcontinent can be traced back to c.1100 BC. In time they came to be used by the Persian empire and Alexander encountered them at the Battle of Gaugamela in 331 BC. So impressed was he by them that he took some to India, but their use was considerably more widespread. The Chinese began to use elephants in the sixth century BC, and they also spread to the Middle East and North Africa. Hannibal's use of elephants during his invasion of Italy during the Second Punic War (218–202 BC) certainly caused consternation among the Romans. It was, however, primarily in south Asia that the elephant was regarded as a major weapon, not least because they were widely available. The war elephant was used in two basic ways. The first was as a weapon of shock action, using their massive weight literally to crush the opposition. Their thick hides, often protected by additional armour, made it very difficult to incapacitate them and the sight of them was often sufficient to cause panic. Horses, in particular, were unnerved by elephants if unaccustomed to their scent. The other use was as a mobile weapons platform, especially for archers. The major drawback was that if an elephant could be panicked through wounds or other means it became a liability. But, as the forces fighting Babur discovered, gunpowder weapons proved the most effective antidote and brought about the elephant's demise as a weapon of war. Even so, they continued to be used for centuries to come for towing heavy artillery and carrying supplies, and as late as the Second World War, were employed on engineering tasks in Burma.

they controlled most of central India. The French and British were also empire building and the Mughal empire had been reduced to merely the region around Delhi. Yet, the Mughal emperor remained in place and it was not until what the British called the Indian Mutiny and the Indians the First War of Independence of 1857–8 that the dynasty came to a final end.

Babur's creation of the Mughal empire in the space of just five years had a significant impact on the history of the subcontinent. For the first time it began to get a sense of nationhood and the Mughal dominance had a lasting influence on culture. In military terms it was specifically Babur who was responsible for introducing gunpowder to the region. Considering the setbacks of his early years, he achieved much in his relatively short life.

✦ ✦ ✦

JAPANESE CIVIL WARS
1560–90

DO YOU REALLY WANT TO SPEND YOUR ENTIRE LIVES PRAYING FOR LONGEVITY? WE WERE BORN IN ORDER TO DIE! WHOEVER IS WITH ME, COME TO THE BATTLE-FIELD TOMORROW MORNING. WHOEVER IS NOT, JUST STAY WHEREVER YOU ARE AND WATCH ME WIN IT!'

The era beginning in 1467 is known in Japan as the period of Warring States. The reason for this was the system of government, which for centuries caused internal unrest. At the top was the emperor, who was regarded as a divine figure, in both Confucian and Shinto terms, and descended from the Shinto sun goddess.

Originally the emperor ruled through the Council of State, and the most powerful clans were constantly vying for office within it, since it was here that the true power lay. The heads of these clans were known as *daimyo* ('great name'). They were landowners and over time came to be province rulers. They also formed their own private armies of *samurai* (see Box). As their political power increased, that of the emperor and his court waned. But the thirst for power among the daimyo resulted in internal strife. During the 11th century the rivalry came down to that between two families. At first the Taira were in the ascendancy before the Minamoto defeated them. By the end of the century, a Minamoto had been appointed *shogun*, a word which literally means 'generalissimo', by the emperor.

Warring States period

The shogun was originally a purely military appointment, but now he was the real power behind the throne. There was a brief period, between 1333 and 1336, when imperial rule was restored, but thereafter the shogunate continued under the Ashikaga clan. However, neither it nor the emperor were able to control the daimyo as a whole. By the 1460s these had grown to some 260 in number and each was in effect head of a private fiefdom jockeying for more power and influence. It was inevitable that conflict would increase, and the opening of the Warring States period in 1467 was marked initially by a struggle between two of the most powerful daimyo families. The fighting started in Kyoto, then the imperial seat, and it was reduced to rubble by the end. It spread across the whole country as the other daimyo sided with one or the other of the two main protagonists.

The Onin War, as it was called, lasted a decade and at the end the daimyo did submit to the shogun. In truth, the Hosokawa family, which had come out on top by the end of the war, now established itself in Kyoto and controlled the Ashikaga shogunate, but other families attempted to take their place and so the strife continued. In particular, the major players would seek to create unrest in the provinces held by their rivals so as to force them to withdraw from the field. There were, too, cases of vassal families betraying their daimyo, often as a result of being bribed. It was this that forced the Hosokawa family to release their hold over the shogunate in 1558. Even so, the clan remained in Kyoto and continued to be a significant force.

OPPOSITE *A depiction of a 16th-century Japanese general ready for battle. His armour is made up of metal plates and his sword represents the high watermark of Japanese sword-making.*

Rise of Oda Nobunaga

By this time the country was exhausted and not many of the daimyo families were left standing. Into this growing vacuum stepped Oda Nobunaga. Born in 1534 in Owari province, today the western part of Aichi prefecture in the central part of Honshu Island, he was the son of the deputy governor responsible for the province. As a youth he was somewhat eccentric – ill disciplined and lacking of awareness of his social position. On the death of his father in 1551 Nobunaga should have succeeded as the ruler of Owari province, but other elements of the Oda clan opposed him. He spent the next eight years fighting for his position, being forced on at least two occasions to assassinate enemies, and also forming alliances with neighbouring daimyo.

By 1560 Nobunaga's hold over Owari was finally secure. But in the spring of that year a major threat came in the form of Imagawa Yoshimoto, one of the leading daimyo. He gathered an army of 25,000 men and began to march on Kyoto in a bid for power. He spread false rumours that he actually had 40,000 men at his back and this persuaded a number of the lesser daimyo in his path not to oppose him. Nobunaga was made of sterner stuff. He did not believe that Yoshimoto had so many men. Even so, he only had some 2000 himself, and his generals believed that he had no chance of victory. Nobunaga overruled them. His scouts had told him that Yoshimoto's army was resting in a narrow gorge near the village of Okehazama and celebrating their victories thus far. Knowing the area well, Nobunaga was convinced that he could surprise his enemy.

Accordingly, he marched out of his castle and halted at a distance from the gorge. He then got his men to construct dummies out of straw and positioned these and a multitude of flags to give the impression of a large army. Having done this, he led his men rapidly round to the rear of the gorge. A sudden thunderstorm now erupted. This sent Yoshimoto's men scurrying for shelter and enabled Nobunaga to deploy his troops without being seen. The storm now ceased as suddenly as it had started. Nobunaga's men charged and such was the surprise that Yoshimoto did not realize what was happening until he was attacked by two samurai, one of whom sliced off his head with a sword. This marked the end of the Imagawa clan as a significant force.

Nobunaga's victory at Okehazama greatly enhanced his reputation. Other clans began to respect him and wanted to ally themselves to the Oda clan. He himself believed that he could, given time, bring the whole country under his thrall, so he set about dealing with the powerful Saito clan, whose base was Mino province (now the southern half of Gifu prefecture). It should be noted that the daimyo, like the nobles in medieval Europe, regarded castles as their power base and Nobunaga usually conducted his campaigns from a castle. In this case he located himself in Komaki Castle and initially conducted a largely psychological campaign. Saito Yoshitatsu, head of the Saito clan and a renowned soldier, had died in 1561. His son Tatsuoki succeeded him, but he was a mere shadow of his father. Nobunaga used this to convince a number of his followers to change sides, considerably weakening the Saito military strength. As a result, Nobunaga captured the Saito stronghold Inabayama Castle in 1567 and sent Tatsuoki into exile. His power was growing, but he still had a long way to go if he was to unify the country. Yet an opportunity now arose to reach the very heart of government, the shogunate.

In 1565 the Miyoshi clan murdered the shogun, Ashikaga Yoshiteru, and installed a puppet in his place whom they controlled. Three years later, after Nobunaga's victory over the Saito clan, he was approached by Yoshiteru's brother Yoshiaki who was seeking revenge and wanted him to march on Kyoto. Nobunaga readily agreed and, quickly brushing aside opposition, soon entered the city. He drove the Miyoshi and Hosokawa clans out and installed Yoshiaki as shogun. This might have produced some much needed stability, but it did not. Nobunaga really wanted the shogun to support him in his aim of bringing the whole country under his control and ensured that his powers were restricted. Yoshiaki resented this and began to create an anti-Nobunaga alliance.

The cornerstone of this new alliance was the Asakura clan, which had traditionally been overlord of Nobunaga's Oda clan. Its head, Yoshikage, had also supported Yoshiaki but had declined the invitation to advance on Kyoto. He was therefore jealous of Nobunaga's success and considered him an upstart. The alliance grew in strength and began to take an increasing toll on the Oda clan. It was also supported by fanatical armed Buddhist monks. Nobunaga was therefore hard pressed to bring matters under control and resorted to ever more brutal methods. In 1571 he stormed the Enryaku-ji monastery just outside Kyoto and put some 4000 people, including women and children, to the sword. Other massacres occurred elsewhere.

RIGHT *Oda Nobunaga was the epitome of a Japanese daimyo. He was ruthless and sly, but realized that Japan would suffer perpetual conflict unless it could be united under strong central rule.*

Defeat of the Takeda clan

1573 was to prove a turning point. The previous year the
Takeda clan, which had been allied to the Oda clan, began
an advance to drive Nobunaga out of Kyoto. It meant that it
crossed territory belonging to Nobunaga's close ally Tokugawa
Ieyasu. At the time Nobunaga was tied up elsewhere and
could not give Ieyasu much help and he suffered a defeat.
Fortuitously, the Takeda clan chief died of an illness shortly
after the battle and his forces withdrew. Nobunaga could now
concentrate on Yoshiaki, whom he decisively defeated in battle
and sent into exile. This marked the end of the Ashikaga
shogunate after nearly 240 years. He then went on to crush
both the Asakura and Azai clans. This confirmed Nobunaga
as one of the leading warlords.

The Takeda clan was still in the field, however, with
Takeda Katsuyori now at its head. He was determined to
finish off what his father had started and in May 1575 began
another advance on Kyoto. Barring his way by threatening his
lines of communication was Nagashino Castle, which was the
main base of Tokugawa Ieyasu. Katsuyori placed it under
siege, but one of the defenders managed to get out with
a message of help. Nobunaga and Ieyasu responded by
leading a relief force.

The two armies met near a village some three miles
southwest of the castle on 28 June. At 30,000 men, the
Oda–Tokugawa forces had twice the strength of their
opponents. However, the Takeda army was renowned for its
cavalry, which had brought about victory several times in the
past and was some 5000 strong. Nobunaga's prized weapon
were his 3000 matchlockmen. This was thanks to the
Portuguese, who had arrived in Japan just over 30 years earlier
and established trading posts, with guns being one of the
commodities on offer. The remainder of the Oda–Tokugawa
army consisted of samurai armed with swords and short
spears and the ordinary foot-soldiers or *ashigaru*, who were
conscripted by the warlords. They were generally armed with long lances, as well as
providing the matchlockmen. Both the opposing sides also employed archers.

Nobunaga and Ieyasu decided to invite Katsuyori to attack them with his cavalry.
They selected a position behind a stream. Some 200 yards beyond this was a wood from

which the Takeda troops would have to emerge. The distance was crucial since this was the maximum range of the matchlock, although it was only effective at 50 yards against men in armour. To protect his gunners Nobunaga had a palisade built in front of them. He then sent out parties to feint frontal attacks in order to provoke Katsuyori into attacking. He duly obliged and his cavalry advanced through the wood and then charged once they emerged. As their horses slowed to cross the stream the matchlockmen engaged them with volley fire, inflicting heavy casualties. Those horses that did get through the palisade were speared, while individual warriors who made it through were tackled by the samurai. By mid-afternoon Katsuyori's men had had enough and broke, only to be ruthlessly pursued by their enemies.

Clans unite against Nobunaga

The humbling of the Takeda clan enabled Nobunaga to continue his expansion. He also laid siege to the militant Buddhist monastery of Ishiyama Hongan-ji on the coast at Osaka. The monks refused to surrender and were encouraged to hold out by the Mori clan, which managed to break the naval blockade and slip in supplies. Nobunaga therefore ordered one of his most promising younger generals, Toyotomi Hideyoshi, who had originally been one of his servants, to move westwards and deal with the Mori clan. It was a task that would tie him up for the next few years. Also prominent in what now became a second anti-Nobunaga coalition was the Uesugi clan under Uesugi Kenshin, who also had a high military reputation. Indeed, he succeeded in defeating Nobunaga at the Battle of Tedorigawa in November 1577. Nobunaga had intended to employ his now routine tactic of inviting his enemy to attack and then to defeat him with his firearms. In this case Kenshin carried out a clever feint. Nobunaga thought that he had divided his forces and decided to take offensive action to defeat them piecemeal. Unfortunately for him, Kenshin had done no such thing and repulsed the Oda attack with heavy casualties.

As it happened, Kenshin, like the head of the Takeda clan in 1573, died of an illness in April 1578 just when he was poised to cause Nobunaga serious problems. Thereafter the Uesugi fought among themselves over the succession and this threat to Nobunaga was lifted. In contrast, The Mori clan was still very much in contention and continued to support the monks besieged in Ishiyama Hongan-ji. Nobunaga organized the building of six powerful new warships and this valuable addition to his fleet enabled him to ward off further Mori attempts to break his naval blockade of the monastery. The siege, however, lasted until August 1580, when, faced with increasing starvation, the monks acceded to a request from the emperor to surrender. Nobunaga in this instance spared the defenders and the fall of the monastery marked the end of Buddhist resistance. Meanwhile, Toyotomi Hideyoshi continued his campaign against the Mori clan, steadily besieging and capturing their castles.

Some more tidying up remained. In 1579 Nobunaga sent his second son Nobuo to subdue the small landlocked province of Iga, which lay between Osaka and Nagoya. He made two attempts to bring it under control, but both failed. Therefore, in 1581, Nobunaga himself took an army of 40,000 into the province and brutally crushed all resistance. The following year saw the final defeat of the Takeda clan. Nobunaga massed a large army and with Tokugawa Ieyasu began rapidly to overrun the Takeda provinces. Katsuyori's followers began to desert him and he eventually committed suicide. That May, Nobunaga returned to Azuchi Castle, which he had built a few years earlier just outside Kyoto. The imperial court offered him the shogunate, but he declined to accept or reject it. It seemed, though, that his dream of control over the whole of the country would soon be realized, but it was not to be.

Soon after Nobunaga's return to Kyoto he received a request for reinforcements from Hideyoshi. He was besieging a Mori castle and had learned that the main Mori army was on its way to attack him. Nobunaga was entertaining members of the imperial court at the Honno-ji monastery in Kyoto and immediately despatched almost all the troops he had with him. During the night one of his generals, Akechi Mitsuhide, surrounded the monastery with his troops. It seems that Mitsuhide had a grudge against his overlord for executing a daimyo whom he had persuaded to surrender without bloodshed a few years earlier. Whatever the reason, at dawn the following day, 21 June 1582, Mitsuhide attacked the monastery. With only a few of his guards available, Nobunaga had little chance. He either committed suicide or perished in the fire that broke out during the fighting.

Nobunaga's legacy

Nobunaga had come close to unifying Japan, but it was left to his successors to make it a reality. As soon as he heard of the death Hideyoshi hastily concluded a truce with the Mori clan, rushed back to Kyoto, defeated Mitsuhide and killed him. This put Hideyoshi in a powerful position, but he still had to contend with his rivals. The Oda succession was the main bone of contention. Nobunaga's eldest son had died with him at Honno-ji and of the two remaining offspring, Hideyoshi supported one while the senior Oda clan general sided with the other. Hideyoshi defeated the general in battle and brought most of the clan elders over to his side. But Oda Nobukatsu, whom the general had supported, remained bitter against Hideyoshi and allied himself with Nobunaga's favourite ally, Tokugawa Ieyasu. After some inclusive actions Hideyoshi made peace with Nobukatsu, while Ieyasu accepted that he was Hideyoshi's vassal.

Hideyoshi was now set on being made shogun, but his humble background meant that he was not eligible. Instead, the emperor conferred the title of *kampaku* (regent) on him. He now set about removing the last vestiges of opposition to him. This culminated in the siege and capture of the Hojo clan's stronghold of Odawara in 1590. With the

The samurai tradition

THE *SAMURAI* WERE ORIGINALLY PROFESSIONAL WARRIORS employed by the emperor and his nobles, but in time they began to become the backbone of the various clans and became *daimyo* themselves. Originally they were regarded as uncouth and uneducated, but by the time of the Warring States period they were becoming upwardly mobile and an elite. A samurai was expected to display absolute loyalty to his daimyo, though there were those who owed no allegiance to a particular clan and offered their swords to whoever might accept their services. They were called *ronin*. The training of a samurai was rigorous. He was taught to empty his mind of pride and fear when fighting and to wield his weapons instinctively. He also had to be prepared to commit ritual suicide (*seppuku*) through self-disembowelment rather than surrender. While he fought with most weapons, his trademark became his two swords, the shorter one being used for fighting inside buildings. Under the Tokugawa shogunate the samurai were drawn away from actual combat and became courtiers and administrators who took an increasing interest in the arts. They were, however, the only class still allowed to bear weapons on a daily basis. With the Meiji restoration in 1868 the samurai rapidly lost their rights and position, but their *bushido* ('warrior way') code of conduct lived on in the Japanese Armed Forces until the end of the Second World War.

country now totally in his grip, Hideyoshi wanted to fulfil a dream that Nobunaga had had of conquering China. In 1592 he invaded Korea as a first step. The Chinese intervened at the request of the Korean government and a drawn-out campaign followed, with the Japanese contained around the port of Pusan. They eventually broke out in 1597 and advanced northwards, but disaster struck in November 1597 when the Chinese defeated the Japanese fleet, sinking half of its ships.

Meanwhile, Hideyoshi, whose only son had recently died, nominated his nephew as his heir in early 1592, but the following year his wife gave birth to another son. To avoid complications Hideyoshi first exiled his nephew and then forced him and his family to commit suicide, with those who refused being murdered. Thus he was able to change the succession, but matters did not go the way he wished. Hideyoshi died in September 1598 and the first action taken by the Council of Five Elders, created by him from the leaders of the most powerful clans, was to withdraw the Japanese forces from Korea. The Toyotomi clan remained in control, headed by the bureaucratic Ishida Masanori, who made plain his low regard for the generals who had fought in Korea. Bitterly resentful, they allied themselves to the still ambitious Tokugawa Ieyasu. His base was in the east of the country, while his enemies drew their forces from the west. The two clashed on 21 October 1600 at Sekigahara. Ieyasu was the winner and became shogun. The title would remain in his family for over 200 years, a period during which Japan turned in on itself, banning foreigners from entry, but one that was relatively peaceful compared to that which had gone before. This was largely thanks to Ieyasu and his successors ensuring that the power of the daimyo and their ability to make war was drastically curbed. Japan was now truly one country.

THE
THIRTY
YEARS
WAR
1618–48

ALL THE WARS THAT ARE ON FOOT IN EUROPE
HAVE BEEN FUSED TOGETHER, AND HAVE BECOME
A SINGLE WAR. Gustavus Adolphus, in a letter, 1630

Religion has been a frequent cause of wars and the Thirty Years War, which so ravaged Europe, is a prime example. Its origins lay in the Reformation, which had begun in 1517 when Martin Luther nailed his *Ninety-Five Theses* to the church door in Wittenberg, Saxony, in protest at what he saw as the endemic corruption of the Roman Catholic Church.

There was also discontent over the political power that the papacy exerted over Europe. Luther was followed by others, including the even more fundamentalist John Calvin. Protestantism, as the new form of Christianity was called, proved more attractive to northern Europe than southern. The Roman Catholic response was the Counter-Reformation, which tried to persuade those who had strayed back onto the true path. Germany, then under the overall umbrella of the Holy Roman Empire, remained the centre of the schism, with the north and east generally opting for Protestantism while the south and the west remained constant to Rome.

Legacy of the Reformation for the Holy Roman Empire

An agreement was reached between the Holy Roman emperor and the Elector of Saxony, the figurehead of the Lutheran church, with the 1555 Treaty of Augsburg, by which Lutheran princedoms would be allowed freedom from papal jurisdiction. The treaty did not embrace Calvinism, which was a rising force, nor allow for the rapid spread of Protestantism. As for the Empire itself, election of the emperor was dependent on seven princes, who were heads of major states within the Empire and known as the Electors. By the beginning of the 17th century, and as a result of the Treaty of Augsburg, there were three Catholics, three Protestants and the king of Bohemia, who was also the emperor. He, of course, was a Catholic, but the majority of his Bohemian subjects were Protestants and it was this that constituted the tinderbox for the conflict to come.

Trouble began to brew after the Catholic Duke Maximilian of Bavaria occupied the city of Donauwörth in 1607. This was a result of the Protestant majority in the city preventing the Catholics from holding a procession. But Donauwörth was a 'free' city, meaning that it was ruled directly by the emperor and so, technically, Maximilian had no right to do what he did. In response, the German Protestants, led by the Elector Palatine and Christian of Anhalt, created the Evangelical Union to protect their interests. Maximilian and the Catholics responded by forming the Holy Catholic League and tension rose. In 1611 Matthias deposed his brother Rudolf as king of Bohemia because of the latter's liberal policies on religion. A year later he was elected emperor. Five years later, and because Matthias was childless, his councillors elected his cousin Archduke Ferdinand of Styria as his successor, but the Bohemian Protestants under Count

OPPOSITE *Gustavus Adolphus, the Lion of the North, leads a cavalry charge against the forces of the Catholic League at the Battle of Lützen, 16 November 1632. He was killed when he ran into enemy cavalry in the fog.*

Matthias of Thurn refused to recognize this. A year later, in 1618, in an event known as the Defenestration of Prague, two of the king's leading councillors were thrown out of the windows of Hradschin Castle and the Protestants established their own government. Count Matthias quickly raised an army, though it was little more than a poorly armed militia, and fanned the flames of revolt to neighbouring states.

As yet this was merely a local conflict, but in March 1619 Emperor Matthias died, leaving two thrones vacant. Bohemia and the neighbouring states of Lusatia, Silesia and Moravia, which made up Greater Bohemia, once more declared the election of Archduke Ferdinand to be invalid. Taking advantage of the vacuum and the fact that much of Austria was now in revolt, Thurn invaded the country and laid siege to Vienna. He did now have some allies, however. He was joined outside Vienna by an army from Transylvania and, more importantly, Savoy, which sent a force of mercenaries under Ernst von Mansfeld to Bohemia. Imperial forces now gathered and defeated Mansfeld. This sent Thurn scurrying back from Vienna and the Transylvanians withdrew back into Hungary. At the end of that August, Bohemia's Protestants duly elected Frederick the Elector of Palatine as their new king. Three days later the Archduke Ferdinand was elected emperor and immediately set about gaining allies to help him remove Frederick from his throne. The war was beginning to broaden.

The forces of the Catholic League now began to deploy. Under Count Tilly an army of 25,000 men went to help Maximilian of Bavaria crush the revolt in Austria and invade Bohemia. In a campaign which began in late July 1620 and ended the following January, the two men were entirely successful. Bohemia lost her independence and Frederick was banished. Meanwhile, the Spanish had also intervened. Ambrogio Spinola set out with an army from the Spanish Netherlands, where the Dutch were trying to throw off the Spanish yoke. Spinola's aim was to prevent the German Protestant states from assisting Bohemia. He feinted towards Bohemia and then occupied the cities of the Palatinate.

In spite of these reverses, the Protestants were not beaten. Mansfeld managed to keep his army intact and withdrew to the Rhine valley, where his men subsisted on pillaging the region, a practice that would become characteristic of the war. Armies became like locusts and starvation in the areas that they occupied was commonplace. Frederick now made an alliance with the Dutch, while Brunswick and Baden-Durlach also rallied to his flag. This did not improve his fortunes. After a few early successes, Frederick and his allies were defeated in a series of battles, and by autumn 1622 had withdrawn into Lorraine. He fell out with Mansfeld and the duke of Brunswick, who then took their armies northwards to help the Dutch, who were being invaded by the Spanish. They succeeded in raising the siege of Bergen op Zoom, but otherwise achieved little. Frederick himself was deposed as the Elector Palatine in February 1623, and the title was given to Maximilian of Bavaria in spite of opposition from the Electors of Saxony and Brandenburg. That August Frederick sought peace with Ferdinand, but Mansfeld and other Protestant princes were determined to carry on fighting. Then, in January 1624, France, which was already at war with Spain, entered the conflict against the Habsburg rulers of the empire. They later formed an alliance with Holland, England, Sweden, Denmark, Savoy and Venice and agreed to disrupt Spanish communications between the Netherlands and Italy.

Danish phase: 1625–9

The focus of the war now switched northwards to Denmark. Lutheran King Christian IV exerted significant influence over the north German states and feared that if they were overrun by the Catholics his own position would be threatened. Financed by England and France, he gathered an army of some 35,000 men, including 20,000 mercenaries, and in 1625 began to advance down the line of the river Weser. Mansfeld, who had formed another army with English help, collaborated with the Danes, but was soundly defeated as he attempted to cross the Elbe in April 1626. His victor was the mercenary general Count Albrecht von Wallenstein, who had been hired by the Emperor Ferdinand. Tilly, the other major Catholic commander, also defeated King Christian that August, a victory that

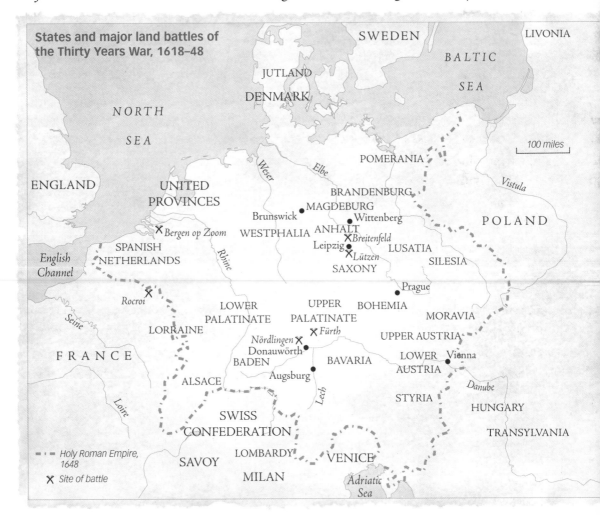

persuaded many Protestant princes to make peace. Faced with a Huguenot uprising at home, France, too, had withdrawn from the Protestant alliance. Furthermore, Mansfeld, who had hoped to combine with the Prince of Transylvania, was forced to disband his army when the latter left the war and he died shortly afterwards. Nevertheless, the Danes made another attempt to advance south in 1627, but were beaten back by Tilly and Wallenstein. They then overran all of Denmark, except for the island of Jutland which they could not reach because they possessed no navy. King Christian was ultimately forced to make peace in June 1629. Furthermore, three months earlier, Emperor Ferdinand had imposed the Edict of Restitution through which all church lands acquired by Protestants since the 1555 Treaty of Augsburg were to be forfeited. It was the nadir of Protestant fortunes, but there were about to be new developments.

Swedish phase: 1630–5

The other major Protestant power in northern Europe was Sweden under its warrior king Gustavus Adolphus. He had stayed out of the conflict because he was at war with Poland over the ownership of Livonia (today's Baltic states). Cardinal Richelieu, the wily chief minister of France, was concerned that the Habsburgs were becoming too powerful in Europe as a result of their victories. He therefore engineered a peace between Sweden and Poland and, even though France was Catholic, agreed to subsidize Gustavus Adolphus in a war against the emperor. The Swedish king was only too willing, since he felt threatened by the Catholic surge. In July 1630 he landed on the Baltic coast and invaded Pomerania. Saxony and Brandenburg, although Protestant, were worried that Gustavus Adolphus might swallow them. They therefore called a conference of Protestant princes who agreed in April 1631 to form their own army under Hans Georg von Arnim. To Swedish eyes, this posed a danger of having to fight the German Protestants as well as the Catholics. Certainly, neither Saxony nor Brandenburg would allow him to enter their territory. Tilly had besieged Magdeburg with the Catholic League army, however. In May, he stormed and sacked it. Some 30,000 of its inhabitants perished in the resultant fire. Protestant anger and fear at this stiffened their resolve and they now accepted that Gustavus Adolphus could do much to help their cause.

Accordingly they demanded that the emperor rescind the Edict of Restitution and make good the other wrongs they had suffered. Ferdinand unsurprisingly refused their demands.

Gustavus Adolphus was determined to bring Tilly to book, but he was short of supplies, so he entrenched himself at Werben on the Elbe in Saxony-Anhalt. Tilly attacked him twice, was repulsed, and set off into Saxony. This persuaded its ruler Prince John George to place his army under the Swedes. Tilly then went to Leipzig, which he captured on 15 September 1631. At the same time the Swedish and Saxon armies linked up 25 miles to the north of the city and moved to engage Tilly. They met at Breitenfeld on 17 September. After an initial artillery bombardment by both sides, Tilly used his cavalry to get round the Protestant right flank, but Gustavus Adolphus merely extended his line and kept it at bay. Tilly therefore attacked the Saxons on the left with the remainder of his cavalry while his infantry pressed forward in the centre. The Saxons broke and it looked as if the day was to be Tilly's, but the Swedish left now counter-attacked, driving the Catholic cavalry back onto their infantry. Gustavus then sent his right wing into the attack and Tilly's forces began to retreat. Tilly himself was badly wounded and Leipzig was quickly recaptured.

After his victory Gustavus quickly secured northwest Germany and then moved on to the Rhine, while the Saxons seized Prague. A shaken emperor now recalled Wallenstein, whom he had sacked to curry favour with the Protestant princes. The following spring Gustavus advanced into Bavaria and met Tilly and Maximilian of Bavaria on the river Lech. He drove them back, with Tilly being mortally wounded, but Wallenstein joined Maximilian with a fresh army after driving the Saxons out of Prague. Wallenstein entrenched near Fürth and invited Gustavus to attack him. This he did at the end of August, but the broken ground and heavy scrub around Wallenstein's position negated the effect of the Swedish artillery and cavalry and Gustavus was rebuffed. With no food left in the area, both sides now withdrew, Gustavus to the northwest and Wallenstein to the north. But the Swedish king was wrong-footed as Wallenstein invaded Saxony and recaptured Leipzig, cutting Gustavus's supply lines with Sweden. Gustavus hurried east and met the imperial forces at Lützen, southwest of Leipzig, on 16 November 1632. Gustavus attacked and for much of the day the battle was in the balance, with each side making numerous cavalry charges. Eventually, the Protestants emerged the victors, forcing Wallenstein to withdraw from Leipzig, but Gustavus himself was killed.

The death of the Swedish king was a severe blow to the Protestant cause and from now on they did not pursue the war with the same fervour. True, the Swedish chancellor, Count Axel Oxenstierna, did create the League of Heilbronn in spring 1633 to continue the fight, and renewed the alliance with France, but fortunes were mixed that year. The Protestants succeeded in occupying Bavaria, but Wallenstein retook Silesia before retiring to winter quarters in Bohemia. There he attempted to gain the throne through a coup d'état, but it failed and he was murdered by his own officers. The emperor now put his

How land warfare changed

THE THIRTY YEARS WAR resulted in significant changes in the conduct of land warfare, not least because of Gustavus Adolphus. In the realm of tactics, artillery became a major weapon, with battles now preceded by a bombardment. Its improving effectiveness also caused a change in infantry tactics. The *tercio*, the large block of pikemen and musketeers that had been introduced by the Spanish during the Reformation, gave way to the more linear Swedish formation. Not only did this reduce casualties from shellfire, but it also enabled musketeers to make more effective use of their weapons. Indeed, the infantryman would soon be armed with firearms only. Gustavus also replaced the *caracole*, whereby cavalrymen merely discharged their pistols at the enemy, with a system in which only the first rank used its pistols and the others their sabres to reintroduce the concept of shock action. Most significant was the coming of the professional standing army. From the late 15th century onwards, European armies had relied heavily on mercenaries, but their brutality, ill discipline and lack of loyalty made them an increasing liability. Gustavus therefore developed the concept of a national standing army organized in regiments with distinctive uniforms, with a formalized code of discipline and rigorous training programme. The regimental system that he introduced would soon become the cornerstone of all European armies.

own son Ferdinand of Hungary in charge of the imperial forces, with Count Matthias Gallas as his principal general. After a largely inconclusive campaign in Bavaria in July 1634, the emperor received a boost in the form of Prince Ferdinand of Spain, brother of the Spanish king. He was en route to Spain from Italy, where he had just been made a cardinal, with 20,000 men at his back when Madrid ordered him to join Ferdinand of Hungary. No sooner had he done so than the two commanders faced Bernard of Saxe-Weimar and the Swedish commander Gustavus Horn at Nördlingen on 6 September. Horn lacked the flair of his late king. He attacked the right wing of the entrenched imperial army and was initially successful. His troops then became confused and were driven back by a Spanish counter-attack. He asked Bernard to cover his withdrawal, but a determined imperialist and Spanish charge broke his troops. The Swedish element was then virtually annihilated and Horn captured. It was time to make peace.

Franco-Swedish alliance: 1635–48

In the May 1635 Peace of Prague, the emperor agreed to delay implementation of the Edict of Restitution for 40 years, and to respect the integrity of the Lutheran states in northeast Germany, but not elsewhere. The German states were not to make alliances with one another or with foreign powers, and their armies were to become part of the imperial army. This might have brought the conflict to an end, but the French had other ideas. A month earlier they had come to an agreement with Sweden, whereby Sweden would recognize France's claim to the left bank of the Rhine in return for France acknowledging Swedish occupation of areas on the right bank and her status as an equal ally. The French agreed to declare war on Spain, which they did immediately, and to make no separate peace. The war would therefore continue.

Cardinal Richelieu's plan was to cut off the Spanish Netherlands from Lombardy in northern Italy, which had been a Spanish possession since the Battle of Pavia in 1525, by clearing the Spanish from their enclaves in eastern France and western Germany. This meant splitting the French armies, and the plan was only partially successful. Some territory was gained in the Rhineland, but invasions of the Spanish Netherlands and Milan failed. The Swedes, however, did enjoy some success against the German states in eastern Germany. In 1636 it was the turn of the emperor and Spain to take to the offensive: they invaded France, enjoying considerable success until they were halted by a newly raised French army at Compiègne. The French won a victory in Italy, but their commander declined to advance to Milan, while the Swedes enjoyed further success in the east.

During the next few years the war continued unabated, but it increasingly went in favour of France and her allies. The Spanish lost ground in the Spanish Netherlands and the French gained further territory in the Rhine region. At sea, too, the Spanish suffered, with defeats at the hands of the Dutch in 1639 and the French the following year. The Dutch also harassed their treasure fleets from the Americas. The Swedes overran Saxony and advanced into Bohemia. In 1640 Portugal declared her independence and broke away from Spain. In 1642 the Swedes gained victory at Breitenfeld for a second time and in 1643 the French turned back another Spanish imperial invasion at Rocroi. Both sides were by now becoming exhausted, physically and economically, and the increasing barrenness of the most fought-over regions made it difficult to maintain armies in the field for any length of time. Neither could find a way of ending the conflict, but cracks had started to appear on both sides.

Peace of Westphalia, 1648

After five years of negotiations, the Spanish and the Dutch made peace at the beginning of 1648. Spain recognized the autonomy of the northern half of the Spanish Netherlands, which became the United Provinces. In August 1648 the French repulsed another Spanish invasion in northern France. The Holy Roman Empire suffered further defeats during the year, with a French-led invasion of Bavaria and Swedish forces entering Bohemia and besieging Prague. But peace negotiations were coming to a conclusion and on 24 October 1648 the Peace of Westphalia was signed. It provided an indemnity and Baltic coast territory to Sweden, while Alsace and a large part of Lorraine went to France. Within the Holy Roman Empire there was a general amnesty, and the German states were granted autonomy, with Catholic and Protestant states given equal status.

Germany would take a long time to recover from the physical ravages of the Thirty Years War. In the most heavily contested areas, as much as two thirds of the population had perished. The result was a desire to make future wars less destructive, which helped to bring about the more formalized warfare of the 18th century. The war marked the beginning of the decline of the Holy Roman Empire and of the power of Spain. It was also the end of the wars of religion in Europe. Finally, it brought about a revolution in military affairs (see Box).

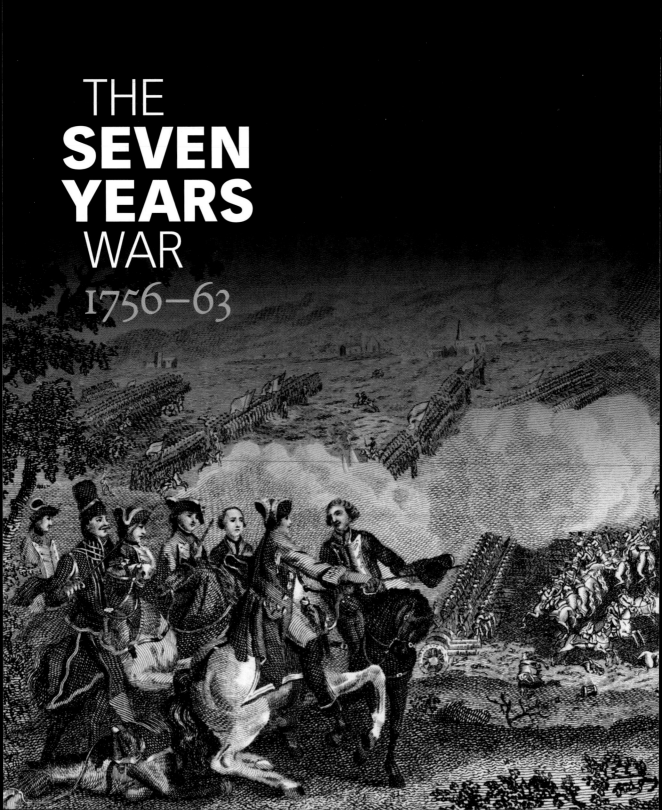

'**THIS HAS BEEN** THE MOST GLORIOUS WAR AND THE MOST TRIUMPHANT PEACE THAT ENGLAND EVER KNEW.'

John Carteret, Earl of Granville, on hearing of the peace terms as he lay dying, January 1763

THE
SEVEN
YEARS
WAR
1756–63

During the first half of the 18th century Europe suffered a succession of major wars. They were primarily concerned with maintaining the balance of power. The first of these was the War of the Spanish Succession, which was caused by the death of the childless Charles II of Spain.

Both France and Austria laid claim to the throne, but Britain and the Netherlands were strongly opposed to France and Spain being united as one. After 12 years of conflict, in which the duke of Marlborough displayed his brilliance as a general, France finally agreed in 1713 that the Spanish and French crowns would not be united. Thirty years later, a new war broke out after the Holy Roman emperor Charles VI, also king of Hungary and Bohemia (loosely known as Austria), died in 1740. In theory the succession to his throne passed down the male line, but Charles had no son and had achieved general agreement that his daughter Maria Theresa should succeed and that her husband would become the next emperor. The young King Frederick II of Prussia was keen on expanding his kingdom and took advantage of the emperor's death to invade Silesia. The subsequent War of the Austrian Succession drew in all the major European powers, each with its own agenda. Charles Albert of Bavaria, hoping to gain the imperial crown and Habsburg lands, also attacked Austria, while the French, sensing an opportunity to become dominant in Europe, sent volunteers to help him. The British and Dutch united against the French, while the Spanish, keen to reclaim territory in Italy, opposed Austria.

The Treaty of Aix-la-Chapelle, which ended the war in 1748, brought about little change to the map of Europe, except that Silesia was now confirmed as part of Prussia. The position of Maria Theresa and the integrity of her kingdom were recognized. But the conflict had not just taken place in Europe. Colonial rivalry caused a tussle between the British and French in North America. The most significant incident was the British capture of Fort Louisbourg on Cape Breton Island. This was handed back to the French under the peace treaty, resulting in much discontent among the British colonists. In India, too, there was growing rivalry between Britain and France, with the French capturing the main British base at Madras, though this was handed back in return for Fort Louisbourg. In addition, the British were challenging the Spanish in the Caribbean. The end of the war did nothing to reduce the tensions in these regions and they would serve to help precipitate the next major European conflict.

Prussia's only ally

The other continental European powers were resentful of Frederick of Prussia's expansionist policies and felt that he must be deterred from further enlarging his kingdom. Accordingly, in summer 1756 the Holy Roman Empire (to all intents and

OPPOSITE *The duke of Brunswick and his staff at the Battle of Minden, 1 August 1759. The linear formations, which armies adopted during the 18th century to reap maximum benefit from firepower, can also be seen.*

purposes, Austria), France, Russia, Sweden and Saxony formed an alliance against him. Fearing that they intended to seize back Silesia, Frederick himself made a pre-emptive strike by invading Saxony at the end of that August. Not only did he overrun the state, but he also defeated an Austrian army that had been sent to help the Saxons. It was an encouraging start and furthermore Frederick had an ally: friction with France in North America and India had prompted Britain to support him. There was also the fact that the House of Hanover, which had ruled Britain since 1714, came from the state bordering Prussia in the west and King George II, who was also the Elector of Hanover, was concerned for its security. Under the duke of Cumberland, 10,000 British troops were sent to protect Hanover, but Prime Minister William Pitt did not want a large British army committed to a protracted land campaign. Instead he agreed to subsidize Frederick with significant sums of money while the main British military effort was concentrated against the French in the colonies.

At this time armies still went into winter quarters, and it was not until April 1757 that the war became active once more. Frederick, with some 175,000 men under arms, now faced multiple threats from the coalition ranged against him. Half his army was deployed along the Bohemian border, where 130,000 Austrian troops were gathered. Forty thousand were in Hanover and the remainder were either facing north against Swedish Pomerania (the present-day German state of Mecklenburg-Vorpommern) or east towards the Russian forces in Poland. As it happened, none of Austria's allies were yet ready and so Frederick again took to the offensive, invading Bohemia, defeating the Austrians and placing Prague under siege. In June the Austrians sent a relief army into Bohemia. This defeated Frederick at the Battle of Kolin and forced him to raise the siege of Prague.

Battles of Rossbach and Leuthen

By now the other members of the alliance had taken to the field. In July a French army invaded Hanover and drove the British and Prussians out. A Russian army brushed aside the Prussians and was now threatening their capital Berlin. Finally, a large Austrian army had crossed the border from Bohemia into Silesia. It looked as though Frederick was facing a crushing defeat, especially since the allies were now converging on Berlin. He was not one to sit on his hands. Leaving a small force in Silesia, he moved quickly to Saxony, where the French who had overrun Hanover had linked up with a combined Austro-French army. Frederick's opponents refused to give battle, and so he dashed eastwards to confront the Austrians in Silesia and the Russians. In October he received news that the Austro-French force in Saxony was advancing once more. In spite of the fact that Austrian raiding forces had briefly entered and looted Berlin, Frederick left merely covering forces in the east and once more moved rapidly westwards. He confronted the allied forces at the village of Rossbach, which lies roughly halfway between Erfurt and Torgau, on 5 November 1757. Frederick had a mere 20,000 men and his opponents had twice that strength, but he outwitted them: when they attempted to outflank him, he feigned a retreat in order to extend the enemy column. His cavalry dashed in from the flank and destroyed the Austro-French advance guard, while his artillery and seven battalions of infantry engaged the head of the main body. His cavalry also attacked the main body from the flank and within a short time the battle had turned into a rout. The allies suffered some 10,000 casualties, the Prussians just over 540.

There was little time to celebrate this shattering victory. In Silesia, the Prussians had suffered a defeat and the Austrian forces were advancing on Breslau. Covering 170 miles in a mere 12 days as he rushed eastwards once more, Frederick met the Austrians near the town of Leuthen on 6 December. Frederick again outgeneralled his opponent, feinting in the centre and making an outflanking movement his main effort. The Austrian line was rolled up and their army virtually destroyed. The Russians made a further, but half-hearted, attempt to invade in January and the fighting then closed down. Thus, and very much against the odds, Prussia was still in the war.

The war overseas

Prussia's survival came as a relief to Britain, especially since there had been significant developments away from Europe during 1757. In Canada, the British had attempted and failed to retake Fort Louisbourg, but in India they had enjoyed some success. The year had begun with the British recapturing Calcutta, which had fallen to the Nawab of Bengal, an ally of the French, the previous June. The crowning success came in June 1757. Robert Clive, a former clerk in the Honourable East India Company – a commercial organization that looked after British affairs in the subcontinent and had its own army – decisively defeated the Nawab of Bengal at Palashi (Plassey) on the Bhagirathi River. The victory was all the more remarkable in that Clive was facing 50,000 men with a mere 3200 of his own troops. The Nawab himself was assassinated a few days later and was replaced on the Bengal throne by a British ally.

The year 1758 witnessed Frederick initially taking to the offensive. He moved into Moravia against the Austrians and laid siege to Olmütz, but had to raise it when the Russians began another attempt at invasion. Luckily, the French were no longer an immediate threat since the duke of Brunswick had driven them back across the Rhine. Frederick attacked the Russians at Zorndorf, east of the Oder, on 25 August and almost annihilated them. Then it was back to Saxony to confront the Austrians. They, however, succeeded in surprising him at Hochkirch in mid-October by surrounding his army during the night. Frederick managed to break out, however. The Austrians then laid siege to Dresden, but withdrew on the approach of Frederick with a reinforced army. Elsewhere, the British did finally succeed in regaining Fort Louisbourg in Canada, but failed to capture Fort Ticonderoga and to advance on the French capital of Quebec. In

India, the principal development was at sea where, in the course of two engagements between British and French naval squadrons in the Bay of Bengal, the French were worsted, leaving the British in command of the seas.

The next year, 1759, was to be the most dramatic of the war. An attempt in the spring by the duke of Brunswick and an Anglo-German force to drive the French out of northwest Germany failed and it withdrew. The French followed up and a battle was fought at Minden on 1 August. It was noteworthy for the performance of six battalions of British infantry, with Hanoverian troops in support. They attacked the French cavalry in the centre of the line, repulsed a charge by it, closed with the French infantry, and defeated it. After this victory the duke pursued the French almost to the Rhine and was only forced to halt because Frederick demanded reinforcements. He was facing invasion by both the Russians and the Austrians. Although outnumbered, Frederick, as usual, attacked at Kunersdorf (today Kunowice in Poland) on 12 August. He attempted a double envelopment, but his infantry columns lost their way in the surrounding woods and the attacks, when finally delivered, were piecemeal and repulsed with some ease. He persisted with them in vain and by the end of the day had lost 40 percent of his army. He suffered a severe loss of self-confidence and even considered abdication. Luckily for him, the Austrians and Russians were very slow to follow up their victory. With reinforcements received from the duke of Brunswick, he made another attempt to drive his enemies back. This came to naught after a Prussian detachment had been decisively beaten by the Austrians at Maxen in November. Both sides then ceased active operations for the winter.

Great Britain's *annus mirabilis*

If 1759 had generally been a bad year for the Prussians, the opposite was true for the British. Prime Minister Pitt had drawn up a three-pronged plan for the conquest of Canada: the capture of Fort Niagara to cut western Canada off from the St Lawrence River, an offensive to secure the river itself and an amphibious assault against Quebec. Both Fort Niagara and Fort Ticonderoga were captured in July 1759. Simultaneously, General James Wolfe, supported by a naval squadron, had set off up the St Lawrence for Quebec. The British arrived off Quebec, but were faced with a quandary. The city itself was on a high bluff overlooking the river and a direct assault up the cliffs seemed impossible. For two months Wolfe and his staff puzzled over the problem, subjecting the city to intermittent artillery fire. The naval commander became concerned that they might have to withdraw to avoid his ships becoming caught in the winter ice, but then a path up the cliffs was discovered. It led to the Plains of Abraham just to the west of Quebec. On the night of 12–13 September Wolfe and 4800 on his troops were landed at this point under cover of a bombardment of the city. Part of the British fleet also sailed past Quebec as a deception. At dawn, the French discovered the British drawn up and ready to fight. They attacked, but were driven off with heavy casualties. Both Wolfe and the Marquis de Montcalm, the French commander, were mortally wounded. The French withdrew into the city itself. Without any hope of relief, it surrendered five days later. Although the war in Canada continued for another year, the loss of Quebec, in spite of a French attempt to retake it in April 1760, was the turning point, and the surrender of France's Canadian possessions became inevitable.

The growing might of British sea power resulted in successes elsewhere. In India the French naval squadron returned and fought another naval action against the British off the main French base at Pondicherry on the Coromandel coast. The French ships suffered such damage that they withdrew, this time never to return. The Royal Navy was also active in operations against French possessions in the Caribbean. Guadeloupe was taken in April 1759, but the British were unsuccessful against the main French base at Martinique. Closer to home, Admiral Edward Hawke decisively defeated the French Brest fleet under Hubert de Conflans at Quiberon Bay on France's Biscay coast on 20 November 1759. It gave the British complete dominance at sea. This was the last of the British successes of the year, which they called the *annus mirabilis*.

On the continent, the allies remained determined to crush Frederick. In Saxony 100,000 Austrians would combine with a further 50,000 in Silesia and 50,000 Russians in East Prussia. Frederick now had fewer than 100,000 men, because of heavy casualties over the past few years, and was unable to concentrate them anywhere because of the

BELOW *The Battle of Quiberon Bay, 20 November 1759. In high winds Admiral Hawke trapped the French fleet and sank or captured seven ships, losing only two of his own. The victory established Britain's command of the seas.*

Frederick the Great

KING FREDERICK II OF PRUSSIA (1713–86) established himself as one of the great captains of war as a result of his performance during the Seven Years War. It was not that he consistently won battles, but that he was able to deal with multiple threats to his kingdom. The basis of his success was the rigid discipline that he instilled in his army. It was this that enabled it to continue fighting in the face of heavy casualties and consistently to carry out forced marches. The latter was especially crucial to his ability to manoeuvre his troops in order to outwit his enemies and catch them off balance. He also appreciated the importance of logistics and much of his manoeuvring was designed to threaten supply lines. At the tactical level he introduced a number of innovations. Most significant was his method of attack. He compensated for his inferiority of numbers on the battlefield not by engaging the enemy along the length of his line, as was conventional practice, but by advancing obliquely against an enemy flank with his infantry in echelon so as to crush it before help could arrive. He classified his cavalry into heavy and light, the former being used for shock action through charging the enemy, while the latter was used for reconnaissance and skirmishing. It was a practice adopted by other armies, as was his introduction of horse artillery – light guns that could accompany the cavalry and deploy quickly. Frederick's *Military Instructions*, originally written in 1748 for his generals, also had a major influence on European warfare until superseded by Napoleon's methods of waging war.

multiple threats he faced. Nor could he call on the 70,000 British and Hanoverians defending Hanover under the duke of Brunswick, since these in turn were tied down by 125,000 French troops. Brunswick, however, did conduct a successful manoeuvre campaign and succeeded in forcing the French back to the Rhine without fighting a major battle. Frederick himself spent the early summer traversing between Saxony and Silesia, but was unable to prevent the allied armies from joining up. At Liegnitz on 15 August he faced the elements of the two Austrian armies and knew that the Russians were not far behind. He got the better of the engagement, but it was not a decisive result. However, he managed, through a false message, to trick the Russians into believing that the Austrians had been annihilated and they withdrew. Even so, Frederick was unable to prevent the allies carrying out a major raid on his capital in October, though he gained his revenge the following month at Torgau by defeating the Austrians, albeit at a very heavy cost in Prussian casualties.

In India, 1760 proved to be the decisive year. Because of the British naval successes, the French had no means of deploying additional troops to the subcontinent and so the writing was probably on the wall. This was aggravated in January when Sir Eyre Coote defeated their troops at Wandiwash and forced them to withdraw to Pondicherry. This was besieged and eventually surrendered in January 1761, leaving the British dominant. In the West Indies the British also managed to capture Dominica.

The most significant event in 1761 was Spain's entry into the war after being bribed by the French with the Mediterranean island of Minorca, which they had captured from the British in 1756. This did not affect the land war in Europe, but would prove to be to

British benefit elsewhere. Otherwise, it was very much a question of whether Frederick of Prussia would survive. Five years of intensive campaigning meant that he was now suffering a manpower crisis and was hopelessly outnumbered. While the duke of Brunswick fought an inconclusive campaign in the west, Frederick was reduced to a summer of desperate manoeuvring in Silesia to keep powerful Austrian and Russian forces at bay. Eventually he was cut off from Prussia and forced to take up position in a fortified camp at Glatz on the present-day northern Czech Republic border. Luckily for him, the allies declined to attack him, but at the end of the year his position remained parlous.

By 1762 all the combatant nations, apart from the British, were becoming exhausted. This became apparent at the beginning of January, when Empress Elizabeth of Russia died. Her successor Peter III, who was an admirer of Frederick, immediately opened peace negotiations with him, which were concluded that May. In that same month Sweden also made peace. Frederick could now concentrate on the Austrians, while Brunswick dealt with the French. This the duke did most successfully, defeating them at Wilhelmstaf in June and then eventually driving them back across the Rhine. The Prussians also achieved two victories over the Austrians, but both were by now so drained that all parties were more than happy to agree an armistice in November.

The British were primarily active in the Caribbean during 1762. Martinique fell early in the year and the French went on to lose Grenada, St Lucia, and St Vincent as well. It was Spain's entry into the war that provided the richest pickings, however. After a 40-day siege, Havana fell. All Spanish trade from the Americas passed through this Cuban port and so the British not only captured 12 ships of the line but considerable amounts of money and merchandise as well. An expedition mounted from India also sailed to the Philippines and captured Manila, as well as, en route, a Spanish treasure ship. Finally, in the Atlantic, the British seized a further treasure ship sailing to Spain. It was all too much for King Charles III and he, too, entered the peace negotiations.

Treaty of Paris, 1763

The Seven Years War was formally brought to an end by the February 1763 Treaty of Paris. In Europe there was little change, with Frederick able to hold on to Silesia. Elsewhere it was Britain that was the sole winner. Its dominance in India was confirmed. Indeed, five years later the French equivalent of the Honourable East India Company was dissolved. Canada, too, passed into British hands. While Guadeloupe and Martinique were handed back to France, Britain was allowed to retain her gains in the Antilles, apart from St Lucia. Spain also gave Britain Florida in exchange for the return of Havana. In truth, the war gave Britain the real foundation of its empire and made it a major economic power. Underpinning both was the fact that it was now the world's foremost maritime power, a position that Britain would continue to hold until well into the 20th century.

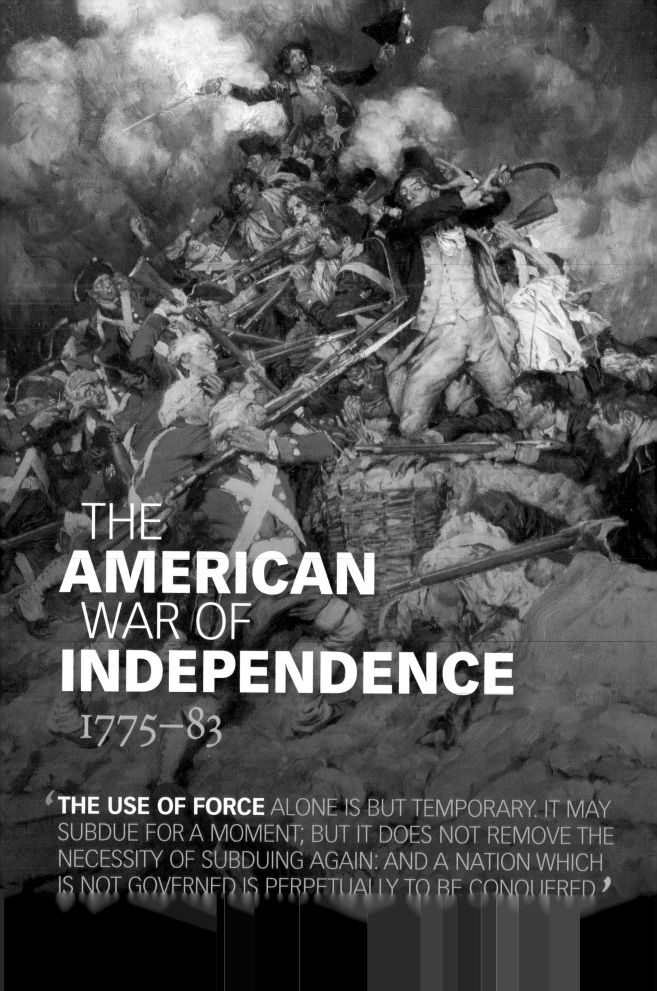

THE **AMERICAN** WAR OF **INDEPENDENCE**

1775–83

'**THE USE OF FORCE** ALONE IS BUT TEMPORARY. IT MAY SUBDUE FOR A MOMENT; BUT IT DOES NOT REMOVE THE NECESSITY OF SUBDUING AGAIN: AND A NATION WHICH IS NOT GOVERNED IS PERPETUALLY TO BE CONQUERED '

To a Britain flushed with success after the Seven Years War, the revolt by the American colonists came as a shock. Yet it should not have been so, since the warning signs were in place. The ensuing conflict would also give France and Spain the chance to gain revenge for the recent losses they had suffered at Britain's hands. Yet, the revolt itself could have been avoided.

The 13 colonies themselves stretched along the eastern seaboard from New Hampshire in the north to West and East Florida in the south and contained a rapidly growing number of inhabitants. Indeed, the population of British North America increased from 265,000 in 1700 to 2.3 million by 1770. In general terms, the quality of life was better than it was in Britain: those colonists who were tax payers paid only a fraction of that levied on their equivalents back in Britain. Each state also had a significant degree of local autonomy by virtue of its assembly. Nevertheless, there was growing discontent.

'No taxation without representation'

In 1765, the British parliament instituted the Stamp Act, which was to apply not only to Britain itself, but to its colonies as well. All printed material had to be on specially stamped paper, the stamp being a form of tax. It was immensely unpopular and was repealed the following year. The principle now was that only external trade would be taxed. In 1768, however, London introduced a new range of customs duties, but as a concession, did cut that on tea – then a very popular commodity in America – by 75 percent. Even so, the colonists were not impressed and were unwilling to pay. British soldiers had to be deployed, notably to Boston, to support the tax collectors, and in March 1770 the so-called Boston Massacre occurred, when a crowd began throwing missiles at soldiers after an altercation between a merchant and a sentry at the Customs House. The soldiers opened fire and killed five people. There was also the famous 'Boston Tea Party' of December 1773 when a group boarded an East India tea ship and heaved its contents into the harbour. This, however, was not actually a protest against the tax on tea, but was instigated by smugglers resentful of the fact that the price of tea had dropped so low. Be that as it may, the main grievance that the colonists had was that of being taxed by a parliament 4000 miles away in which they had no direct representation. Hence their slogan, 'No taxation without representation', which became a formalized demand when elements from each of the colonial assemblies met in Philadelphia in autumn 1774.

In Britain, some forward-thinking men sympathized with the colonists' position, but the government of Lord North proved resistant to any form of compromise. The colonists therefore began to organize themselves for an armed rebellion, stockpiling arms and ammunition and doing additional militia training. Conflict became increasingly inevitable. On 18 April 1775 General Thomas Gage, the governor of Massachusetts, sent 700 troops to seize arms and ammunition being kept by the colonists at Concord, 20 miles northwest of Boston. Paul Revere, and others, made their now celebrated 'midnight ride' to call out the Minutemen (see Box) and when the troops reached Lexington next morning, they were confronted by armed men. Firing broke out, some colonists fell and the remainder scattered. The soldiers then went on to Concord, found most of the munitions had been removed, and destroyed the rest. On their return march, however, they were harassed all the way by militiamen and suffered nearly 300 casualties. The revolt had begun.

British besieged at Boston

The Massachusetts Provincial Congress immediately authorized the raising of a militia of nearly 14,000 men and, with help from neighbouring states, placed the British in Boston under siege. Elsewhere, the colonists scored another success when they captured Fort Ticonderoga, the gateway to Canada. The British sent out reinforcements, but Boston was still under siege and the 7000-man garrison was not strong enough to break it. Then, on 17 June, the first proper battle of the war occurred. A detachment of militia had been ordered to fortify Bunker Hill, which dominated Boston harbour – since the colonists possessed no navy the British were able to keep the garrison supplied by sea. By mistake, they occupied a lower and more vulnerable hill and built an earth rampart. General Gage sent a force of 2200 men under General William Howe across the bay to seize the hill under cover of a naval bombardment. He eventually succeeded on his third attempt, but by then his casualties amounted to almost half his force. It showed that the militia were a match for the British regulars.

At this point, what was called the Continental Congress, which was meeting in Philadelphia, agreed to create a proper army, to be called the Continental Army. Colonel George Washington, a Virginia landowner with plenty of experience in fighting the French and the Indians, was appointed to command it. He took over the conduct of the siege of Boston, at the same time working hard to create a disciplined and well-trained army.

For the remainder of 1775 the focus was on Canada. With Ticonderoga now in their hands, the colonists pressed on northwards, capturing Fort St Jean (St John) at the beginning of November and then occupying Montreal in the middle of the month. The next objective was Quebec. A force of 1100 under Benedict Arnold had left Cambridge, Massachusetts, in mid-September and after a long and punishing march 600 men eventually arrived before Quebec on 8 November. They linked up with 300 men from the force that had taken Montreal. On the last day of the year, they attacked the city in a blizzard, but were repulsed with heavy casualties and spent the remainder of the winter outside the city walls.

The Minutemen

THE ORIGINS OF THE MINUTEMEN go back to the middle of the 17th century. The New England confederation arranged for its four member colonies to raise militias that would be prepared to operate anywhere within the confederation. In Massachusetts this was taken a stage further, with a number of men being selected who were prepared to turn out fully armed and equipped within half an hour of being ordered to do so. This was especially important because of the constant threat from marauding Native American tribes. In time, a system of riders and signals to spread the alarm through the townships was also developed. Up until the 1770s they, and the militias as a whole, saw service not just against the Native Americans, but in the conflicts with the French as well. They also assisted the civil authorities in times of unrest. Eventually armed with rifled muskets, the Minutemen became adept at irregular warfare and were often used as scouts and skirmishers. After General Gage began to crack down and actively search for munitions stockpiled by the increasingly hostile militias, it was the Minutemen who monitored their movements and gave warning so that the arms could be moved to safety. It was also they who faced the British troops at Lexington. Once the Continental Army had been formed and the militias brought under its umbrella, though not made part of it, the Minutemen lost their special identity.

During this time Washington had increased his strength in front of Boston to some 26,000 men, supported by cannon that had been removed from Ticonderoga. Howe, now commanding the British garrison, recognized this, and in mid-April 1776 evacuated the city and sailed north to Halifax. Washington, rightly believing that New York would be the next British target, took his army off to defend it. The British were now pouring reinforcements into Canada. This frustrated further colonist attempts to take Quebec and forced them to withdraw to Ticonderoga. To all intents and purposes this marked the end of the attempt to drive the British out of Canada.

Declaration of Independence, 4 July 1776

The British plan for 1776 had been drawn up in London. It called for a landing at New York by Howe with a large force. The reasoning behind this was that the theatre of war was geographically a long one, stretching 1200 miles from the St Lawrence in Canada to Florida, but on average only 150 miles wide. Lacking the resources to deal with each region simultaneously, it seemed to make sense to deal with the opposition in the north first. Howe himself set out from Halifax by sea in June, the fleet that transported his 32,000 men being commanded by his brother. He landed on Staten Island on 3 July. The following day the Continental Congress, meeting again in Philadelphia, issued the Declaration of Independence. This had two immediate effects. First, it made anyone supporting the British crown a traitor. This divided the colonists into two groups, the Patriots who supported independence, and the Loyalists, who hoped that a way could be found to dissuade the colonies from breaking away. The Declaration also transformed the situation from one of rebellion to that of open war.

Congress had instructed Washington to hold New York at all costs. He had constructed a series of earthworks and employed part of his army on Long Island and the remainder in Manhattan. Howe took his time and it was not until the end of August that he succeeded in forcing Washington to evacuate Long Island. Two weeks later he abandoned the city itself. The British were slow to follow up, but in a series of actions bested the Americans. Washington withdrew behind the Delaware River, but he was in a difficult position. His army was down to 10,000 men and half of them were sick. Howe, though, decided that the time had come to go into winter quarters. These were covered by a series of posts, with that at Trenton held by Hessian mercenaries, whom the British had brought across from Germany. Undeterred by the state of his army, Washington decided to attack this post and overran it on 26 December. Six days later, on 1 January, he did the same to another post at Princeton. These two actions, small as they were, were an enormous boost to American morale.

General John Burgoyne, who had been with the British forces in Canada, conceived the plan for 1777. It was an ambitious one, with the aim of splitting the American forces by occupying the Hudson valley. He himself would move south from Canada, while Howe would advance north from New York and meet him at Albany. A third column consisting of regulars, Loyalists and friendly native Americans, would proceed up the St Lawrence to Lake Ontario, cross to Oswego and then join the others at Albany. The plan required very careful coordination, but London did not emphasize this and did not make clear to Howe that his priority was meeting up with Burgoyne. Even worse, it failed to appoint an overall commander. The fact, too, that orders from London took months to arrive did not help matters.

As it was, Howe saw his priority as bringing Washington to battle. After some fruitless manoeuvring during the spring and early summer in New Jersey, he set out from New York with 18,000 men and sailed south and then into Chesapeake Bay in an attempt to get behind Washington. He landed in late August at Elkton, southwest of Philadelphia. He then fought Washington at Brandywine on 11 September, forced him back and entered Philadelphia before the month was out. Washington then attacked Howe at Germantown on 4 October, was repulsed and withdrew, eventually coming to rest for the winter in Valley Forge, 22 miles northwest of Philadelphia. While Howe had enjoyed some success – though hardly decisive – he had, to its detriment, totally ignored the overall plan.

The advance from Canada had begun well, with Ticonderoga being recaptured at the beginning of July. Burgoyne pressed on southwards pursuing the Americans, who made life difficult for him by wrecking the roads that he wanted to use. In early August he learned that Howe was too tied up to meet him at Albany, but Burgoyne resolved to carry on, hoping that he would at least link up with the Oswego column. This, however, became involved in the siege of Fort Stanwix, which delayed its progress. Meanwhile

OPPOSITE *George Washington was largely self-taught as a soldier but proved to be a natural leader of men, especially during his army's grim winter sojourn at Valley Forge in 1777–8. He would later become one of America's greatest presidents.*

Burgoyne was becoming short of supplies. He sent a detachment to Bennington to capture stores known to be there, but this was defeated on 16 August. Five days later the Americans relieved Fort Stanwix and the British withdrew. Burgoyne was now very much on his own, but he pressed on, crossing the Hudson River near Saratoga on 13 September. The Americans under General Horatio Gates were waiting for him on the other side and repulsed his attempt to drive them back at Freeman's Farm six days later. Burgoyne had sent a message to Sir Henry Clinton, the British commander in New York, for help. The latter therefore took 4000 men up the Hudson and captured two forts. He thought that this was enough to distract Gates, and returned to New York. Still on his own, Burgoyne made another desperate attack on the American positions on the Bemis Heights. It failed and, now with less than 6000 men, he began to withdraw back to Saratoga. Gates quickly followed up and surrounded the British. Burgoyne's surrender followed on 17 October. It was to be the turning point of the war.

French encouragement

The news of Saratoga may have cheered Washington, but the winter in Valley Forge was a grim one. In spite of repeated requests to Congress, his army remained short of rations and clothing, and sick rates were high. Yet, it survived intact. Good news for the Americans came in February when France signed an alliance with them. The French and Spanish, delighted to see their old enemy Britain discomfited, had been supplying money from the outset, and France had been the first to recognize America's independence. It was followed in June 1778 with the French declaration of war on Britain and the subsequent sending of forces to America. Spain did the same a year later, though it refused to recognize American independence.

It was not until June 1778 that the war really became active once again. Clinton had succeeded Howe in command and decided to evacuate Philadelphia and return to New York to launch another offensive from there. This was not to be, since Washington followed up and hemmed the British in at New York. He was helped for a time by the French fleet, which arrived in July. It then went off to assist in the capture of Newport, Rhode Island. In the process of this Admiral Howe tried to bring the French to battle, but was frustrated by a storm. This also forced the French to withdraw to repair damage to their ships and the Newport attack was abandoned. The French fleet then left for the West Indies, where their local forces had captured Dominica, the British countering this by taking St Lucia in November.

The war moves south

Frustrated in the north, the British now turned to the south, where for two years Patriots and Loyalists (also called Tories) had been indulging in guerrilla warfare with one another. They began by landing at Savannah in December 1778. The force then advanced northwards and seized Augusta at the end of January. After some further actions, during which the Americans were reinforced, the British withdrew to Savannah. There they were put under siege by Admiral d'Estaing and the French fleet, which had returned from the Caribbean with 4000 troops. But the French admiral was concerned about seasonal storms and was not prepared for a long siege. Accordingly, after five weeks, he launched a premature attack on 8 October. It was repulsed with heavy losses and the French and Americans then withdrew.

Clinton himself moved south in December 1779, after withdrawing his troops from Newport but still retaining New York. He landed near Charleston and besieged it. The port fell in May 1780 and Clinton returned to New York, leaving Lord Cornwallis with 6000 men to begin an advance northwards. He overwhelmed a largely militia force at Camden in mid-August, but, in spite of stern measures, found it difficult to control the territory that he had captured. One of his Loyalist columns was then defeated at King's Mountain in October and Cornwallis withdrew to Winnsborough, North Carolina, to take up winter quarters.

Washington now appointed Nathaniel Greene to command in the south and reinforcement provided him with a force of 3000 men with which he took to the offensive against Cornwallis just before Christmas 1780. He divided his forces, as did Cornwallis. There was one clash at Cowpens in January, with Greene's troops being victorious. He then withdrew into southern Virginia, closely followed by Cornwallis. Once the latter reached the unfordable Dan River he withdrew again. Greene, reinforced once more, came on and the two met at Guilford Court House in mid-March. Cornwallis won a pyrrhic victory and, deciding that Georgia and the Carolinas were untenable, withdrew to Wilmington on the coast. He left some scattered garrisons in the south. Greene moved against them, and after a number of clashes, they all fell back on Charleston.

The final act was now about to be played out. Both Clinton in New York and Cornwallis, and the British government, believed that Virginia now held the key to improving their now very tenuous hold on the southern states. There was a protracted three-way correspondence on this, with several letters inevitably crossing one another. In the meantime Clinton sent troops under Benedict Arnold, who had won eternal opprobrium among Americans by changing sides, to Virginia, with orders to interdict Green's supply lines. He captured and burnt Richmond and then returned to Portsmouth. In March he was reinforced by General William Phipps and the combined force then moved south and met Cornwallis at Petersburg. Washington had reacted to these moves by sending a force under the French volunteer Marquis de Lafayette to Virginia. During May–July Cornwallis unsuccessfully tried to draw Lafayette into battle, but then received orders from Clinton to occupy the tip of the Virginia Peninsula. Accordingly, he took up position at Yorktown and Lafayette settled down to watch him, passing the news to Washington.

The French had a strong fleet under Admiral de Grasse in the West Indies and he was persuaded by Washington and Jean-Baptiste Comte de Rochambeau, commanding the French troops in America, to cooperate with them. Rochambeau joined Washington outside New York and they marched south, leaving just 2000 men to contain Clinton. On 30 August de Grasse arrived off Yorktown and disembarked the troops he had on board to reinforce Lafayette. A British naval squadron rushed from New York to intercept the French, but they had been joined by further ships and siege artillery. Totally outnumbered, the British ships withdrew to New York, leaving Cornwallis to his fate. Washington and Rochambeau arrived with their troops during the second half of September. Cornwallis, now besieged, hoped that Clinton would come to his rescue, but the siege artillery now deployed against him proved too powerful. Rather than face annihilation, he surrendered on 19 October. It was the beginning of the end.

The peace treaties

The British now evacuated their ports in the south and concentrated in New York. Lord North's government collapsed in March 1782 and the new administration sued for peace, which was agreed through the November 1782 Treaty of Paris. Its terms would not come into effect, however, until the present conflict between Britain, France and Spain had ended. This had been fought in the Mediterranean, where Britain lost Minorca but retained Gibraltar after a three-year siege, and in the eastern Atlantic, where the Royal Navy enjoyed a number of successes. A French naval squadron even entered the Indian Ocean and had the best of a number of encounters with the British squadron based there. There was, too, the West Indies, where the British eventually ended on top after Admiral George Rodney decisively defeated de Grasse in the Battle of the Saints, which took place between Guadeloupe and Dominica, in April 1782. Peace was eventually agreed through the January 1783 Treaty of Versailles.

Thus America won its independence. Its watchword of *liberty* would continue to attract immigrants in increasing numbers, many disillusioned with life in Europe. American territory would expand south and westwards to the Pacific and the enterprise of the citizens of the United States would eventually create the superpower that it is today.

✦ ✦ ✦

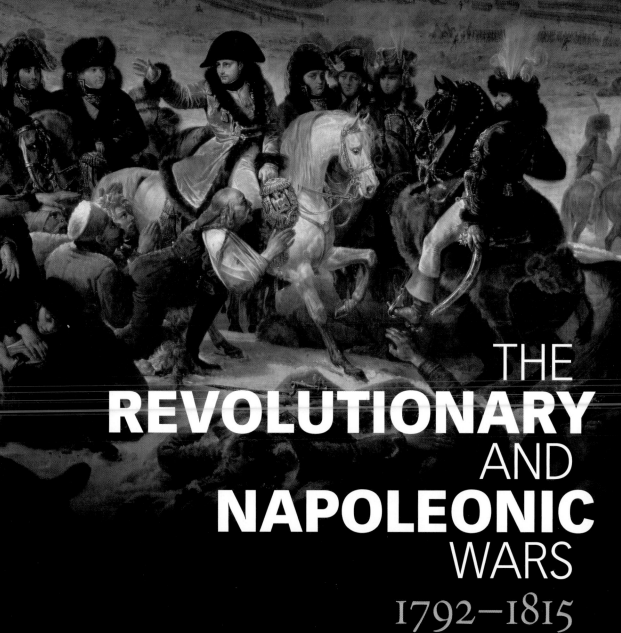

" **HE ALWAYS APPLIED ALL HIS MEANS,** ALL HIS FACULTIES, ALL HIS ATTENTION TO THE ACTION OR DISCUSSION OF THE MOMENT. INTO EVERYTHING HE PUT PASSION. HENCE THE ENORMOUS ADVANTAGE HE HAD OVER HIS ADVERSARIES, FOR FEW PEOPLE ARE ENTIRELY ABSORBED BY ONE THOUGHT OR ONE ACTION AT ONE MOMENT. " General Armand de Caulaincourt, on Napoleon

THE
REVOLUTIONARY
AND
NAPOLEONIC
WARS
1792–1815

The conflicts that wracked Europe during the closing years of the 18th century and first part of the 19th were as much as anything a struggle between the old and new orders. They came to be dominated by one man, Napoleon Buonaparte, whose armies marched to and fro across the continent and for a time created an empire, the like of which had never before been seen.

In the aftermath of the French Revolution of 1789 the crowned heads of Europe feared for their thrones. King Frederick William II of Prussia and Emperor Leopold II of Austria declared that they were prepared to restore Louis XVI to his throne and asked other European states to join them. Early in 1792 they began to mass their forces. Feeling threatened, the revolutionary government in France declared war that April. It was the beginning of a conflict that would rage, with just one small break, for more than 20 years. Initially the revolutionaries appeared to stand little chance as they faced invasion across their eastern frontier. Yet their fervour managed to keep their enemies at bay and indeed drove the Austrians out of Belgium and the Prussians back across the Rhine.

The First Coalition

In January 1793 Louis XVI was executed and, fearing that France might now be intending to export its revolution abroad, Britain, Holland, Austria, Prussia and Spain formed the First Coalition. This scored a series of victories and these, combined with royalist uprisings within France itself, created a sense of panic across the country. The result was the so-called Reign of Terror – the purging of elements suspected of not being wholly behind the revolution – in the late summer of 1793. Creating fresh armies through conscription, the French managed to repulse their enemies once more. One of their successes was at Toulon, a major French naval base, which had been seized by royalists with the support of allied warships. Republican forces laid siege and, thanks to a plan put forward by a young Corsican artillery officer, Napoleon Buonaparte, recaptured the forts dominating the harbour and forced the allied naval force to withdraw. It was the beginning of his meteoric rise to power.

During the next few years the French armies continued to enjoy success, creating a number of buffer states to keep their enemies at bay. Buonaparte himself played a lead role in this. In October 1795 he had been instrumental in putting down a counter-revolution in Paris with the aid of some guns he had seized. What he called 'the whiff of grapeshot' gave him command of the Army of Italy. In the course of a brilliantly conducted campaign during 1796–7 he drove the Austrians out and set up further puppet republics. This helped to establish him politically and he had little difficulty in persuading the Directory, which governed France, to allow him to lead an expedition to Egypt, then part of the Ottoman empire, with the aim of improving French trade and threatening the British in

PREVIOUS PAGE *Napoleon with some of his marshals at the Battle of Eylau, 8 February 1807. Though he heaped honours on the marshals who formed his inner circle, he trusted few of them to wage campaigns without his close supervision.*

India. Successfully evading the British navy, Napoleon duly landed and decisively defeated the indigenous Mamelukes. The British Mediterranean Fleet, led by Horatio Nelson, caught Napoleon's supporting warships at anchor in Aboukir Bay, however, and all but destroyed them. This left Napoleon and his men stranded.

Napoleon consolidates power in France

Back in Europe, France was becoming politically unsettled, especially in the face of a number of victories by the allies, who once again appeared on the brink of invading France. Consequently, in August 1799, Napoleon was summoned back, leaving his army in Egypt. As a result of a coup he became First Consul, which gave him the reins of political power. This enabled him to begin overhauling the machinery of government. In particular, his Code Napoleon totally reformed French law, replacing the largely feudal structure with a modern system. Further French victories removed the threat of invasion, but Napoleon was angered that the Austrians had retaken northern Italy while he had been in Egypt. Therefore, in spring 1800, he launched his second Italian campaign, decisively defeating the Austrians at Marengo, although it was not until they had been further defeated the following year at Hohenlinden by the veteran General Jean Victor Moreau that they actually recognized Napoleon's gains and sued for peace. With Russia having previously left the war and the remaining members of the Coalition unwilling to pursue hostilities further, only Britain remained defiant.

In 1800 the British had seized the strategically important Mediterranean island of Malta, which the French had captured two years before, and then, a year later, defeated the army that Napoleon had left in Egypt. They had also made colonial gains at the expense of the French. Yet, both sides were becoming war weary and through the Treaty of Amiens of March 1802 Britain agreed to give up the French overseas possessions that it had recently occupied in return for the evacuation of the Papal States and Sicily. It was to be a shortlived peace. The main bone of contention was Malta, which the British refused to hand back because of the continued French occupation of Piedmont in northern Italy, Switzerland and Holland. Negotiations proved fruitless. The conflict thus resumed in May 1803, but to begin with it was merely between Britain and France, to whom Spain became allied in November 1804 with the promise that Napoleon would grant it sovereignty over Portugal. Just before this, and as a result of the discovery of a royalist assassination plot against him, he had himself crowned emperor of France and henceforth discarded the name Buonaparte.

Planned invasion of Britain

Napoleon was determined to invade Britain and crush 'Perfidious Albion' once and for all. He therefore began to gather a large army opposite the English Channel and assembled invasion craft at the mouth of the Rhine in Holland. In Britain, the sense of determination to resist the invader was as great as it would be in summer 1940, with defences rapidly being constructed along the south coast and volunteers flocking to enlist in the army. Diplomatic efforts were also made to persuade Britain's erstwhile continental allies to rejoin the war. Napoleon knew that he would have little chance of success unless he could lure the British fleet away from home waters. But, with the French and Spanish ports under close blockade, this was easier said than done. Not until the end of March 1805 was Admiral Pierre-Charles Villeneuve able to slip out of Toulon, pass through the Straits of Gibraltar and link up with a Spanish squadron off Cadiz. He then drew Admiral Horatio Nelson's fleet to the West Indies and back, only to find himself trapped in Cadiz. Meanwhile there had been developments elsewhere.

Britain had managed to persuade Austria and Russia to re-enter the conflict. This and the fact that he had been unable to deploy the Franco-Spanish fleet to a position where it could support the invasion of Britain caused Napoleon a change of heart. His Grand Army doused its campfires on the English Channel coast and marched eastwards. Given that the Russians would take longer to deploy, he decided to deal with Austria first. Crossing the Rhine on a broad front at the end of September 1805, Napoleon headed for Bavaria, which an Austrian army under the Archduke Ferdinand had already entered. Napoleon located them at Ulm on the river Danube and forced them to surrender on 20 October, before pursuing the remnants into Austria itself. It was an inauspicious beginning to the Third Coalition, as the alliance was called, but there was hope elsewhere.

Villeneuve had remained bottled up in Cadiz with his fleet, but was ordered by Napoleon to take troops to Italy as reinforcements for Marshal André Massena, who was outnumbered by the Austrian forces facing him. The French admiral reluctantly set sail early on 19 October. Nelson was waiting for him and two days later the two fleets met. Superior British gunnery and tactics (see Box) soon began to tell, and by the end of the day over half of Villeneuve's ships had been forced to strike their colours. It was a decisive victory that confirmed Britain's naval supremacy, though its architect did not live to enjoy it, Nelson being mortally wounded on board his flagship HMS *Victory*.

Allied defeat at Austerlitz

The French defeat at Trafalgar could not, however, influence events on land. In Italy, after learning of the disaster at Ulm, the Austrians began to withdraw, with Massena following them up. Napoleon himself entered the Austrian capital Vienna on 13 November, but was mindful that his men had been constantly on the march for three months and that his supply lines were becoming overstretched. He therefore decided to concentrate his army at Brünn, some 120 miles north of Vienna, so that it could be reorganized. The Russians, who had now appeared on the scene, did not consider themselves strong enough to continue their advance yet. They and the Austrians also hoped that they could persuade the Prussians to join in, but they were fence sitting and expecting to receive some reward from Napoleon for doing so. The allies then became convinced that Napoleon was fearful of attacking them and so decided to assault. What became known as the Battle of Austerlitz was fought on 2 December 1805 in the presence of three emperors – Napoleon, Francis of Austria and Alexander of Russia. It ended in a devastating defeat for the allies, eliminating Austria as a protagonist. When the news reached British prime minister William Pitt in London he was devastated. Indeed, it sent him to his grave. 'My country! How I leave my country,' he murmured as he lay dying.

Yet, the Russians were still in the war. In addition, Napoleon's intention to bind the German states into a Confederation of the Rhine increasingly angered a Prussia bent on creating a Greater Germany. The last straw came when Napoleon offered Hanover to Britain as a carrot to make peace with him. In October 1806 the Prussians declared war, but Napoleon had been prepared for this and immediately invaded. He rapidly outmanoeuvred and defeated them at the twin battles of Jena and Auerstadt on the 14th

Major battles of the Napoleonic Wars

of that month. Before October was out the French had entered Berlin and King Frederick William had fled to Russia. Napoleon now advanced into Poland to prevent any Russian attempt at rekindling Prussian resistance. He went into winter quarters at the end of the year, but the Russians soon mounted an offensive, which culminated in the bloody but indecisive Battle of Eylau in early February 1807. After this there was a lull until the spring, when Napoleon successfully laid siege to Danzig (present-day Gdansk). In June the Russians launched another offensive, which was quickly repulsed by Napoleon, who then decisively defeated them at Friedland. He now met Tsar Alexander and King William Frederick on a barge on the river Niemen at Tilsit. Prussia was forced to cede western Poland to France, recognize the Confederation of the Rhine, and pay a huge indemnity. French troops would occupy the country until this was done. In addition, the Prussian army was to be reduced to 42,000 men. Russia had to recognize the Duchy of Warsaw, as French-occupied Poland was called, and join France in the war against Britain.

The Continental System isolates Britain

The Treaty of Tilsit left Napoleon master of much of western and central Europe. Only Britain remained in the field against him, but Napoleon had plans to throttle the obstinate island nation. His Continental System was designed to attack Britain's lifeblood – mercantile trade. To this end he sought to close all continental European ports to British ships, but one country, Portugal, refused to take part. Its punishment was a French invasion in November 1807. The Spanish had provided half-hearted support, but Napoleon no longer trusted their degenerate royal house and corrupt government and decided that the time had come to bring the country firmly under his heel. In early 1808 the French secured the Spanish frontier fortresses and then advanced rapidly to Madrid. The king of Spain abdicated and Napoleon's brother Joseph took his place. Horrified by these events, the people of Spain rose in open revolt and the French found themselves hard-pressed to bring the country under control. The same situation applied to the limited French forces in Portugal.

The British viewed the events unfolding on the Iberian peninsula with hope. Since Trafalgar, they had been reduced very much to nibbling around the edges of the conflict, apart from the continuing naval blockade of French ports. They had made some pinprick forays into mainland Italy and bombarded the Danish capital and port of Copenhagen to dissuade the Danes from siding with Napoleon, without success. In the West Indies, South Africa and India, they had increased the size of their overseas territory at the expense of France and its allies. But with Spain and Portugal in uproar it seemed a good opportunity to re-enter the continent and so in mid-July 1808 a force was despatched to Portugal under the up-and-coming Sir Arthur Wellesley. He defeated the French, who were allowed to evacuate their forces by sea. Further British reinforcements now arrived, but an attempt to invade Spain came to naught. Napoleon personally took charge and forced the British to withdraw. They endured a grim retreat through the mountains at the height of winter and were only rescued by the Royal Navy at Corunna in mid-January 1809 after fighting a desperate rearguard action outside the port.

Napoleon had, however, already returned to Paris. He had heard that Austria, heartened by what was happening in Spain, was about to take up arms again and liberate Germany. Indeed, in April 1809 the Austrians not only invaded Bavaria, but Italy as well. These events were accompanied by an uprising in the mountainous Tyrol. Napoleon arrived at Stuttgart on 16 April to find his armies in disarray, but quickly grasped the situation and, after a series of battles, entered Vienna once more on 13 May. The Austrians still fought on and it was not until Napoleon defeated them yet again at Wagram in early July that they sought an armistice. The subsequent peace they made was at the price of surrendering territory and breaking off all contact with Britain, which once again was virtually on its own. Indeed, apart from at sea and in the Iberian peninsula, continental Europe was in a state of relative peace.

For Britain, Portugal beckoned once more. In April 1809, scarcely three months after the evacuation from Corunna, British troops under Wellesley landed there again. While he soon drove the French out, hopes that he could expel them from Spain as well were dashed when Napoleon sent reinforcements and decisively defeated the Spanish army in November. For the next two years Viscount Wellington, as Wellesley had become, was forced to remain on the defensive in Portugal.

Napoleon reaches Moscow

Concentrating on the business of governing his European empire, Napoleon left fighting the British in Spain to his marshals. Cracks, however, were beginning to appear in his relations with Russia. Apart from growing resentment towards the Duchy of Warsaw, since the Russians traditionally regarded Poland as their backyard, they were also lukewarm about applying the Continental System. Matters came to a head when the Russians began to concentrate troops on their Polish border. In response Napoleon massed an army of nearly 600,000 men. The final aggravation came in June 1812 when Britain made peace with Russia and Sweden. Napoleon crossed the river Niemen in the last week of the month. The Russians fought a series of delaying actions, but it was not until the French were 70 miles from Moscow that they really stood and fought. The Battle of Borodino took place on 7 September. Both sides suffered heavily, but it was the Russians who withdrew at the end of the day and a week later Napoleon was in Moscow. Ominously, just after his troops entered, fires began to break out in the city.

Napoleon was now faced with a dilemma. Even though Moscow was in his hands, the Russians had not surrendered. Rather, they were reorganizing their armies and also beginning to harry his now overstretched supply lines. Worse, there was the prospect of the Russian winter. Eventually Napoleon decided to withdraw to Smolensk and his troops began to leave Moscow on 19 October. Five days later he clashed with a rejuvenated Russian army, which forced him back onto his original line of advance. Because this had been laid waste during the summer fighting, keeping the French troops supplied became a nightmare. They began to straggle, even more so when the first snows arrived at the beginning of November. Realizing that he was in danger of losing his empire, Napoleon returned to Paris in early December. Ravaged by both the weather and the marauding Russians, the remnants of his army struggled back into Prussia leaving some 400,000 of their comrades behind as casualties.

Napoleon retreats to Paris

Encouraged by the disaster that had befallen the French, Prussia and Austria once again declared war on Napoleon and, with the Russians, they began to advance towards the main French defence line on the river Elbe in spring 1813. During the summer a number of battles were fought, with Napoleon attempting to defeat the allied forces one at a time. The campaign culminated in the three-day Battle of Leipzig in October, which ended with Napoleon being forced to withdraw back into France. He hoped that the allies would now pause and enable him to rebuild his exhausted armies. It was not to be. The allies began to cross the French frontier in the last weeks of 1813. Although Napoleon defeated elements of them in various small battles, he could not halt their remorseless advance on Paris. Worse, there was also a threat from the southwest. With his Portuguese and Spanish allies, Wellington had taken to the offensive in 1812 and, in a series of battles and sieges, steadily drove the French forces northwards to Spain's frontier with France.

On 31 March 1814 the allies entered the French capital. Although Napoleon was still determined to keep fighting, many of his marshals were not, and a week later he abdicated. The allies sent him to the Mediterranean island of Elba, while in Paris the monarchy was restored. It seemed as though Napoleon's star had finally been extinguished, but this was not so. In late February 1815 he escaped and landed in the south of France.

Crossing the T

THE STANDARD PRACTICE FOR FLEETS engaged in battle during the 18th and early 19th centuries was to deploy in parallel lines and exchange volleys of cannon fire known as 'broadsides'. Indeed, this is why warships of the day were called 'ships of the line'. The French practice was to aim for the masts and rigging, while the British concentrated on the hull. Inevitably, through dismasting or heavy casualties, opposing ships would become locked together and boarding parties would be sent across to force the opponent to 'strike its colours', which meant surrender. A battle could thus be almost as costly to the victor as it was to the vanquished. An alternative to this was first propagated by a Scottish amateur strategist called John Clerk. He argued that if the attacking fleet's line approached the enemy line at right angles it would present far less of a target. Once it closed it could also engage the opposing ships with both its port and starboard broadsides, doubling its firepower, while the enemy ships could only engage with the broadside facing the attack. This was the tactic that Nelson used at Trafalgar, penetrating the Franco-Spanish line in two places, which became known as 'crossing the T'.

He began an increasingly triumphant march on Paris, his veterans flocking to his standard. The French king fled to Belgium and Napoleon once more held the reins of power. The allies branded him an outlaw and on 13 March declared war once again. Recognizing that it would take time to mobilize their armies, and believing that Napoleon would remain on the defensive, they planned a broad front invasion at the end of June.

The emperor had other ideas, however. Although he had to deploy considerable forces to cover the Rhine and France's southern frontiers, he was able to assemble a strike force of some 130,000 men in the north and intended to attack the Anglo-Belgian force under Wellington and Gebhard von Blücher's Prussians, both of whom were assembling in Belgium. On 16 June Napoleon attacked both at Quatre Bras and Ligny respectively. Wellington withdrew to Waterloo, while Blücher did so to Wavre, thereby splitting the allied forces. Two days later Napoleon attacked Wellington at Waterloo. The British and their Dutch-Belgian allies held firm until the Prussians arrived on the scene in the evening. Forced to withdraw, Napoleon returned to Paris, which was again under threat, and was made to abdicate a second time. He tried to flee by sea, but surrendered to a British frigate and was eventually taken to the remote South Atlantic island of St Helena, where he died in 1821.

Congress of Vienna

The subsequent peace settlement drawn up at the Congress of Vienna resulted in much redrawing of the map of Europe. It also provided the continent, which had been so fought-over for centuries, with 100 years of relative peace. The French practice of conscripting men to maintain the strength of its army came to be adopted by other European powers. But the greatest legacy of the Napoleonic Wars was left by Napoleon himself. Not only did he establish himself was one of history's 'great captains', whose campaigns are still studied by today's soldiers, but his Code Napoleon also continues to provide the framework for many European legal systems.

'**DO NOT COMPARE** YOUR PHYSICAL FORCES WITH THOSE OF THE ENEMY'S, FOR THE SPIRIT SHOULD NOT BE COMPARED WITH MATTER. YOU ARE MEN; THEY ARE BEASTS; YOU ARE FREE, THEY ARE SLAVES.'

General Simon Bolivar, 1814

LIBERATION CAMPAIGNS OF **BOLIVAR** AND **SAN MARTIN**

1813–25

The make-up of South America today is due largely to two remarkable men, Simon Bolivar and José San Martin. By the turn of the 19th century the continent had been under Spanish rule for more than 250 years, with the exception of Brazil, which was under Portuguese control, and the three small colonies of British Guiana, Dutch Suriname and French Guiana in the north. The indigenous population had observed the American and French revolutions and, like the American colonists, had become increasingly resentful at being ruled from so far away.

At the time Europe was at war. Spain was allied to France and Britain was opposed to both. In this context, the British launched two expeditions against Buenos Aires, then capital of the River Plate viceroyalty, in 1806 and 1807. On both occasions, the local militia forced the British contingent to surrender and this gave it confidence that it could defeat European troops. Indeed, with Napoleon's invasion of Spain, the colony was largely left to look after itself and became independent in all but name. In 1811, though, part of the River Plate viceroyalty broke away from the regime in Buenos Aires. This was Paraguay, which declared independence and then came under the rule of the dictator José Rodriguez de Francia, who adopted a policy of isolationism. The area between Paraguay and the Atlantic Ocean was known as the *Banda Oriental* and was claimed by Portugal, though it was part of the River Plate viceroyalty. Local revolutionaries and a force from Buenos Aires wrested it from the Spanish, only to lose it a few years later to Brazil.

In the northern part of South America, agitation was centred on Venezuela. Unlike in the south, this colony was rich in plantations, the Creole owners of which feared that a revolt would be detrimental to their well-being. Spanish troops were also more in evidence. The revolutionary driving force was Francesco Miranda, a soldier who had served with the French during the American War of Independence. On his return home he began to plot a revolution, but was discovered and forced to flee the country. He made his way to Europe, where he spent much time trying to enlist support for revolution. At one point he served as a general in the French Revolutionary army, but was then imprisoned and thrown out of France. The British showed some sympathy, but no more. He tried the United States, again to no avail. Eventually, in 1806, he landed with a small group of foreigners near Caracas and proclaimed the Colombian Republic. He was supported by a British naval squadron, but this backed off after a false report of peace between Britain and Spain. Miranda therefore had to withdraw. In 1811 he landed again, this time encouraged by the fact that the South American governors were mixed over where their loyalties lay: to the

OPPOSITE *José San Martin (1778–1850) and his army cross the Andes in early 1817 to liberate Chile from Spanish rule. The crossing took 21 days in extremes of heat and cold, and many men perished.*

Spanish throne. This time Miranda declared a republic in neighbouring New Granada (present-day Colombia) as well. His revolt was crushed, however, and Miranda died in Spanish captivity in 1816.

Simon Bolivar leads the revolt in the north

One of Miranda's lieutenants was Simon Bolivar, who came from a wealthy Creole family in Caracas. Like Miranda, he had spent much time in Europe and was well educated. After the failure of the revolt, Bolivar fled across the border to New Granada, which was still in rebel hands, although a conflict was raging between rival groups. In 1812 he wrote his first political manifesto, arguing that a strong government, headed by a president for life, was needed if the revolution was to be secured. He also saw the liberation of Venezuela as but the first step in freeing the whole continent. The revolutionary New Granadan government now set about removing the remaining Spanish strongholds on its territory. Although he had received no military training, Bolivar took part and distinguished himself to such an extent that he was made commander of the army.

In May 1813 Bolivar re-entered Venezuela at the head of a mere 650 men. The Spanish strength was some 4000, but Bolivar won a series of quick victories against various detachments of the Spanish force. Many of the local population joined him, enabling him to swell his ranks to 2500 men. After scoring a more significant victory against a force half his size he entered Caracas in August. He was declared ruler, with dictatorial powers, and set about securing the remainder of the country. This was easier said than done. The Spanish still enjoyed superior strength and were much better equipped than Bolivar's army. They had also recruited the *ilaneros*, nomadic cowboys from the Amazon grasslands. The conflict became ever more ruthless and war weariness set in among the civilian population. Bolivar won further victories, but none were decisive and his army was suffering from the endless marching as it pursued one royalist band after another. Then, on 15 June 1815, Bolivar met the ilaneros leader, an embittered revolutionary called José Tomas Boves, at Santa Mara, and was badly beaten. Boves then marched into Caracas and subsequently almost annihilated the remnants of Bolivar's army. Grabbing a large amount of church silver and other treasure so that he could buy more arms, Bolivar fled to Cartagena, New Granada. There he was given troops to continue the process of driving the remaining Spanish out and bringing the country under control. But, with the war in Europe now over, the Spanish were able to send out considerable reinforcements to the Americas. They crossed the border from Venezuela and Bolivar was forced to flee once more, this time to the British colony of Jamaica.

Again he tried to enlist the support of European governments, but without success. Only Haiti, independent since 1805, was prepared to provide money and men. For Bolivar, this was enough, and in March 1816 he sailed to Venezuela once more. But he only had 250 men and was quickly driven out. Undaunted, he made a further attempt at the end of the year, this time with 500 men. Basing himself in the interior of the country, he launched a skilful propaganda campaign and managed to quadruple the size of his force in a very short space of time. At the same time he successfully dealt with attempts by some of his subordinates to usurp his position. With the inclusion of cavalry along the lines of the ilaneros in his ranks, Bolivar set about reducing Spanish garrisons, with some considerable success. The Spanish still vastly outnumbered him, however, and eventually they caught him at La Puerta on 15 March 1818 and decisively defeated him.

Recruitment of European veterans

This setback still did not deter Bolivar. He remained just as driven by the dream of a confederation of South American states respected by the rest of the world. He set about rebuilding his army, but this time, to provide a backbone of discipline and experience, he sent his agents to Europe to recruit former soldiers, especially British ones, who had been discharged at the end of the Napoleonic Wars (see Box). At the same time he continued to wage guerrilla warfare against the Spanish, mainly with his cavalry. He also hatched an ambitious and audacious plan. Republican guerrillas under Francisco de Paula Santander had been operating successfully against the Spanish in northern New Granada and had secured a significant area. Bolivar decided to join him, but to do so meant marching over the inhospitable Andes. He set out in early June 1819 and, after crossing several swollen rivers, his men struggled through the frozen wastes of the mountains. They lost all their horses and cattle, and 1000 of his scantily clothed men

The British mercenaries

WHILE THE SAILOR THOMAS COCHRANE is undoubtedly the most well-known mercenary to take part in the wars of liberation, the vast majority fought under Bolivar in the British and Irish Legions. The liberators themselves consistently looked to Europe for material support and Bolivar in particular wanted military expertise to help him defeat the Spanish. He looked especially to Britain, because of its by then high military reputation and also because the British government was generally sympathetic to his cause. Realizing that the British army was demobilizing after the end of the Napoleonic Wars, Bolivar established an agent in London in spring 1817. He looked specifically for ex-officers and non-commissioned officers, promising them the same rates of pay and the former a rank higher than that they had previously held. Fear of poverty, the promise of adventure, and genuine belief in the cause motivated the volunteers. The first contingent of some 120 officers and 660 NCOs, organized into four battalions and an artillery detachment, set sail in December 1817. So impressed was Bolivar with them that he immediately organized the raising of the 2nd British Legion. This totalled nearly 2000 men, including Germans who had been in the British army's King's German Legion, and sailed during the early part of 1819. An Irish Legion was simultaneously raised. On arrival the units were brought up to strength with local men. They took part in all of Bolivar's battles and after the Battle of Carabobo in June 1821, which secured Ecuador's independence, he called them 'saviours of my country'. Many, however, perished from disease and hardship, as well as on the battlefield.

also perished. Once they were through the mountains and into the valley below, they found the local population only too willing to take care of the survivors, and they quickly recovered their strength. After a few skirmishes with the Spanish, Bolivar's men found their way south to Bogota barred by 3000 enemy troops in a well-entrenched position. Bolivar attacked on 24 July and, although repulsed, inflicted sufficient casualties on his opponents to persuade them to withdraw. Then, on 7 August, he fought another battle at Boyaca. Bolivar managed to get between the Spanish and Bogota and then attacked, his British Legion making a devastating frontal assault. The Spanish were routed and three days later Bolivar entered Bogota. As the Spanish hastily began to evacuate their colony, Bolivar established the Republic of Colombia, with himself as president. It also embraced Venezuela and present-day Ecuador.

Bolivar had enjoyed his first concrete success and it was clear that the tide was beginning to turn. But there was still much to do, especially in finally ridding Venezuela of the Spanish. He was helped in this by unrest back in Spain, which was caused by increasing friction between the autocratic King Ferdinand and some of his more liberally minded subjects. This prompted the Venezuelan Spanish to sign a six-month armistice with Bolivar in November 1820. Nothing favourable came out of this, so Bolivar renewed hostilities. On 25 June 1821, he fought another decisive battle at Carabobo and then entered Caracas. Cartagena then fell after 21 months' siege. All that now remained was to remove the Spanish from the province of Quito (Ecuador). In late May he forced the surrender of the Spanish army there, which meant that the whole of the northern part of Spanish South America had now been liberated. Peru was next on Bolivar's agenda, as it was for South America's other great liberator.

José de San Martin leads the revolt in the south

José de San Martin was five years older than Bolivar, having been born in 1778 at Yapeyu in the far northeastern region of Argentina bordering Brazil. He had studied in Madrid, and, after the French invasion of the country in 1808, had joined the Spanish army and fought in a number of battles. At the same time he came into contact with South Americans bent on liberation, and as a result returned home in 1812 and offered his services. At the time, the river Plate viceroyalty was ruled by a revolutionary junta. In theory this was still subservient to Spain, but in practice it operated as an independent state. At the time, the junta was waging a campaign in the northwest of the territory, the area known as Upper Peru. This bordered the Peruvian viceroyalty and contained a significant Spanish presence. San Martin himself was given the task of raising a mounted regiment and used his experience fighting in Spain to train it. His first opportunity to prove himself came at the end of January 1813. A small Spanish force had crossed over to the west bank of the river Plate near the town of San Lorenzo. San Martin had been ordered to bring such raids to a halt. He moved quickly and easily defeated the Spanish.

Impressed by this, the junta promoted San Martin to general. The war in the north now began to go badly, with the junta's forces suffering a series of defeats. Fears that Buenos Aires might be attacked resulted in a supreme director, Gervasio Antonio de Posadas, being appointed to govern in place of the junta in January 1814. One of his first steps was to create a small fleet under William Brown. The son of Irish immigrants to the United States, he had much experience both as a merchant seaman and with the British Royal Navy, but had settled as a merchant based in Montevideo. Two months later he bested the Spanish naval squadron off Montevideo and removed the maritime threat to Buenos Aires. Matters, however, continued to go badly in the north where, by the end of 1815, the Spanish had regained Upper Peru and incorporated it in the Peru viceroyalty.

The refusal of King Ferdinand of Spain to rule as a constitutional monarch had gone down badly in the colonies. In July 1816, all the provinces of the River Plate viceroyalty bar three, and the *Banda Oriental* (present-day Uruguay), convened a special assembly. This declared Argentina's total independence from the Spanish crown and began to draw up a new constitution. The three absent provinces later incorporated themselves in the new republic. The question of Upper Peru remained, however, and San Martin was appointed to command a new invasion of the region. He soon realized that this might be easier said than done and, fearing another reverse, decided on an alternative plan. This was to get to Peru via the General Captaincy of Chile. There was already an insurrection taking place there under the leadership of Bernardo O'Higgins, with whom San Martin had become friendly when he was in Spain, so cooperation between the two would not be a problem.

On 24 January 1817 San Martin set off from Mendoza, which was on the opposite side of the Andes to Santiago, the Chilean capital, and to the northeast of it, with a force of 3000 infantry, 700 cavalry and 21 guns. He crossed the mountains, arrived on the Chilean coastal plain and met up with O'Higgins. They then advanced towards Santiago, but on 12 February were confronted at Chacabuco by a Spanish force of 1500 infantry, 500 cavalry and 7 guns. In the early hours of the following morning O'Higgins deployed his men to tie the Spanish down frontally. San Martin then turned the Spanish left flank. The result was a rout and O'Higgins and San Martin entered Santiago in triumph two days later. There was still much to be done to liberate the entire country, especially since the Spanish deployed an additional 9000 troops from Peru. There were also the indigenous Marpuche, who inhabited a region south of Santiago and who had managed to remain largely independent of Spanish rule. Indeed, they would not be properly incorporated in the Chilean state until the 1880s.

Chilean independence was eventually declared on 12 February 1818. A month later San Martin and O'Higgins fought the Spanish force from Peru, which was commanded by General Mariano Osorio, at Cancha-Rayada. The Spanish won, capturing most of San Martin's guns, although their casualties in personnel were higher. A major reason for the defeat was that O'Higgins' troops panicked after a false rumour was spread that he had been killed. After this reverse O'Higgins handed over total command of the joint army to San Martin. In April he met Osorio again on the banks of the Maipo River, which runs close to Santiago. This time San Martin had his revenge: using his favourite tactic of turning his opponent's flank, he totally destroyed the Spanish force, killing some 1000 men and capturing 2300 prisoners. Osorio had no option but to take the remnants of his army back into Peru, and the future of Chile's independence was assured.

San Martin could now deal with Peru. A land invasion of Peru from Chile was out of the question since it meant advancing up the spine of the Andes. Therefore it would have to come from the sea, but as the Spanish still had command of this, it would have to be wrested from them first. The Chileans had managed to organize a small navy, whose centrepiece was a captured Spanish frigate, and it was now that a particularly colourful character appeared on the stage. Thomas Cochrane had been an outstanding frigate captain in the British Royal Navy and a perpetual thorn in the French side during the Napoleonic Wars. He had been knighted for his services and had become a Member of Parliament. He was then, however, charged with fraud on the London Stock Exchange and sentenced to a year's imprisonment, stripped of his knighthood, and dismissed from the Royal Navy. The Chileans invited him to take command of their navy and he accepted with alacrity. Arriving at Valparaiso at the end of November, he quickly got to work.

Cochrane put to sea in January 1819, making the frigate *O'Higgins* his flagship. The Spanish squadron was based at the ports of Callao, close to the Peruvian capital Lima, and Valdivia in southern Chile. Cochrane tried to tempt it out so that he could engage it, but without success. He continued to cruise the coasts of Chile and Peru, which at least kept the Spanish ships in port. Finally, in June 1820, he carried out an operation typical of those which had won him fame during the war against France. He sailed into Valdivia harbour, bombarded the fort there, and sent a party ashore to overrun the defences. It was enough to make the Spanish abandon their last outpost on the Chilean coast.

San Martin now felt confident enough to mount his invasion of Peru. Cochrane transported his army to Pisco, 150 miles south of Lima, where it landed on 8 September 1820. At the end of October he moved his army, again by sea, to Huacho, north of Lima. Cochrane then went off to blockade Callao. San Martin gained two victories over the Spanish forces and then, after isolating Lima, tried to negotiate with the Spanish governor of Peru, but without success. His patience finally exhausted, his troops entered Lima on 12 July 1821. Two weeks later, Peruvian independence was declared, with San Martin being made Protector. Callao surrendered a few weeks later.

Liberation movements meet in Peru

With Bolivar having just liberated Quito (Ecuador) there remained the final task of driving the Spanish from their last footholds in northern Peru. To this end, Bolivar and San Martin met for the first time on 26 July 1822. No one knows precisely what occurred at this meeting, but it is clear that the autocratic Bolivar and the more liberally minded San Martin did not personally get on. The upshot was that San Martin bowed out and, after the death of his wife two years later, exiled himself to Europe, where he lived for the rest of his life. It was therefore left to Bolivar to bring the curtain down on the long drama. He forced the Spanish to surrender at the Battle of Ayacucho in December 1824 and then moved on to establish independent Bolivia the following year.

Thus, in the space of 12 years, and operating from the two extreme ends of the continent, Bolivar and San Martin ended Spanish rule and created the South America that we know today.

ABOVE *Simon Bolivar (1783–1803) rose to become president of the Federation of Gran Colombia, which covered the northernmost region of South America, as well as president of Bolivia, which was named after him, and Peru.*

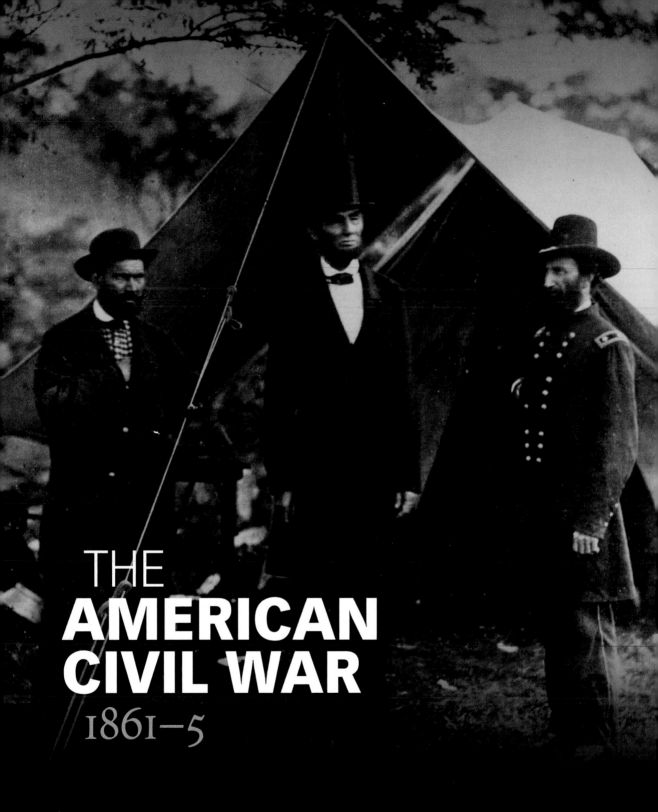

THE
AMERICAN
CIVIL WAR
1861–5

'**WE MUST MAKE THIS CAMPAIGN** AN EXCEEDINGLY ACTIVE ONE. ONLY THEN CAN A WEAKER COUNTRY COPE WITH A STRONGER; IT MUST MAKE UP IN ACTIVITY WHAT IT LACKS IN STRENGTH' General 'Stonewall' Jackson, April 1863

The conflict that tore America apart during the first half of the 1860s has often been called the first of the modern wars because of the new technology that was employed during it. It is also perhaps the most important event in the history of the United States in that before the war the country was a collection of states; afterwards it became a unified nation.

The schism between the North and the South had its origins in economics. The South had one major staple – cotton – while the North had, as a result of the Napoleonic Wars, begun to create an industrial base. To protect these new industries against European competition, tariffs were introduced in 1828, but this did not suit the Southern states and they agitated for their removal. In 1832 Congress removed the duty on a long list of imports, but this did not satisfy the South, and South Carolina even declared both the Tariff Act and its 1832 amendment null and void. A compromise was achieved, but mutual suspicion remained and, indeed, was aggravated. The reason for this was slavery. It had been abolished in the North at the beginning of the century, but the South remained dependent on it, especially on the cotton plantations. During the first part of the 19th century the status quo was maintained by the fact that there was an equal number of slave and non-slave states, but with expansion westwards there was an unwillingness in the North to give new territories statehood unless they were against slavery. This served to put the Southern states in a minority. At the same time their white populations were beginning to decrease through a desire to join the march westwards and the realization that the North was enjoying rapidly increasing prosperity. Besides which, few of the steady flow of immigrants to the New World were settling in the South.

The South secedes from the Union

The result of all this was that the Southern states increasingly adopted a siege mentality and sought vociferously to defend slavery, while the North became determined to have it abolished. Matters began to escalate rapidly when a small group under John Brown, a fanatical Abolitionist, seized the arsenal at Harper's Ferry, Virginia, in October 1859 with the intention of starting a slave revolt. Brown was hanged and there was an outcry in the North. For the South matters went from bad to worse with the 1860 presidential election. It was won by a senator from Illinois, Abraham Lincoln, on the platform that the nation's situation of being 'half slave and half free' could not be allowed to endure. He received no electoral votes from the Southern states. Their reaction was swift. In rapid succession they declared their secession from the Union. They called out their local militias and seized Federal forts, arsenals and customs houses. On 4 February 1861 representatives of the seven states in the Deep South met in Montgomery, Alabama, and

OPPOSITE *Abraham Lincoln visiting his army at Antietam in 1862. He stands alongside General John A. McClernand and (left) Allan Pinkerton, the Union's head of intelligence during the first part of the war.*

formed the government of the Confederate States of America, with President Jefferson Davis at its head. In March, President Lincoln made a final plea for peace. The Confederate response came on 12 April when it bombarded Fort Sumter in Charleston harbour, which was still in Federal hands. Lincoln responded by calling for 75,000 volunteers to crush the insurrection and imposing a naval blockade on the South.

Four more states – Virginia, Arkansas, Tennessee and North Carolina – joined the Confederacy, while Kentucky declared its neutrality. In terms of states, the South was outnumbered two to one. As for population, the North had 22 million, while the South contained a mere 9 million, of whom more than a third were black slaves. Even so, it managed to raise 200,000 volunteers for its army by August 1861, while the North had 300,000 under arms by July. The South, however, had no navy, though a quarter of the US navy's officer corps rallied to the Confederacy, and one of the first acts of the Virginia militia was to seize the Norfolk naval yard. As for the US army, its strength was a mere 16,300 all ranks at the outbreak of war, and it was scattered in frontier posts and coastal forts. A third of its officer corps also went south. Where the North enjoyed a massive advantage was in its industrial base, which made it self-sufficient in terms of waging war. The Confederacy had some industry, but not enough, and would have to supplement its arsenal with munitions from abroad.

The commander-in-chief of the US army, the elderly Wingfield Scott, had proposed a strategy for bringing the South to heel. Named the Anaconda Plan, it called for an advance down the Mississippi to cut the South off and squeeze it into submission. The Northern politicians believed that this would take too long and called for an immediate invasion of Virginia, provoked by the South's decision to move its seat of government from Alabama to Richmond, Virginia, just 100 miles from Washington DC. The focus therefore switched to Virginia. While Union forces succeeded in overrunning the western part of the state, their half-trained army suffered a reverse at Bull Run on 21 July, when Thomas J. Jackson, commanding a Confederate brigade, gained his nickname of Stonewall. The Union troops withdrew, but the Confederates failed to follow up their victory. The Union recognized that it would need to carry out further training before it took to the offensive once more in the east.

Theatres of the war

On account of the Appalachian Mountains, the war on land was fought in two separate theatres – the eastern in Virginia and the western largely in Kentucky, Mississipi and Tennessee. In the latter, 1861 saw both sides win victories. The Union was able to secure Missouri, but was unable to make any significant advance southwards. At sea the Union's blockade was initially not very effective and the South began to operate privateers to prey on merchant vessels. The North did, however, have two amphibious successes. In August a Union flotilla seized Hatteras inlet on the North Carolina coast and then, in November, another expedition secured Port Royal, between Savannah and Charleston. Both these actions helped to tighten the blockade. On 8 November, however, a Union warship's crew boarded the British packet boat *Trent* and took off two Confederate commissioners en route to Britain. British sympathies were, in any event, with the South on account of its cotton, and only some adroit diplomacy averted a British declaration of war.

General George B. McClellan had taken over from Wingfield Scott as commander-in-chief, but he was more concerned to continue training and protect Washington than venture once more into Virginia. Pressured by Lincoln, he eventually began an operation to turn the Confederate flank through an amphibious landing at Urbana on the Rappahannock River. Learning of the plan, J.E. Johnston, the Confederate commander, withdrew behind this river. McClellan then decided to land on the peninsula formed by the rivers York and James and advance on Richmond. The operation opened with a naval battle in the Hampton Roads. On 8 March the Confederate ship *Virginia* ventured out of Norfolk. She had originally been the USS *Merrimack* and had been captured when the Norfolk yard was seized. The Confederates had armoured her and when she took on the Union blockading squadron, she sank three of its six wooden-walled ships, using her metal ram to great effect. She retired to repair some damage and then set out again the following day to destroy the rest of the squadron. Overnight the Union navy had deployed its own ironclad, the *Monitor*. The two fought a four-hour, but inconclusive, action before the *Virginia* withdrew to port. Even so, it marked the end of the wooden warship. More immediately, it meant that McClellan could now land on the Peninsula.

Lincoln now decided to take over the military conduct of the war. He was concerned that sufficient troops be left to protect Washington and would also have preferred another direct attack into Virginia. As it was, McClellan's troops landed on the Peninsula on 22 March and closed with the Confederates. He was intending to bring another 25,000 men from Washington to reinforce his Army of the Potomac, but Lincoln prevented this from happening. This was in part because Stonewall Jackson, who was operating in the Shenandoah Valley between the Allegheny plateau and the Blue Ridge Mountains, was presenting a further threat to the Union capital. Indeed, Robert E. Lee, the overall Confederate commander, decided that Jackson should maintain this threat in order to prevent the forces threatening Richmond from becoming too strong. Jackson conducted a highly skilful campaign during May and early June with 16,000 men, and succeeded in tying down 70,000 Union troops. Meanwhile, McClellan advanced cautiously up the Peninsula, fighting a number of actions with the Confederate rearguard. At Seven Pines on 1 June, with McClellan in sight of Richmond, the Confederates counter-attacked, but without success, their commander being seriously wounded. Jefferson replaced Johnston with Robert E. Lee, who ordered Jackson to withdraw from the Shenandoah Valley and join him. In a sequence of actions collectively known as the Seven Days, Lee launched a series of attacks on McClellan and drove him back to the James River.

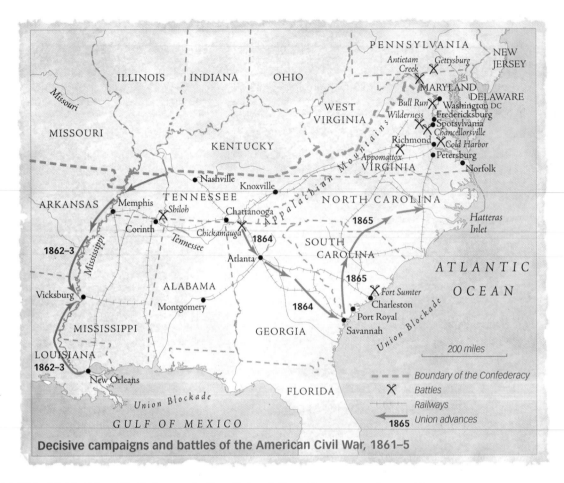

Decisive campaigns and battles of the American Civil War, 1861–5

Battle of Antietam and the Emancipation Proclamation

This reverse of Union fortunes caused Lincoln to embark on another reorganization. He ordered the Army of the Potomac to evacuate the Peninsula and return to Washington and formed a new army, that of Virginia under John Pope. Learning of all this, Lee decided to attack Pope before McClellan could join him. A successful invasion of the North might also encourage Britain and France, also sympathetic to the South, to join the war. He set off into Maryland at the head of his Army of North Virginia in early September 1862. Lincoln, however, had merged Pope's army with McClellan's and the latter, with 97,000 men, set off to confront Lee's 55,000. The Confederates were initially successful, partially thanks to McClellan's hesitation. He finally confronted them at Antietam Creek (Sharpsburg) just east of the Potomac River on 17 September. In the course of what was the bloodiest battle of the whole war, with nearly 20 percent of those engaged becoming casualties, Lee repulsed McClellan and then withdrew back across the Potomac. It marked the end of his invasion attempt and encouraged Lincoln to issue his preliminary Emancipation Proclamation, which announced the freedom of all slaves in the South. McClellan failed to follow Lee up with any energy and so Lincoln replaced him with Ambrose E. Burnside. He attempted another advance on Richmond, but was badly beaten at Fredericksburg in mid-December.

Elsewhere, the Union carried out some more successful amphibious operations on the North Carolina coast and also captured Charleston in April. In the Western theatre there were some significant developments. West of the Mississippi the Confederates enjoyed some early successes, but they eventually failed to secure Arkansas. To the east, Ulysses S. Grant began the year by driving the Confederates out of Kentucky. On 6 April Johnston retaliated by attacking Grant at Shiloh, initially taking him by surprise. At the end of the day the Union line was still firm and Johnston had been wounded. The following day Don Carlos Buell, who had taken Nashville, joined Grant and they followed the Confederates to Corinth, which finally fell to Grant in October. Meanwhile the Confederates had mounted a further invasion of Kentucky in July. This campaign lasted for the remainder of the year with no significant results. It was characterized by deep penetration cavalry raids by both sides. There was also a campaign on the Mississippi itself. Federal forces, assisted by gunboats, advanced south and captured Memphis in June. Simultaneously, a combined force arrived in the Mississippi estuary in March and entered New Orleans at the end of April. Admiral David G. Farragut, commanding the naval element, then made two forays up to Vicksburg and bombarded the forts that protected it. Finally, at the end of the year, Grant began to advance on Vicksburg, which was now the key to securing the river.

Tide turns against the South

1863 was to prove the pivotal year. The naval blockade on the South was becoming ever tighter and little in the way of imports was getting through. In the west the focus was on Vicksburg. After a series of preliminary operations Grant outwitted the Confederates, marching 200 miles in 19 days and living off the country, and placed Vicksburg under siege on 19 May. The defenders held out as long as they could, but with starvation staring them in the face, they surrendered on 4 July, Independence Day. The Confederacy was now isolated.

The fighting continued in Kentucky and Tennessee. After a summer of manoeuvring, the Confederates were driven into Georgia. Then, reinforced, they turned and struck the Union forces at Chickamauga on 19 September. They drove them back to Chattanooga on the Tennessee River and besieged them there. Grant, whom Lincoln had now placed in command of the whole of the Western theatre, rushed post haste from the west and got supplies through to his beleaguered troops via the river. Confident that the Federal troops were trapped, Braxton Bragg, the Confederate commander, sent 20,000 men off to besiege Knoxville. Grant now sent William T. Sherman to relieve Chattanooga. He attacked the Confederates on Lookout Mountain and Missionary Ridge and lifted the siege.

If the tide had turned for the Confederates in the West during 1863 it was even more so in the East. In April Joseph Hooker, now commanding the Army of the Potomac, moved to attack Lee in the Fredericksburg area of Virginia. Lee, although heavily outnumbered, went out to meet him and during the first week in May, in what came to be called the Battle of Chancellorsville, outfought Hooker and forced him back behind the Rappahannock River, but at the cost of losing his outstanding lieutenant Stonewall Jackson. Lee then mounted a second invasion of the north. Brushing aside the Union detachment in the southern part of the Shenandoah Valley, Lee crossed the Potomac and entered Pennsylvania. Hooker's cavalry shadowed the advance north, but he himself made no attempt to intercept Lee's strung-out army. The bulk of Lee's cavalry under J.E.B. Stuart had been screening the Confederate right flank, but now went off into Maryland on a raid round the rear of Hooker's army. Hooker now resigned. George C. Meade replaced him and moved to bring Lee to battle. On 30 June a Union cavalry brigade met one of Lee's brigades near the village of Gettysburg. Both sides quickly reinforced and the result was the Battle of Gettysburg, which began the next day. The key Union position was Cemetery Ridge. For three days the Confederates hammered at it, but failed to break Meade's line. Accepting defeat, Lee withdrew back into Virginia. Coming at the same time as the surrender of Vicksburg, Gettysburg indicated that the writing was on the wall for the Confederacy.

In March 1864 Lincoln appointed Grant general-in-chief on the grounds that he had demonstrated the will to fight and win. Grant's strategy was to wear down Lee's army, while in the west Sherman advanced into the Deep South. Active operations in Virginia began in May. Some punishing battles followed. The first was fought on 5–6 May amid the tangled undergrowth of the Wilderness south of the Rapidan River. Grant then tried to slip round Lee's right but was blocked at Spotsylvania. He tried again and then attempted to split Lee's army. The result was the ten-day Battle of Cold Harbor, just north of Richmond, in early June, in which Lee repulsed Grant. Undeterred, Grant maintained the pressure: he swung westwards and then south to outflank Richmond and its defences and eventually confronted Lee in front of Petersburg on 18 June. He attacked, was again repulsed and placed Petersburg under siege.

Petersburg kept Grant tied down for the remainder of the year, but he kept Lee's army pinned down. Yet, the South was not wholly on the defensive in the Eastern theatre. Jubal Early, who was operating in the Shenandoah Valley, was ordered into Maryland in an attempt to draw off troops from Grant's army. He crossed the Potomac on 2 July, brushed a Union force aside and almost reached the outskirts of Washington. Grant was forced to rush troops to the city to help defend it. Early then withdrew, but made another foray at the end of the month. Grant organized an army under Philip Sheridan to destroy Early. Sheridan laid waste to the Valley and by the end of October had driven Early almost out of it.

It was in the Western theatre that the greatest impact on the war was seen, however. On 5 May 1864 Sherman, at the head of the Union Armies of the Cumberland, the Tennessee and the Ohio, set out from Chattanooga to advance into the Deep South. Facing him was J.E. Johnston's Army of Tennessee, Johnston having recovered from his wounds. Using a series of turning movements Sherman tried to trap and destroy the

Confederate army, but, keen to keep his army intact, Johnston was always too quick for him. His delaying tactics were not, however, popular with the Confederate government and he was replaced in mid-July by John B. Hood. He immediately counter-attacked, was repulsed and forced to withdraw behind the defences protecting the Georgia state capital, Atlanta. No sooner had he done so than he attacked twice again, each time without success. Then, at the end of August, Sherman executed a great wheel round to the south of the city, cutting Hood's lines of communication. Hood was therefore forced to evacuate the city. But Sherman's lines of communication were by now very stretched and vulnerable. He therefore sent one of his armies back to Nashville and Chattanooga. Vowing to live off the land, he set off towards Savannah with the remainder of his troops in mid-November. Sherman's March to the Sea cut a 300-mile swathe of scorched earth through Georgia before it ended with the capture of Savannah on 21 December. It brought the war home to the South like nothing else before it.

On 31 January 1865 Lincoln held a peace conference with the South. He offered total amnesty if it rejoined the Union and abolished slavery. Although now on its knees, the Confederacy insisted on total independence. The war therefore went on. While Grant was still preoccupied around Petersburg, Sherman turned north and began to drive the Army of Tennessee through the Carolinas. Meanwhile, Lee and Grant exchanged blows with little result, apart from steadily weakening the Confederate army. In late March, having finally destroyed Hood's army, Sheridan joined Grant, who decided that the matter must be ended. After two preliminary attacks elsewhere against the defences, he struck directly at Petersburg on 2 April. Lee was forced to abandon his position and now aimed to meet up with Johnston in North Carolina. The Union forces prevented him from making a clean break and, on 9 April, after a final skirmish at Appomattox, Lee surrendered. America had become one nation again.

The role of the railroads

IN 1825 THE FIRST RAILWAY LINE, running between Stockton and Darlington in the north of England, was opened. Over the next few decades the railway rapidly became the most important means of transportation in the Western world. By 1860, the United States could boast of 30,000 miles' worth of track, though only a third of this was in the South. Both sides in the Civil War immediately recognized the military value of the railway in the speedy transport of both troops and supplies. An early instance was the Confederate use of trains to rush troops from the Shenandoah Valley to Manassas to take part in the First Battle of Bull Run in July 1861. The South, however, lacked the industrial resources to maintain and expand its railway system to any great extent – it built only nine of the 470 engines constructed in the USA before 1860. The railways were always vulnerable to attack and were a prime target of the deep penetration cavalry raids mounted by both sides during the course of the conflict. Sherman, too, made a point of destroying all the railways he came across during his campaign in the Deep South and this contributed significantly to the decline in the ability of the Confederacy to maintain the war.

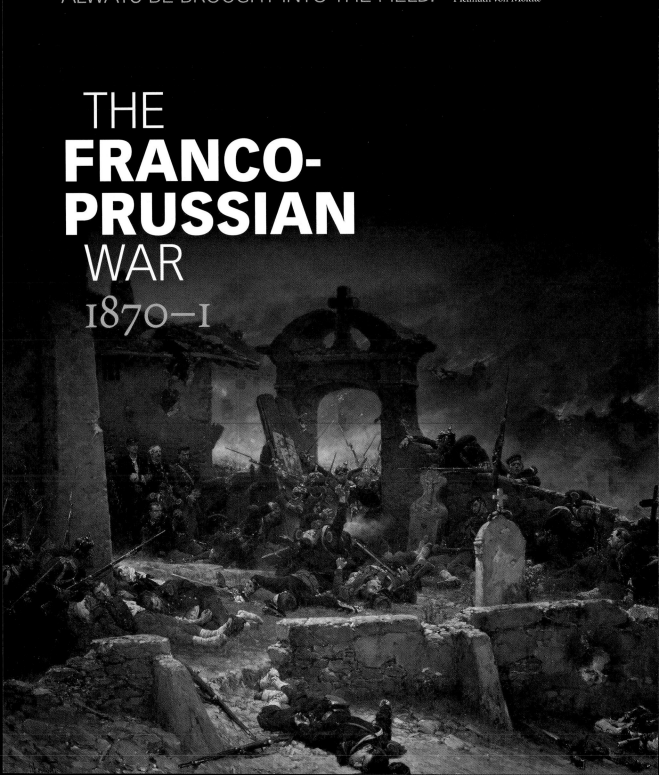

'**ABOVE ALL** THE PLAN OF THE WAR WAS BASED
ON THE RESOLVE TO ATTACK THE ENEMY AT ONCE,
WHEREVER FOUND, AND KEEP THE GERMAN FORCES
SO COMPACT THAT A SUPERIOR FORCE COULD
ALWAYS BE BROUGHT INTO THE FIELD.' Helmuth von Moltke

THE
FRANCO-
PRUSSIAN
WAR
1870–1

After the end of the Napoleonic Wars in 1815, Europe enjoyed a period of peace such as it had hardly known before. It was not until the 1850s that tensions began to surface once again. Britain and France were siding with Turkey, which was under threat from Russia. The result was the Crimean War (1854–6), but apart from some naval action in the Baltic, the battleground was outside Europe.

At the time France was ruled by Louis Napoleon, nephew of the great Buonaparte. He had overthrown the democratic government at the end of 1851 and a year later was elected emperor of France by the French people. Six years later a plot to assassinate him was hatched in London by a revolutionary called Felice Orsini. Not only did this create friction between Britain and France, but it also convinced Louis Napoleon that he must go to war with Austria for the sake of Italian liberation to avoid further assassination attempts. He therefore willingly entered into an alliance with the Italian state of Piedmont and fought the Austrians in 1859. His victories there, following the performance of his troops in the Crimean War, convinced him that he could make France as great as it had been under his uncle.

Re-emergence of Prussia stokes Franco-German enmity

During the 1860s, however, another European state began to flex its muscles. Prussia had become a shadow of what it had been a century before under Frederick the Great. In 1850 it suffered the humiliation of having to surrender its claim to lead the German states and had to accept Austria's leadership of the German Confederation, which was an association of the German states, all of which still enjoyed a significant degree of autonomy. In 1861 William I ascended the Prussian throne. He had had a military education and his first speech from the throne avowed that 'the Prussian army will, in the future, also be the Prussian nation in arms.' A year later he appointed Otto von Bismarck, a professional politician and at the time ambassador to France, as his president-minister. With Count von Roon as war minister and Helmuth von Moltke as chief of staff, William now had a triumvirate that could transform into reality his dream of making Prussia great again.

The Prussian army used conscription for a short term of service in order to build up a trained reserve rapidly. As for Prussia's political ambitions, the first task was to remove Austrian influence from Germany. Schleswig-Holstein, which borders the present-day Danish province of Jutland, had been disputed territory for some time. Although under Danish control, it contained a large German minority, and Bismarck wanted to bring it into the German fold. On 1 February 1864, Prussian troops, with a small Austrian contingent, invaded. There was a two-month truce brokered by Britain in the middle

OPPOSITE *The French defence of St Privat against the cream of the Prussian army on 18 August 1870. Either side could have won the battle, but the French nerve gave way first, with dire consequences for France.*

of the campaign, which ended on 1 August with Denmark surrendering Schleswig-Holstein to Prussia and Austria. They agreed that the Prussians would occupy Schleswig and the Austrians Holstein. Bismarck now sought to isolate Austria. He made an agreement with Louis Napoleon that France could have a free hand in Belgium and the Rhenish provinces if the emperor could persuade Austria to sell the province of Venetia to Italy, which was still pursuing unification. Bismarck also made an alliance with Italy and began to raise the question of Austrian domination of the German Confederation. Finally, he sent Prussian troops into Holstein. It was all too much for the Austrians, and in June 1866 they broke off diplomatic relations with Prussia. The Prussians immediately attacked. The aim was not to crush Austria, but simply to point out forcibly that German nationalism was a fact that Vienna had to accept. The war itself was short and demonstrated only too well what an effective force the Prussian army had become. After a decisive Prussian victory at Königgrätz on 3 July, the Austrian emperor asked Louis Napoleon to intervene, which he did by brokering a peace. Austria renounced all interest in the German states, a North German Confederation – with Prussia at its head – was formed, while the southern German states – a number of which had sided with Austria – formed the Southern Union.

Given that Franco-German enmity had existed for centuries, the formation of the North German Confederation and Prussia's clear desire to unify the whole of Germany made Louis Napoleon feel threatened. The immediate cause of the conflict that was soon to happen came, however, from an unexpected quarter. In 1868 the Spanish Queen Isabella was deposed. A leading soldier was appointed regent and, as there was no Spanish candidate, he looked for a foreign prince to take the throne. Bismarck proposed a distant relative of the Prussian royal house. When the news broke that he was acceptable to Spain, Louis Napoleon was furious, since this brought about the possibility of Prussia and Spain initiating a two-front war against France. He demanded that King William forbid the German candidature and give an assurance that it would never be revived. The father of the candidate had by then withdrawn him and William considered the matter closed. He was therefore irritated at the French demand and declined to see the French ambassador. This was expressed in the so-called 'Ems telegram', which was sent by Bismarck to Paris on 13 July 1870. When it was published Louis Napoleon called a meeting of his council. This also had a calming dispatch from the ambassador himself, but it was now the Paris mob that took over, demanding war. The pressure was too great, and on 19 July France declared war on Prussia.

Military mobilizations

The French army, unlike that of the Prussians, was based upon a system of selective conscription on a long term of service. This seemed suitable at the time since France had a growing empire in Africa and Indo-China, which necessitated troops being overseas for

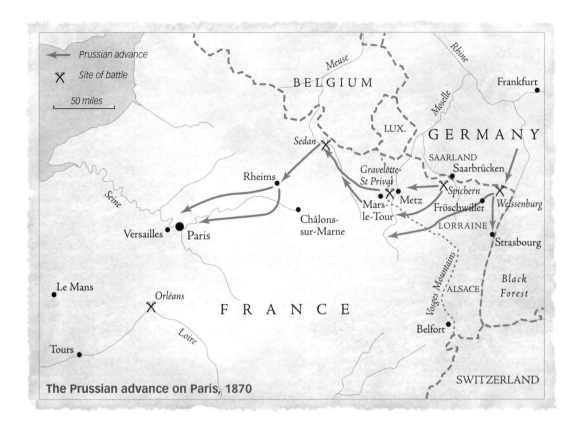

The Prussian advance on Paris, 1870

lengthy periods. It did mean, however, that the availability of trained reserves was much more limited than in the Prussian model. Even so, the army was widely respected abroad, so much so that several foreign armies had adopted its style of uniform, both sides in the American Civil War being a case in point. In France there was a widespread belief that it was its magic quality of *élan* or dash that set it apart from other armies and that this would enable it to secure a quick victory over Prussia. But the French army had a major weakness – a lack of a professional general staff. This was in direct contrast to the Prussians. For decades they had given their staff officers professional training and their work was of very high quality.

The Prussians mobilized in line with plans for war against France that had been drawn up three years earlier. They had concluded that the French would always have a problem with their eastern frontier because the existence of the Vosges Mountains meant that their armies would be physically separated. They also expected the French to make a pre-emptive strike. Making maximum use of the German railways, von Moltke therefore deployed his three armies on the middle Rhine so that they could quickly come to one another's aid in the event of a French attack. As for the overall aim, it was to invade France and march on Paris.

The French plan was grandiose, to say the least. They had calculated that by the ninth day of mobilization they could have 150,000 men deployed in Lorraine and 100,000 in Alsace. They were aware that the Prussians would outnumber them by 100,000 men. Louis Napoleon therefore decided to concentrate the bulk of his army around Metz and Strasbourg and then strike east, forcing the southern German states into neutrality and then linking up with Austria, which he hoped would regard this as an opportunity to gain revenge for 1866. The joint forces would then advance on Berlin, while the French fleet dominated the Baltic. Matters did not turn out as he hoped, simply because the French, unlike the Prussians, did not have a clear-cut mobilization plan. The result was utter confusion, with formations deploying without essential equipment and troops unsure about their deployment positions. Louis Napoleon himself assumed overall command on 28 July. Realizing that none of his scattered army corps were ready, he cancelled the invasion of southern Germany, though the fleet did sail to the Baltic. Instead he formed two armies, one of 55,000 men under Marshal MacMahon around Strasbourg and 128,000 under himself around Metz. One corps remained at Châlons and an additional force was at Belfort to cover the approaches from the Black Forest.

French attack and defeat

Sensing indecision, the Paris mob once more took a hand in affairs and clamoured for an immediate attack. Louis Napoleon obliged and on 1 August Marshal Achille Bazaine, with three corps, began to advance into the Saarland, seizing the heights above Saarbrücken the following day. MacMahon advanced as far east as Weissenburg (Wissembourg), where one of his divisions was surprised by the advancing German Third Army. On 6 August there were two significant actions. At Fröschwiller the Prussian crown prince's Third Army enveloped MacMahon, forcing him to retreat, a retreat that took him all the way to Châlons-sur-Marne in the space of a week. Simultaneously, the other two German armies, which were advancing into Lorraine, clashed with Bazaine at Spichern. Although the German losses were heavier, their continuing attempts to envelop the French ended in Bazaine also withdrawing. Aghast at these defeats, Louis Napoleon relinquished command on 12 August, leaving Bazaine in charge of the Army of the Rhine. He was now withdrawing in the direction of Metz, while MacMahon reorganized at Châlons.

Von Moltke was not prepared to give the French any respite. A clash with Bazaine forced the French commander across the Moselle and denied him the possibility of linking up with MacMahon. On the following day, part of the German Second Army struck him in the flank between Gravelotte and Mars-le-Tour. The battle itself was a draw, characterized by numerous cavalry charges and both sides remaining on the field that night. The next day Bazaine continued his withdrawal towards Metz, but then took up a new position facing west on a ridge between the Moselle and Orne rivers in an attempt to fend off the Prussians. This was the scene of the Battle of Gravelotte-St Privat, which was fought on 18 August. It was a day of furious German attacks, especially against the village of St Privat la Montaigne, which held out against the Prussian Guard until nightfall, when the defenders withdrew into Metz. On the other flank the situation for the Germans became desperate at one point and a French counter-attack only narrowly failed. Bazaine had the resources to mount another blow, but the loss of St Privat dissuaded him and he withdrew the rest of his army into the ancient fortress town.

With Bazaine now bottled up and under siege by the First and a large part of the Second Army, von Moltke now turned his attention to MacMahon, who set out from Châlons on 21 August to relieve the beleaguered Bazaine. He was accompanied by Louis Napoleon, but his move was widely reported by the French press. He also took a northerly route, which invited interception by the Prussians, who advanced on both sides of the Meuse and forced Bazaine northwards towards Sedan and away from Metz. There were a number of clashes. MacMahon was wounded and replaced by Auguste Ducrot. By now the army was at Sedan, had its back to the Belgian frontier and was surrounded on three sides. On 1 September the French tried desperately to break out of the trap, but without success. Louis Napoleon went out under a flag of truce and surrendered himself to the Prussian king. The army, too, laid down its arms. With Bazaine still shut up in Metz the road to Paris was now open.

Declaration of the Third Republic and unification of Germany

While German reinforcements set about reducing the remaining French frontier fortresses, von Moltke advanced with the First and Second Armies to the French capital. Here, on 4 September, the government of the Second Empire was overthrown and the Third Republic declared. A provisional government was established under Léon Gambetta, with General Louis Trochu as president. Trochu was also the governor of Paris and organized a motley body of some 120,000 men – reservists, serving marines, and a large number of untrained recruits – to defend the city. Von Moltke had no wish to incur casualties through an immediate assault and so, on 19 September, he placed Paris under siege and settled down to starve the inhabitants into submission. This was what happened at Metz, which Bazaine and his 170,000 men surrendered on 27 October. It seemed that the war was about to end, but it was not to be, particularly since the day before the siege of Paris began Gambetta had rejected the Prussian peace terms as being too harsh.

Von Moltke's long lines of communication were under constant threat of attack by guerrillas known as *francs-tireurs*. A new French army was also assembling in the Loire valley and Gambetta made an audacious escape from Paris in a hot air balloon to establish a new seat of government at Tours. Trochu also adopted an active defence, making a number of sallies against the besieging forces. The Army of the Loire scored an early success when on 9 November it defeated a Bavarian corps and liberated Orléans.

But the army commander then made the error of dividing his force, sending half away to relieve the French garrison of the frontier fortress of Belfort. Consequently, the Second German Army was able to defeat the remainder and reoccupy Orléans at the beginning of December. The Army of the Loire, its two parts now respectively commanded by Antoine Chanzy and Charles Bourbaki, continued to fight on. Chanzy was defeated at Le Mans in the Loire valley in early January 1871. Bourbaki reached Belfort and fought a three-day battle against the invading force in mid-January. He lost and attempted suicide. German reinforcements then arrived, trapping his army with its back to the Swiss frontier. There was no option but to cross the border, after which the 80,000 survivors were interned by the Swiss.

Outside Paris, meanwhile, von Moltke was becoming impatient and on 5 January began to bombard the city. Two weeks later Trochu made another sally. It was thrown back largely because the ill-disciplined and anarchist-minded middle-aged recruits of the *gardes nationales* fired on their comrades. With starvation beginning to take hold, Trochu sought an armistice on 26 January. Two days later the city surrendered. The garrison marched into captivity, apart from the *gardes nationales*, whom the French asked to retain as the city's police force – a mistake, as it would turn out. Only Belfort, which had been under siege since the beginning of November, still held out. Its garrison did not capitulate until 15 February, and then only after being given an express order to do so by the National Assembly, which was now at Bordeaux.

France's defeat shocked the rest of the Western world. For Prussia, and indeed Germany as a whole, it had much greater significance than just a stunning military

Weapons of the Franco-Prussian War

LIKE THE AMERICAN CIVIL WAR, the conflict between France and Prussia demonstrated rapidly evolving military technology. The principal development during the mid-19th century was that of breech-loading, as opposed to muzzle-loading weapons. For the infantry, the main advantage of this was that they could reload while lying down behind cover and were therefore not so vulnerable. The Prussians used the Dreyse needle gun, so-called because it had a needle, operated by a spring, to strike the base of the cartridge. By 1870 it had been in service for 30 years and was inferior to the French *chassepot*, which had an effective range of 1200 yards. Where the Prussians did enjoy a major advantage was in artillery. Their guns were rifled breech-loaders, but the French retained muzzle-loaders, which took longer to reload. There was a reason for this. Shortly before the outbreak of war in 1870, the French army had begun to introduce a revolutionary new weapon. This was the Reffye *mitrailleuse*, a weapon that consisted of 25 barrels encased in bronze, mounted on an artillery chassis. Using two worm screws, one to move the firing mechanism backwards and forwards and the other to line up the barrels with the firing plate, it could produce automatic fire and was in this sense an early machine gun. Unfortunately, French doctrine viewed it as an artillery piece, rather than an infantry weapon, and it was often employed at its extreme range, which drastically reduced its effectiveness.

victory, however. On 18 January 1871, while Paris was still under siege, an historic event took place in the Hall of Mirrors in the palace at Versailles. King William I was proclaimed emperor of all Germany. The dream of a united nation, with Prussia at its head, had finally been realized.

The Paris Commune

Although the fighting was now at an end, Paris had to endure further agony. On 18 March 1817 the *gardes nationales* rose in revolt and overthrew the city's government. With Paris dissolving into chaos the National Assembly, which had returned from Bordeaux, fled to Versailles. The Paris Commune that was now established began to carry out a programme of radical socialist reforms: to a large extent it had distinct echoes of the 1789 revolution. The National Assembly was not prepared to accept the situation, but there was little that it could do until released prisoners of war had returned and were rearmed. Even so, the government forces, under Marshal MacMahon, began operations as early as 2 April. They steadily reduced the forts surrounding Paris, while the German army of occupation sat back and watched. Finally, on 21 May, they entered the city itself. There followed a week of bitter fighting against the Communards, who barricaded streets and murdered hostages. Many prominent buildings were burned. For their part, the government troops were equally ruthless and when resistance was finally crushed some 20,000 people had lost their lives. The scars of the whole episode would take a long time to heal.

By the time the Paris Commune ended the Treaty of Frankfurt had been signed, formally bringing the Franco-Prussian War to an end. France was forced to hand over the eastern provinces of Alsace and Lorraine to Germany and also had to pay a substantial indemnity. The German army of occupation remained until this had been fully paid, only finally leaving in September 1873. France was left burning with a desire for revenge at the loss of its easternmost provinces and this enmity would contribute to the conflict that would embroil Europe just over 40 years later. By the same token, the new Greater Germany looked set to dominate the continent, contributing further to the friction that was to develop across it.

✦ ✦ ✦

THE
RUSSO-
JAPANESE
WAR
1904–5

'**THE FATE OF THE EMPIRE** RESTS UPON THIS
ONE BATTLE; LET EVERY MAN DO HIS UTMOST.'

Admiral Heihachiro Togo's signal to the Japanese fleet at Tsushima, 27 May 1905

The Russo-Japanese War was in many ways a dress rehearsal for the First World War. Apart from the aeroplane, most of the weapons that would be employed in 1914 were present on the battlefield a decade earlier. As a result, the war gave a good indication of what conflict in the immediate future might be like. It also propelled Japan onto the world stage.

In July 1853, the American commodore Matthew Perry appeared off the Japanese coast near Tokyo. Nine months later he succeeded in getting the Japanese to sign a trade agreement with the United States. This was noteworthy because it ended over 200 years of isolationism during which the Japanese had purposely turned their backs on the Western world. Britain and Holland signed similar treaties, as did Russia shortly afterwards. The result was that the more liberally minded Japanese became keen to acquire Western technology, though not all were happy. Not only did some of the clans fire on Western vessels, but civil war also broke out between those who supported reform and the conservatives. Eventually the reformers won and their success was sealed at the beginning of 1869 when Emperor Mutsuhito adopted the name *Meiji* ('enlightened one'). The Japanese saw modernization of their armed forces as a priority. As a result of their victory over France, they looked to the Prussians when it came to forming a national army, and the model for their fleet was Britain's Royal Navy. Japanese officers were very soon visiting Europe, noting in meticulous detail how things were done so that they could be copied at home.

Beginning of Japanese expansionism

The first test of the new Japanese army came in 1877 when the samurai rebelled against the concept of a modern force based on conscription. The revolt was quickly crushed. Shortly after this, Japan embarked on an expansionist policy, annexing the Ryukyu Islands to the south in spite of Chinese protests. It then turned its attention to Korea, which had been under Chinese influence for centuries. In 1876 the Japanese navy forced the Koreans to sign a trade treaty. This opened several ports to the Japanese, who in turn recognized Korea's independence from China. In the early 1880s unrest culminated in an attack on the Japanese legation in the Korean capital Seoul. Troops were sent in to protect Japanese interests. The Chinese did the same in order to re-establish their suzerainty, and war was only avoided through an agreement by which both countries withdrew their troops and would let each other know if either felt the need to intervene in Korea again. In 1894, however, there was an uprising by anti-foreign elements in Korea. The Koreans requested help from China, which acquiesced. This brought protests from Japan. The result was a war in which the Japanese proved themselves superior both on land and at sea.

OPPOSITE *A Russian gun crew engaging Japanese ships during the siege of Port Arthur. Each gun crew adjusted its own fire, though it was often difficult to judge a gun's accuracy among the shell splashes created by other guns.*

China was forced to recognize the independence of Korea and to cede to Japan Formosa (present-day Taiwan), the Pescadores and the Liaodong peninsula, which lay on the west side of Korea Bay and was part of Manchuria. There was, however, another nation that was taking steps to secure a hold on the region.

Scramble for Manchuria

As soon as the peace treaty had been signed, Russia, France and Germany stepped in. All had interests in China, and Russia, in particular, had designs on Port Arthur (today Lushunkou) at the tip of the Liaodong peninsula as a warm-water port. It demanded that Japan give up its claim to the peninsula, which it felt forced to do in return for an increased Chinese indemnity. The Russians now began to construct a railway linking Port Arthur with Harbin in northeastern China, aiming to connect the line to the Trans-Siberian railway. The Chinese made strong protests and eventually the Russians agreed to lease Manchuria instead of annexing it. The Japanese were not best pleased, but their discontent increased when Russia then tried to exert influence over Korea, obtaining timber concessions in the north of the country and sending in troops to protect them. The Japanese offered to respect the Russian hold over Manchuria in return for recognition that Korea was in Japan's sphere of influence. The Russians ignored this and the Japanese considered that they had no option but to go to war.

Both sides had plans in place for this eventuality. In Japanese eyes, command of the sea was the prime requirement. The Russian Far Eastern Fleet was based at Port Arthur and built around seven elderly battleships and nine armoured cruisers. The Japanese fleet under Admiral Heihachiro Togo was superior in that its ships were more modern and better armed, with the crews better trained. The plan was therefore to try to engage the Russian fleet. If it refused to fight, it was to be blockaded. Port Arthur itself could only be taken from the landward side and so the plan was to land three armies on the north shore of the Bay of Korea. These would advance north and form a blocking position while a fourth army dealt with Port Arthur itself.

The Russians recognized their naval inferiority, but there were conflicting schools of thought about how to deal with the problem. The war minister, General Alexei Kuropatkin, worked on the assumption that the Japanese would mount a major invasion of southern Manchuria. Their likely superiority in strength meant that to attempt to hold the Liaodong peninsula would be foolish. Better, he argued, to withdraw north to Harbin and there await the arrival of reinforcements before going over to the offensive. He accepted that this would leave Port Arthur isolated, but was confident that it could hold out. The Russian navy thought differently. It believed that the Japanese navy could be defeated by reinforcing the Far Eastern Fleet with the Baltic Fleet, even though this would have to steam halfway round the world. The navy also discounted the possibility of Japanese amphibious landings.

As it happened, the Japanese struck before formally declaring war. On the night of 8–9 February 1904 they sent torpedo boats into the harbour at Port Arthur and sank three ships. Simultaneously, Admiral Togo bombarded the Russian shore batteries. On the following day a Japanese cruiser squadron surprised two Russian cruisers in the Korean port of Chemulpo (present-day Incheon), close to Seoul, sinking one and forcing the crew of the other to scuttle her. Only on 10 February did they then declare war. A week later Japanese forces landed at Chemulpo and began to advance northwards to the Yalu River. In early March 1904 Admiral Stepan Makarov arrived to take command of the Russian fleet and launched a series of attacks on the blockading Japanese ships. Unfortunately, in mid-April his flagship struck a mine while returning from one of these sorties and was lost with all hands. Thereafter the Russian ships remained in port.

It was now that the Russian differences over the concept of operations came home to roost. General Kuropatkin was appointed to command the Russian forces in the Far East and set in train his own plan. He began to concentrate all available forces to the south of Mukden (present-day Shenyang) and at the base of the Liaodong peninsula. He then intended to fight a delaying action back to Harbin, while reinforcements were despatched along the Trans-Siberian railway. The tsar, however, had appointed Admiral

BELOW *The beginning of the 1905 Russian Revolution, when workers marching to present a petition to the tsar at the Winter Palace, St Petersburg, on 22 January 1905 were fired on by troops. Uncoordinated uprisings took place elsewhere during the year, but resulted in only modest political reform.*

Evgeni Alekseev, the Far East viceroy, as generalissimo. He had a low opinion of the Japanese and demanded immediate offensive action. The result was that when the Japanese First Army, which had landed at Chemulpo, reached the Yalu, the Russian force covering the river gave battle and was destroyed. This was immediately followed on 5 May by the Japanese Second Army landing on the Liaodong peninsula. It then turned south towards Port Arthur, 40 miles' march away. This landing was followed by that of the Fourth Army to the west of the Yalu.

The Japanese Second Army found its way barred by a Russian position based on Nanshan Hill astride the narrowest part of the peninsula. After a frontal attack had failed, the Japanese took to the surf and outflanked the Russian left, forcing a withdrawal. The Fourth Army then landed and invested Port Arthur, while the Second turned northwards to face the offensive that Alekseev had ordered. The two sides met at Telissu, 80 miles northeast of Port Arthur, on 14 June. The Russians let the Japanese attack them and then withdrew to avoid being outflanked. There were further clashes before Kuropatkin began to pull all his forces back to Liaoyang, some 50 miles south of Mukden, at the beginning of August. Three out of the four Japanese armies under Field Marshal Iwao Oyama concentrated against him there. Reinforced by troops from Russia, Kuropatkin attacked on 25 August. He was repulsed and the Japanese counter-attacked, but without success. The Russians made another unsuccessful assault. Then, even though the Japanese had suffered the heavier casualties, Kuropatkin gave up the excellent defensive position that he held and carried out a systematic withdrawal back towards Mukden, his rearguards keeping the Japanese at bay. He was, however, continuing to receive reinforcements and by early October his army had grown to 200,000 men, outnumbering Oyama's 170,000. Kuropatkin therefore took to the offensive once more and during the first half of the month faced the Japanese at Shaho, 15 miles southwest of Liaoyang. Both sides made attacks, but the result was inconclusive and they dug in where they were.

Siege of Port Arthur

The Port Arthur defences were in three lines. The innermost consisted of a trench system and protected the Old Town. In the middle there was a chain of concrete forts linked by entrenchments and ramparts, while the outermost was made up of a chain of fortified hills. None of these systems was complete, however. The garrison itself consisted of some 40,000 men and 506 guns, but supplies were limited. The besiegers of the Japanese Third Army increased to a strength of some 85,000 men by July and had 474 guns, but this was not enough to guarantee early success. The blockading Japanese fleet also had a problem in that it had been weakened by accidents and the mining of two of its battleships. It was this that concerned Togo, especially when the Russian ships sallied out on 23 June. They evaded action, however, and returned to port. On the landward side the Japanese ground forces made a number of probing attacks during July.

Then, on 7 August, they made a determined assault on the hill defences in the eastern sector and, after bitter fighting, captured them.

The tsar now ordered the Russian fleet to break out of Port Arthur and link up with four cruisers that were based at Vladivostok. Six battleships, five cruisers and eight destroyers set sail on 10 August. They initially managed to evade the Japanese blockading ships, but by afternoon Togo had caught up with them. In the clash that followed the Russian flagship received a direct hit, killing Admiral Vilgelm Vitgelt, who had succeeded Makarov in command. Subsequent orders from the ship were confused and the Russian ships became scattered. One cruiser was sunk and a number of other vessels sought refuge in neutral ports and were interned. The remainder then returned to Port Arthur. One of Togo's cruiser squadrons followed this up three days later by sinking one of the Vladivostok squadron's ships. All this gave Togo mastery of the seas.

The Japanese made a second assault on Port Arthur on 19 August. During the course of five days of bitter fighting, in which their casualties were very heavy, they succeeded in making only small gains. General Maresuke Nogi, who was in command, therefore called for siege artillery. This would take time to arrive, but during the second half of September he made yet another costly attempt to break through the defences. His siege artillery did then materialize. It included massive 280 mm howitzers firing 500-pound shells. Nogi subjected Port Arthur to continuous bombardment throughout October and mounted another assault at the end of the month. This, too, was beaten back by machine-gun fire, artillery and grenades. Yet the garrison's food supplies were dwindling and, with Kuropatkin blocked at Shaho, the prospects of relief appeared slim. But the beleaguered garrison then heard news that the Baltic Fleet had finally sailed.

Awaiting the Baltic Fleet

When war had broken out back in February 1904, the Baltic Fleet was in such a poor state that it was virtually non-operational. There were debates over where it should be sent and the wait for the commissioning of four new battleships also delayed its departure. It finally set sail on 15 October under the command of Admiral Zinovi Rozhdestvenski. It was made up of some 50 ships, but some were very old and mechanically unreliable, while the newest had not completed their sea trials. The quality of both officers and men was generally poor and they faced a further problem. The ships needed to take on coal en route, but most of the coaling stations en route belonged to Britain, which had signed a defensive pact with Japan in 1902. Hence they were barred to the Russians. As a result they were forced to cram the ships with spare coal. Not only did living conditions suffer, but this measure also affected the handling of the ships. This was borne out when the fleet set sail. One ship ran aground and another collided with a torpedo boat.

Once into the North Sea, the fleet ran into British fishing boats in fog. Convinced, for some reason, that Japanese torpedo boats were among them, the Russians opened

Tsushima's influence on warship design

THE BATTLE OF TSUSHIMA was the first proper fleet versus fleet action since Navarino in 1827, when the combined fleets of Britain, France and Russia defeated those of Turkey and Egypt during the Greek War of Independence. Consequently, there was much analysis of the battle and a number of significant lessons were drawn. The general conclusion was that it was the superior speed and firepower of the Japanese ships that had won the day. The result was a new breed of battleship called the Dreadnought, after the first of this type to be built, though the British had conceived her design before the battle took place. The battleships of the day had a variety of armament, but the largest guns, usually 10- or 12-inch, were housed in just two turrets, fore and aft. Tsushima clearly demonstrated that it was the largest guns that had done the damage, especially since the initial and decisive phase had taken place at long range. Hence the new battleships had four or five large-calibre twin turrets with much-reduced smaller armament, primarily to counter the threat of the torpedo boat destroyer. There was also a radical change in fire control. Up until Tsushima, a ship's guns were usually fired individually, with the crews making their own corrections. It was often difficult to identify the splash of their own guns and therefore hard to bring the guns onto the target. The new system therefore called for centralized fire control. The guns were fired in a broadside and corrections for range and direction were made centrally. To maximize the advantage of speed, another new type of ship was also introduced – the battle-cruiser, which had much the same armament as the battleship but sacrificed armoured protection for speed.

fire, sinking some of them. The affair was very embarrassing for the Russians and they had to pay a large indemnity. Rozhdestvenski then sent his slower ships through the Mediterranean and Suez Canal, while the remainder went via the Cape of Good Hope. Arriving off Madagascar, where the fleet was to come together again, the admiral received bad news.

The Japanese had launched another attack on the Port Arthur defences on 26 November 1904. It was as costly as the previous assaults, but eventually they managed to capture the vital 203 Metre Hill, which overlooked the harbour. They continued their attacks and the remaining defences quickly crumbled. On 2 January 1905 the 10,000 members of the garrison who were still standing surrendered. With no Far Eastern Fleet to link up with, and acknowledging that his command was not strong enough on its own to gain a decisive victory, Rozhdestvenski now proposed to his government that he break through to Vladivostok and then threaten the Japanese lines of communication to Manchuria, where Kuropatkin was still fighting. The Russian government agreed to this.

It took considerably longer than expected for the Russian fleet to reunite, and it was not until 10 March that it set sail across the Indian Ocean, but that day also witnessed another reverse for Russian arms. In late January, having built his army up to 300,000 men, Kuropatkin went over to the offensive once more, aiming to destroy Oyama's three armies before Nogi, fresh from his victory at Port Arthur, could join him. The battle took place in a snowstorm and the Russians very nearly broke through, but they failed to capitalize on early success and Oyama counter-attacked. The result was a stalemate. Kuropatkin then withdrew to Mukden and entrenched there. The Japanese began to attack on 21 February, concentrating on the Russian right wing of the 40-mile front. During the next two weeks, and in spite of several Russian counter-attacks, it gradually crumbled. Kuropatkin's communications with the homeland eventually came under threat, and on 10 March he began to fall back on Harbin. Russia's hopes for salvaging the situation were therefore now solely dependent on Rozhdestvenski.

The Admiral decided to take the direct route to Vladivostok. This would take him through the Tsushima Straits (now better known as the Korea Strait), which separate Korea from Japan. He first called into Van Fong Bay in French Indo-China and prepared his ships for battle. He sent his colliers to Shanghai to obtain more coal and entered the South China Sea on 9 May. News of the Russian colliers arriving at Shanghai alerted Togo to the fact that the Russians were likely to pass through the Tsushima Straits and he deployed his fleet accordingly. Rozhdestvenski entered the Straits in a line ahead formation on 27 May. Togo was in a similar formation to the northwest and enjoyed the advantage of being able to steam at almost twice the speed of the Russians. He now turned to cross the Russian line. The Russians altered course, but in vain. The firing then began.

Battle of Tsushima

Superior Japanese firepower, gunnery skills and seamanship quickly made themselves felt. By nightfall, three of the Russian battleships had been sunk and Rozhdestvenski himself had been wounded. The remainder of the Russian ships were desperately trying to escape, pursued by Togo's cruisers and torpedo boats. The destruction was completed on the following day. All that got away were six ships interned in neutral ports, one that reached Madagascar, and one cruiser and two destroyers that eventually made it to Vladivostok. It was a defeat of epic proportions.

At this juncture the United States stepped in to broker a peace. This was sealed through the Treaty of Portsmouth of August 1905. Japan gained everything she had wanted – Russian evacuation of Manchuria, including the handing over of the Liaodong peninsula to Japan, and recognition of Japan's influence over Korea. Japan also gained the southern half of Sakhalin Island to its north. Disgust in Russia at the conduct of the war as a whole manifested itself in revolution, which began on 22 January 1905 when troops fired on strikers in St Petersburg and lasted for the remainder of the year before it was finally crushed. It had, however, sowed the seeds for the more momentous upheaval that followed 12 years later. The war made the world recognize Japan as a major power. It also demonstrated to the peoples of the then-undeveloped world that the 'white man' was not invincible. Finally, the Battle of Tsushima Strait brought about a revolution in warship design (see Box).

'YOU WILL BE HOME BEFORE THE LEAVES HAVE FALLEN FROM THE TREES.'

Kaiser Wilhelm II, addressing his troops, August 1914

THE
FIRST
WORLD
WAR
1914–18

Some have argued that the Napoleonic Wars were the first world conflict in that, while the main fighting took place in Europe, it also spilled over into other continents as well. The Great War of 1914–18 better deserves the title because of the number of nations that eventually became involved. It is, however, more often remembered for the heavy battlefield losses suffered both by sides.

As in other European wars opposing alliances were a major cause. In 1879 Germany formed an alliance with Austria-Hungary, and Italy joined three years later. This became known as the Triple Alliance. To counter this, France and Russia created a pact in 1894, but matters became complicated when, eight years later, Italy declared that it would never go to war with France provided it was allowed a free hand in Libya, which it aimed to wrest from the ailing Ottoman empire. German anti-British propaganda during the war in South Africa against the Boers, and the realization that Germany was now a serious rival in terms of world trade encouraged Britain to sign an entente with France in 1904 and another with Russia three years later. Tension was increased through an arms race: essentially between Britain and Germany, this involved the building of a new breed of battleships, the Dreadnoughts. Kaiser Wilhelm II also had ambitions to enlarge the German footholds in Africa, but this could only be at the expense of the British and French empires.

There was also tension in another part of the Europe – the Balkans. The rivalry there was principally between the Ottoman empire, which had slowly been forced to release its grip on the region, and the Austro-Hungarian empire, but Russia was also involved. When Austria-Hungary annexed Bosnia and Hercegovina to keep these provinces out of Turkish hands, Serbia, one of the independent states, objected with Russian support. This set Austria against Serbia. The Balkan states themselves fought two wars during 1912–13 to rid the region of the Turks. Bulgaria and Turkey came off worst. Serbia's success during the conflicts encouraged it to foster nationalist feeling among the Slavs of Bosnia and Hercegovina, and it was this that produced the spark that lit the fuse.

Balkan spark

On 28 June 1914, Archduke Franz Ferdinand, heir to the Austro-Hungarian throne, and his wife were assassinated by a member of a Bosnian secret society while on an official visit to the capital Sarajevo. Convinced that Serbia was behind it, the Austrians, after consulting with Berlin, issued an ultimatum on 23 July. Among the demands was one that Serbia allow them to conduct their own judicial investigation into the murders. The Serbs refused and so five days later Austria-Hungary declared war. A chain reaction now began. Germany warned Russia against mobilizing in support of Serbia, but when Austrian guns began to

OPPOSITE *British troops on the Western Front, autumn 1916. The desolation, caused largely by artillery fire, is typical of the landscape that marked the battle zone of France and Flanders.*

bombard Belgrade on 30 July, the Russians ordered a full mobilization. Germany followed suit, and France gave full backing to its Russian ally. On 3 August, Europe was at war.

Both sides had plans in place. Germany's principal aim was to avoid a war on two fronts. Assuming that Russia would take longer to mobilize than France, the plan was to strike westwards first. The defeat of France was to be achieved through a scheme that had been perfected during the preceding 20 years. Known as the Schlieffen Plan, after the chief of Germany's general staff who had originally conceived it, it rightly assumed that France's first action would be an attack to regain the provinces of Alsace and Lorraine, which had been lost to Germany in 1870. The Germans therefore intended to attack with seven armies. They would operate like a swinging door with the hinge on the Swiss border. Taking in neutral Belgium and Luxembourg to give themselves more room, the intention was to sweep southwestwards, enveloping Paris and the Channel coast, and then attack the rear of the French armies engaged on the eastern frontier.

The main theatres of war, 1914–18

The German mobilization operated like clockwork. Even before they had declared war, German troops had entered Luxembourg to secure the railways and then demanded free passage of Belgium. The Belgians refused and invasion followed. This prompted Britain, which had stood on the sidelines, to declare war on the strength of an 1839 treaty guaranteeing Belgian neutrality. The German armies swept through much of Belgium, with the only significant resistance coming from the forts around Liège. Leaving Antwerp partially under siege, they then swung south to confront the western French armies and a small British expeditionary force. Meanwhile, on 7 August, the French had executed their Plan XVII: the assault into Alsace and Lorraine. The ten-day Battle of the Frontiers proved to be a disaster. Advancing in Napoleonic style formations they suffered grievously from the German machine guns and artillery, and achieved little or nothing.

After initial clashes, the German wheel forced the Allied left wing into retreat, but their high command was beginning to find it difficult to exercise control over so many armies on such a large canvas. The result was that the wheel passed east of Paris instead of west, exposing the German flank. The French counter-attacked into this on 5 September, and they and the British then followed up the German withdrawal to the river Aisne. Everywhere the front was beginning to solidify, but the Germans now attempted to outflank the Allies in the north. This precipitated the so-called Race to the Sea, which ended on 20 October at Nieuwpoort on the Belgian coast. By that time what remained of the Belgian army had withdrawn to the area between Nieuwpoort and Ypres. It was towards the salient based on the latter that the Germans now mounted repeated attacks. It was the British, who were holding the nose of the salient, who took the brunt, but they managed to cling on, and by late November the Germans had had enough.

Eastern theatre

In the eastern theatre, the Russians aimed to take advantage of the Polish salient by striking from the east with one army in order to pin down the German Eighth Army and then strike from the south to cut it off before advancing on Berlin. The Russian First Army crossed the border on 17 August and started to drive the Germans back. The Second Army began to move up from the south and the German commander decided to withdraw behind the river Vistula. The German high command was not impressed. Paul von Hindenburg was brought out of retirement to replace him and was given Erich Ludendorff, fresh from triumphing over the Liège forts, as his chief of staff. They decided that the Russian Second Army posed the more immediate threat. Leaving just a screen to cover the slow-moving First Army, they moved the bulk of their troops by rail and struck the Russians at Tannenberg on 25 August. In the course of the next five days they shattered the Second Army. A week later they did the same to the First Army.

If the Germans were enjoying success their Austrian ally was not. The Austrians had invaded Serbia but were thrown back across the Danube by mid-December. They also advanced into Galicia, ran headlong into the Russians, who were bent on invading Silesia, and were sent reeling backwards. The newly formed German Ninth Army was sent south to help the Austrians. It drove the Russians back, almost to Warsaw. This helped the Austrians halt the Russian advance on Cracow.

World at war

Campaigns had opened up elsewhere. Far away in China lay the German colony of Kiaochow, with its fortress city of Tsingtao. Honouring their alliance made with the British in 1902, the Japanese laid siege to it in early September, capturing the city two months later. They and the Australians and New Zealanders also occupied Germany's Pacific possessions. German commerce raiders were hunted down and the German Far East naval squadron was eventually cornered and destroyed by British warships near the Falkland Islands in December. In Africa British and French indigenous troops quickly overran Togoland, but Cameroon, also in West Africa, held out until February 1916. South African troops were sent into German South-West Africa (present-day Namibia), which finally surrendered in July 1915. German East Africa proved much harder to crack. The German commander Paul von Lettow-Vorbeck conducted an extremely skilful manoeuvre campaign that lasted for the remainder of the war.

At the end of October 1914 the Central Powers gained a new ally. Turkey had signed a secret treaty with Germany just before the outbreak of war but had hesitated to join in. The Turks were eventually persuaded and on 28 October their fleet, assisted by two German cruisers, bombarded Russian Black Sea ports. The Turks then invaded the Caucasus in late December. Inadequately equipped and supplied, they lost one third of their strength in the mountains before battle had been joined, and their advance was brought to a halt in front of Kars in mid-January. With the Suez Canal vulnerable to Turkish attack from Palestine, the British sent reinforcements to Egypt. A force from India also opened a new front by landing at the head of the Persian Gulf and then advancing to Basra in what was then called Mesopotamia.

In the West, the year 1915 saw both sides attempting to get to grips with trench warfare. The Germans, however, were content to remain on the defensive, except in April, when they attacked the Ypres salient using a new weapon – gas. This enabled them to make some initial gains, but the Allies were able to stabilize the situation. With the British still building up their strength in France and Flanders, the offensive action fell mainly on French shoulders. They launched two offensives in Champagne and two in Artois with no significant success. The British did mount some attacks during the spring and summer and a larger effort at Loos, in support of the second French attack in Artois, in the autumn.

On the Eastern Front, it was the Russians who attacked first, launching one offensive into East Prussia and another towards the Carpathians. They were quickly thrown back in the north, but achieved some success against the Austrians, capturing the important fortress of Przemysl. The Central Powers then launched two counter-offensives. In the north, the Germans almost reached Riga, while in Galicia the Germans and Austrians achieved an immediate breakthrough. Not only was Przemysl recaptured, but the twin offensives also threatened to engulf the Russian centre. The Russians had no option but to withdraw, leaving Poland in the hands of their opponents. The Central Powers also enjoyed success in the Balkans. Bulgaria joined the alliance and in October the Austrians and Bulgarians invaded Serbia, driving its army out of the country. The Austrians, however, had found themselves committed to another theatre. After persuasion by Britain and France, Italy entered the war in May 1915, determined to wrest south Tyrol, with its largely Italian-speaking population, from Austria. Anglo-French forces were also deployed to Salonica in northeastern Greece in October 1915 to counter Bulgaria, but little was to happen here until the very end of the war.

As for Turkey, its fortunes were mixed during 1915. Recognizing the temporary stalemate on the Western Front and wanting to give more direct support to Russia, especially in the Caucasus, the British conceived the idea of forcing their way through to the Black Sea. After naval bombardments against the fort protecting the Dardanelles, which connected the Aegean to the Sea of Marmara, British, Australian and New Zealand troops landed on the Gallipoli peninsula on the north side of the narrows on 25 April, while the French landed on the south side. By now surprise had been lost and a bloody stalemate ensued for the remainder of the year, after which the Allies withdrew their forces. In Mesopotamia the British began an advance up the river Tigris and reached a point 15 miles south of Baghdad in mid-November, but their lines of communication had become overstretched and the Turks forced them to retreat to Kut-al-Amara, which was then put under siege. In Palestine, in February 1915, a Turkish attempt to get across the Suez Canal and invade Egypt had failed. Thereafter this front remained quiet.

A significant development during 1915 concerned the war in the air. In 1914 the primitive aircraft of the time were primarily regarded as a reconnaissance tool. The Germans, however, possessed Zeppelin airships, which had a considerably longer range. They bombed Liège, Antwerp and Warsaw in 1914 and the following year attacked southern England. While the damage they did was slight they did instil uncertainty among the civil population. This turned to fear in mid-1917 when the Germans sent bombers against England and France. The Allies retaliated with raids against western German targets. What all this meant was that a means had been developed to put civilian populations immediately in the firing line.

Western Front, 1916

The Allied plan for 1916 was to be simultaneous offensives on the Russian, Italian and Western fronts. But the Germans, too, were planning an attack. Erich von Falkenhayn, their chief of staff, concluded that Russia was now exhausted and that it was time to concentrate on the West. He chose Verdun, one of the ancient French fortress towns, as the place of attack, in the belief that the French would commit everything to prevent it falling into German hands. The initial assault took place on 21 February 1916. It soon developed into a battle of attrition, as both sides threw in increasing numbers of men into the charnel house, and lasted for the remainder of the year. By then each side had suffered over 300,000 casualties. The French commitment to Verdun meant that the main Allied offensive on the chalklands of France's Somme region became a largely British affair. After a seven-day bombardment the attack was mounted on 1 July. The British army suffered almost 60,000 casualties on that first day, although some gains were made. The battle would continue until late November. Even though an overall advance of no more than eight miles was achieved, the German army also suffered heavy casualties and, taken with those at Verdun, would never be quite the same again.

Eastern Front, 1916

The Russian offensive was conducted by General Alexei Brusilov. He made careful preparations and struck against the Austrians in two places. The northern prong attacked just south of the Pripet marshes on 4 June and in two months drove the Austrians back some 30 miles. In the south the attack was even more successful, destroying one Austrian army and advancing to a depth of 100 miles. The Germans once more came to the help of their ally and the offensive came to a halt by mid-October. One effect of the Brusilov offensive was that it encouraged Romania to join the war on the Allied side and invade Austria-Hungary. This proved a mistake. German forces were deployed and by the end of 1916 had overrun the country. The Italians, who had spent 1915 battling with little success against the Austrian defences in the Isonzo region in the extreme northeast, had their offensive delayed by an Austrian attack in the Trentino east of Lake Garda in May 1916. They lost some ground, but stabilized the front by the end of June and then launched a further series of virtually fruitless attacks in the Isonzo.

In the Caucasus, the Russians launched an offensive in early 1916 and captured Erzerum and Trebizond on the Black Sea. The Turks enjoyed better success in Mesopotamia, however. Despite desperate attempts to relieve it, the British force at Kut-al-Amara was forced to surrender at the end of April. The Suez Canal remained the British priority in Egypt. To ensure its security, they advanced into Sinai and in August rebuffed a Turkish attack at Romani. They also fostered an Arab revolt against Turkish rule in Arabia.

The war at sea saw a significant event on 31 May 1916. Apart from blockading Germany, the British aim was to draw the German High Seas Fleet into battle in the North Sea. There were a number of skirmishes, but it was not until the late spring of 1916 that the Germans set sail. Their plan was to lure the British Grand Fleet out from its anchorages in Scotland and the North Sea and defeat it in detail. In the event, the Battle of Jutland saw the British lose more ships, but the High Seas Fleet returned to port and did not venture out again except to surrender at the end of the war. Instead, the German navy concentrated on submarine warfare. The object was to strangle Britain's maritime communications, which were its lifeblood, and Germany subsequently announced in January 1917 that it would no longer be bound by international conventions and that its U-boats would wage unrestricted warfare.

USA enters and Russia exits, 1917

To the Americans, the war up until now had been seen as just a European problem. The new German announcement provoked them into breaking off diplomatic relations with Berlin. Following this came revelations that the Germans were bent on stirring up trouble in Mexico, the USA's southern neighbour. The result was that on 6 April 1917, the USA declared war. The US navy was able to make an immediate contribution to the war against the U-boats in the Atlantic, which was beginning to have a severe effect on British food imports. On land it would take a considerable period of time before it made its presence felt. This was especially since the US armaments industry was very small and its army would have to be largely equipped by the French and British.

Because of their casualties in 1916, the Germans decided to shorten their line in the west by withdrawing to pre-prepared defences at the base of a large salient stretching from

Restoring mobility to the battlefield

TRENCH WARFARE DEVELOPED EARLY ON the Western Front because the volume of fire produced by machine guns and magazine rifles made defence more powerful than offence, in its ability to inflict heavy casualties on the attacker. During 1915–17 the belief developed that artillery was the means of breaking the deadlock. Preparatory bombardments became prolonged in an effort to pulverize the opponent's defences so that a breakthrough could be achieved, but this meant loss of surprise and sacrifice of mobility because of the churned-up ground. The British answer was the tank, which made its debut in September 1916 during the Battle of the Somme. Early models were, however, very slow and unreliable and too dispersed across the front to make a decisive contribution. The British use of tanks en masse finally demonstrated their potential at Cambrai in November 1917. The battle also showed that the science of artillery had been so developed that it was now possible to lay down accurate fire on a target without having to register the guns beforehand and thus lose surprise. The successful German counter-attack at Cambrai indicated another way of restoring mobility. Their stormtroops were trained to infiltrate through the lines, bypass strongpoints, and penetrate deep enough to cause the maximum confusion. Their supporting artillery concentrated on boxing in the forward defences and attacking communication centres in order to inhibit the movement of reserves. Both methods also relied on close air support. The early 1918 German offensives and the Allies' attack at Amiens that August came close to achieving decisive breakthroughs. That they were unable to do this was because the necessary momentum could not be maintained. The tanks were still too slow and exhausting for their crews to operate. The stormtroops on their feet were also limited in speed, and efficient battlefield communications were still wanting. Emerging technology would overcome these drawbacks during the interwar years and enable the Blitzkrieg tactics of the Second World War.

Arras south to the river Aisne. They did this during the early months of 1917, which slightly wrong-footed an Allied offensive planned for April. The French were to attack between Soissons and Rheims, while the British made a subsidiary effort at Arras. The British made some progress, but the French attack was a disaster, to the extent that there were mutinies, with the French troops refusing to carry out any more attacks. It was therefore the British who had to carry the burden for the remainder of the year. They launched an offensive at Ypres at the end of July, aiming to outflank the Germans with an advance along the Channel coast. Unseasonably wet weather turned the ground into a morass, but the attacks continued until early November amid indescribable conditions. Morale was raised by an initially successful tank attack at Cambrai as soon as the offensive was closed down, after which the Allies went over to the defensive. The reason for this was developments on the Eastern Front.

Coming on top of the disasters they had already suffered, the losses the Russians had endured during the Brusilov offensive were almost the last straw. In March 1917 leftwing and moderate socialist representatives came together in Petrograd (St Petersburg, but renamed in 1914 to sound less German) and established a provisional government. The tsar abdicated and was then arrested. The Germans merely watched and waited, but did transport Bolshevik revolutionary Vladimir Illyich Lenin from exile in Switzerland to neutral Sweden, from where he was able to enter Russia. The Provisional Government tried to honour its obligations to the Allies by launching an offensive in July 1917, but it soon faltered. As agitators increasingly infiltrated the armed forces they began to disintegrate. The Bolsheviks soon had conditions in place for a coup. On 7 November they seized power and then agreed an armistice with the Central Powers. A peace was eventually signed at Brest-Litovsk in March 1918, but not before Ukrainian nationalists had allowed German troops into Russia's 'bread basket' in order to secure foodstuffs to feed their now near-starving peoples.

Germany had begun to transfer troops to the Western Front from the moment the armistice with Russia was agreed. Some also went to help the Austrians against Italy. These struck at the Italians in the Isonzo in late October and sent them reeling back to the river Piave, 120 miles to the southwest. The British and French had to send troops from the Western Front to prevent their ally from collapsing under this assault. It was a grim time for the Allies, but worse was to come.

With American troops now arriving in France, the Germans reasoned that they had to attack before the Allies gained overwhelming strength. They did so in March 1918, driving the British right wing back across the old 1916 Somme battlefield and aiming to split the British from the French. With help from the latter, the offensive was eventually brought to a halt. In April they struck in Flanders, this time to cut the British off from the Channel ports and to bring southeast England within artillery range. Again, the attack ran out of momentum. The Germans then turned against the French, launching three attacks between late May and mid-July. None were decisive and after the last they had to accept that it was now the Allies' turn. Beginning at Amiens on 8 August, the Allies launched a series of rolling offensives, which steadily pushed the Germans back.

Elsewhere the sun was also setting on Germany's allies. In Mesopotamia the British had begun another advance towards Baghdad before the end of 1916, capturing it in May 1917 and reaching as far north as Mosul by November 1918. In Palestine they had advanced steadily through Palestine, entering Jerusalem in December 1917. Sir Edmund Allenby, the British commander, was then forced to send some of his troops to France and not until September 1918 did he attack again. With help from the Arabs, led by T.E. Lawrence, he decisively defeated the Turks at Megiddo and pursued them north to the Sea of Galilee before they sued for peace on 30 October. In September 1918 the Allies also struck at Bulgaria from Salonica and forced it to seek an armistice at the end of the month. In Italy, too, autumn 1918 brought victory. After holding an Austrian attack on the Piave in June, the Allies went over to the offensive in October and rapidly regained the ground lost the previous November, entering Austro-Hungarian territory before an armistice came into effect on 4 November.

Collapse of the old order in Europe

In Germany, 1918 had seen ever-increasing disillusion with the war, its population debilitated by shortages caused by the Allied blockade and the Spanish influenza then sweeping across Europe. Its troops continued to fight bravely on the Western Front, but the Allied pressure was remorseless. The Germans began to put out feelers for peace, but the Allies were firm that they must agree to terms that had been put forward by US President Woodrow Wilson in January 1918 – the so-called Fourteen Points. Leftwing elements began to influence the armed forces and there was mutiny in the High Seas Fleet. A socialist government was then installed, the Kaiser abdicated and an armistice was signed. It came into effect at 11 a.m. on 11 November.

1914–18 brought about enormous upheaval in Europe. Three of the major monarchies came to an end. Russia not only underwent revolution, but also saw Finland, the Baltic states and Poland granted their independence. The Austro-Hungarian empire was broken up, with Hungary, Czechoslovakia and Yugoslavia being created in its place. Germany lost its overseas possessions and the Ottoman empire was no more. It was not, however, to be 'the war to end all war' as people had hoped.

'**DEATH AND SORROW** WILL BE THE COMPANIONS OF OUR JOURNEY; HARDSHIP OUR GARMENT; CONSTANCY AND VALOUR OUR ONLY SHIELD.'

Winston Churchill, House of Commons speech, 8 October 1940

THE
SECOND
WORLD
WAR
1939–45

The Second World War is without doubt the most all-encompassing conflict that the world has ever known. It was a war fought between creeds and often with great ferocity and intense ruthlessness. There were few areas of the globe that were untouched by it. It was also in many ways two separate wars running in parallel – that against Nazism and fascism in Europe, and the conflict against Japanese militarism in the Far East.

The origins of the war lay to a large extent in the peace treaties that had formally brought the Great War of 1914–18 to an end. As far as Germany was concerned, the crippling financial reparations that it was forced to pay had had a grievous effect on its economy. The Allied occupation of the Rhineland and the loss of much of Germany's eastern territory to the newly independent Poland rankled, especially the so-called Polish Corridor. This had been created to give the Poles access to the sea but it physically cut East Prussia off from the rest of the country. Weak government did not help matters and many Germans began to embrace either communism or the new Nazi creed preached by Adolf Hitler. Two of the victors of the Great War, Italy and Japan, were also dissatisfied with the peace treaties. Italy had failed to gain territory in the Balkans, while Japan had hoped for Tsingtao (Qingdao), formerly a German treaty port in China. In Italy's case this resentment, combined with weak government and leftwing-fuelled unrest, resulted in Benito Mussolini and his fascists seizing power in 1922. Japan's political system was bedevilled by corruption. This drove many towards rightwing nationalism, which in turn fed a desire for territorial expansion that was already aggravated by a lack of natural resources and a population explosion.

Legacy of Versailles

The road to war truly began when Hitler came to power in Germany in 1933. He was determined to make the country great again and began by tearing up the Treaty of Versailles, which had ended the First World War. He began a major rearmament programme and sent his troops into the demilitarized Rhineland. Mussolini, keen to expand his African empire, invaded Abyssinia (Ethiopia) in 1935. Hitler and Mussolini sent contingents to help the Nationalists in the Spanish Civil War, while the Soviet Union did the same for the Republicans. Japan, too, had been flexing its muscles. While it had had some rights over southern Manchuria since the Russo-Japanese War, a trumped-up incident in 1931 provided an excuse to take over the remainder of the territory. The League of Nations had been established to prevent aggression such as this, but it proved powerless. Thus, while the League censured Japan, there was little else it could do and Japan promptly left it, as Germany also later did over moves towards global disarmament. The two countries then formed a pact in 1936, which Italy then joined.

OPPOSITE *A Nakajima B5N2 Type 97 torpedo-bomber (US codename Kate) overflying Pearl Harbor, 7 December 1941. The smoke from burning US warships can be clearly seen.*

Britain and France could have acted against this aggression, but proved themselves unwilling to do so.

Hitler, in particular, was encouraged by the lack of positive opposition to his expansionist plans. In March 1938 his troops marched into Austria and *Anschluss* (union) between the two countries was proclaimed. He then turned to Czechoslovakia's western border area, the Sudetenland, which had a significant German population. The Czechs prepared to resist. Britain and France were not yet prepared for war and appeased Hitler by allowing him to annexe the region in return for a declaration that he had no further territorial ambitions. It was an empty promise. In early 1939 Hitler dismembered the rest of Czechoslovakia and then concentrated on Germany's greatest irritation – the Polish Corridor. Britain and France now accepted that Hitler must be stopped and formed an alliance with Poland. They then attempted to get the Soviet Union to join, playing on Hitler's loathing of communism. He turned the tables by signing a pact with the Soviets on 23 August 1939. A secret clause acknowledged Moscow's right to annexe the Baltic states and eastern Poland.

Germany invades Poland

After a fake border incident, the Germans invaded Poland on 1 September. The British and French issued an ultimatum calling on them to withdraw, and two days later were at war with Germany once again. Mussolini, who had annexed Albania in 1939, told Hitler that his country was not yet ready for war. The Poles fought bravely, but could not cope with the pace of the German *Blitzkrieg*, which involved swiftly moving armoured formations operating with close air support. They hoped that the French and British would invade Germany from the west. The French did make a cautious advance into the Saarland, but refused to advance beyond the range of the guns on the Maginot Line, which they had constructed between the wars to protect their eastern frontier. Polish hopes were finally dashed when the Soviet Union invaded from the east on 17 September.

The Germans now turned westwards but did not attack France. Their generals needed time to assimilate the lessons from the Polish campaign. Then winter set in, and it was one of the coldest in Europe on record. Little therefore happened in the west and the period became known as the 'Phoney War'. This also applied to the air, with both sides strictly observing the rule that only military targets could be bombed. At sea there was more activity. Germany had a relatively small, but modern fleet and the policy was to attack Britain's commerce, using both surface ships and U-boats. It was the former that made the greatest impression during the opening period of the war. One vessel, the pocket battleship *Graf Spee*, wreaked havoc in the South Atlantic before eventually being brought to bay off Uruguay.

In the east the Soviets attempted, without success, to obtain a lease on Finnish ports. They therefore attacked Finland at the end of November 1939. The Soviet Union's armed forces were not in a good state, thanks largely to Stalin's purges of the late 1930s, and the

Finns succeeded in holding them. Britain and France hatched plans to send forces to Finland and attention switched to neutral Norway, since troops would have to pass through it to reach Finland. They were also concerned that the Germans might secure Norway's valuable iron-ore deposits. Finland was eventually forced to come to terms with the Soviet Union in March 1940. The following month the Germans invaded Norway, swallowing up Denmark as well. The Allies sent forces by sea to help the Norwegians, but their efforts were poorly coordinated and could not prevent a rapid German advance northwards. The last Allied troops were evacuated from the northern port of Narvik in early June.

The long-awaited German attack against France and the Low Countries finally took place on 10 May 1940. While one army group overran Holland and northern Belgium, a second, with the bulk of the armour, advanced rapidly through the heavily wooded Ardennes region of southern Belgium and cut off the northern Allied armies, as well as outflanking the Maginot Line. Attacks on Allied airfields gained the Germans immediate air superiority, and the use of airborne troops in the Low Countries added to the surprise and confusion. In less than three weeks the German *Blitzkrieg* conquered Holland and Belgium and trapped the northern Anglo-French forces. Some, including the bulk of the British troops, were evacuated by the Royal Navy from Dunkirk. The Germans then dealt with the remainder of France, forcing the French to sign an armistice on 22 June.

Britain stands alone

Britain was now alone, but Hitler's hope that it would seek terms was firmly rebuffed by Prime Minister Winston Churchill. The Germans therefore prepared to invade, but first they needed to obtain air superiority over the English Channel and southern England. During the late summer and early autumn of 1940 a desperate air battle was waged, but the Royal Air Force proved the victor. Hitler therefore postponed invasion and subjected Britain's cities to a winter of bombing, which became known as 'the Blitz'. At sea the situation was equally grim. The German U-boats began to operate from the French Atlantic ports and they and the surface warships caused severe losses to Britain's merchant shipping.

The only place that British ground forces were in action was North Africa. Ten days before the French armistice, Mussolini entered the war. He was determined to enlarge his African empire at the expense of the British. In early September 1940

timeline

1933
Nazis seize power in Germany.

1938
German *Anschluss* with Austria and annexation of Sudetenland.

1939
Invasion of Poland; Britain and France declare war on Germany.

1940
Germany occupies France and Low Countries; Blitz begins on London.

1941
Germany invades USSR; Japan attacks USA.

1942
German Sixth Army surrenders at Stalingrad; Japan occupies Burma and Malaya.

1943
Axis powers defeated in North Africa.

1944
Allies land in Normandy; Paris liberated; Warsaw uprising.

1945
Auschwitz liberated; Allied victory in Europe; atomic bombs dropped on Japan.

Italian forces from neighbouring Libya invaded Egypt, but halted after three days. Three months later the British counter-attacked and drove the Italians back, deep into Libya. They then invaded Italian Eritrea and Abyssinia, both of which were eventually liberated. The British also enjoyed naval successes against the Italians in the Mediterranean.

While Churchill believed that Britain, with the help of its empire, could hold out against the Axis powers, he was certain that the war could not be won without US involvement. Yet most Americans were convinced isolationists and had no wish to become involved in another European squabble. President Franklin Roosevelt was a realist, though, and was certain that the USA would eventually be drawn in. He therefore began to give what help he could to Britain. Principally this was through an arrangement called Lend-Lease, by which Britain would receive munitions, foodstuffs and other material that would be paid for after the war. A similar arrangement also applied to China, which had been under attack from Japan since 1937. This enabled the United States to establish its war industry and become 'the arsenal of democracy'.

Operation Barbarossa

Meanwhile, Hitler had turned his eyes eastwards. Even though he had made a pact with the Soviets it was merely one of convenience and he was determined to crush the USSR. First he needed to secure his southern flank. To this end he launched a diplomatic offensive in southeastern Europe. By March 1941 all the states in this region had allied themselves to Germany, apart from Greece. Mussolini, determined to expand into the Balkans, had attacked Greece from Albania the previous autumn, but his initial invasion had been repulsed. Now faced by the fact that British forces were arriving from North Africa to help the Greeks and an internal coup that removed Yugoslavia from the alliance, Hitler decided he must strike. In early April he invaded both Yugoslavia and Greece and quickly overran them. The invasion of Russia could now go ahead.

Operation Barbarossa, as the invasion was codenamed, was launched in the early hours of 22 June 1941. It caught the Soviet Union totally unprepared and the advance was rapid, with the Soviet forces being trapped in huge pockets. It seemed that nothing could stop the Germans, but Hitler began to interfere with the conduct of operations, changing his mind over whether the main objective was Moscow, Leningrad or the Ukraine. The autumn rain and mud slowed the advance and soon after this the winter snows appeared. The Germans were ill equipped for the intense cold and the advance finally came to a halt, just 20 miles from Moscow, in early December 1941.

Barbarossa lifted considerable military pressure from Britain, but there was little it could do to help its hard-pressed ally, except to intensify its bombing of Germany. Only in the Middle East were British ground forces engaged, and they were experiencing problems. Hitler had sent German troops to help Mussolini in North Africa and under

Erwin Rommel they had driven the British back into Egypt. Britain's traditional naval dominance of the Mediterranean, especially that centred on the vital base of Malta, was also under serious threat from the Axis air forces.

Japan attacks Pearl Harbor

December 1941 brought a dramatic development: the Japanese attack on the US Pacific Fleet base at Pearl Harbor, Hawaii. Although still deeply embroiled in war with China the Japanese had cast envious eyes towards southeast Asia, especially the resource-rich British and Dutch possessions. To ward off any threat from the north they formed a neutrality pact with the Soviet Union in April 1941 and then occupied the now defenceless French Indo-China. But to realize the rest of their dream the Japanese needed to neutralize US naval power in the Pacific. While the Pearl Harbor attack did destroy a number of capital ships, the US aircraft carriers were not present. This would prove critical. The Japanese also attacked US-held Pacific islands, invaded Hong Kong and northern Malaya (today Malaysia) and hit airfields on Singapore and in the Philippines.

The first half of 1942 was grim for the Allies. The Japanese swept all before them, conquering Malaya, Burma, the Dutch East Indies (Indonesia) and the Philippines. At sea the U-boats enjoyed a second 'Happy Time', especially off the poorly defended US eastern seaboard. On the Eastern Front the Germans launched a fresh offensive in the south designed to secure the industrial area between the river Donets in the Ukraine, the Volga in southern Russia, and the oilfields in the Caucasus. North Africa, too, saw Rommel attacking once more. He drove the British back to within 50 miles of Alexandria before his supply lines became overstretched.

Yet the tide did begin to turn. The Americans and Australians thwarted a Japanese plan to secure Port Moresby in Papua New Guinea. More significantly, in June 1942 the Japanese fleet was decisively defeated at Midway, confirming that the carrier had superseded the battleship as the principal naval weapon. Midway forced Japan onto the defensive. That August the long fightback began when US forces landed on Guadalcanal in the Solomon Islands. The German offensive in Russia also ran into trouble. While it reached the Caucasus, Hitler became increasingly mesmerized by the city of Stalingrad (today Volgograd) on the Volga. Stalin ordered it to be defended to the last and a bitter battle ensued. Then, in early November, Anglo-US forces landed in French North-West Africa, coinciding with a decisive British victory over the Axis forces at El Alamein in Egypt.

The tide turns in Europe

February 1943 witnessed a major turning point in the war on the Eastern Front. A Soviet counter-offensive in November 1942 had totally cut the German Sixth Army off at Stalingrad and, after efforts to relieve it had failed, it was forced to surrender. The Soviets also managed partially to lift the siege of Leningrad, which had been invested by German and Finnish forces since summer 1941. In July 1943 the Germans attempted to eradicate the Kursk salient in order to shorten their line. They failed, after what was the largest tank battle of the war, and the Soviets began to move westwards, liberating Kharkov in August.

In western Europe there had also been significant developments. The Axis forces in North Africa were eventually trapped in Tunisia by the British First Army, which included US and French troops, and the Eighth Army, which had pursued Rommel through Libya. They finally surrendered in May 1943. That same month also saw the turning point in the Battle of the Atlantic. Thanks largely to the fact that the Allies now had air coverage over the whole of the North Atlantic, improved anti-submarine tactics, and an increasing ability to decipher the German military codes produced by their Enigma encoding machines, sinkings of U-boats rose significantly. After some disagreement, the Anglo-US strategy was now to knock Italy out of the war and to mount a cross-Channel invasion of the Continent in 1944. To prepare for the latter the British and US air forces now mounted a sustained 'round the clock' bombing offensive on Germany. Anglo-US forces landed on Sicily in July 1943. Mussolini was then deposed and when the Allies landed in Italy itself in early September the country surrendered, though the Germans quickly moved troops into southern Italy to ensure that the Allies would have to fight their way north.

The war against Japan saw the development of two Allied axes of advance in the Pacific during 1943. That in the southwest Pacific worked its way up through the Solomon Islands and along the New Guinea coast through a series of amphibious assaults, while the second moved eastwards across the central Pacific. US submarines were also deeply engaged in a campaign against merchant vessels sailing between southeast Asia and Japan. So successful was this that they ran out of targets during 1944. The British, too, had re-entered Burma.

The principal concern of the Western Allies with regard to the war against Germany in 1944 was the cross-Channel invasion. The Normandy landings of 6 June 1944 were the culmination of some three years of preparation. Not least was the gathering of intelligence, a significant amount of which came from the various resistance movements in the German-occupied countries, and the elaborate deception plans put into effect. There was, however, two months' grim fighting before the Allies were able to break out and liberate northern France. But their supply lines became overstretched and the advance ground almost to a halt, allowing the Germans time to recover.

On the Eastern Front, where the Red Army continued to face the bulk of the German army, the Soviets launched a major offensive to coincide with D-Day. This shattered the German Army Group Centre and took the Soviets to the river Vistula. As they approached it, the Poles in Warsaw rose up against the Germans in the hope that the Red Army would come to their aid. It did not and the uprising was crushed. In the south, Romania was overrun, and in the extreme north the Soviets invaded Finland once more.

In the Pacific the Allies were starting to close in on the Japanese mainland, with the capture of the Marianas putting Japan within range of US strategic bombers. In Burma the Japanese launched a further offensive aimed at invading India. The battle to contain this lasted into the summer. The British then launched their own offensive directed at Rangoon, the capital, while largely Chinese forces moved to reopen the main supply route from India to China in northern Burma.

Germany and Japan surrender

In December 1944 Hitler launched a major counter-offensive in the west through the Ardennes. It initially caught the Americans by surprise, but once the weather cleared and the Allies were able to take advantage of their air superiority, the attack was brought to a halt and the Germans driven back. The Western Allies then advanced to the Rhine, which they crossed in mid-March 1945. The Soviets overran the remainder of eastern Europe and on 13 April they entered Vienna. East Prussia was isolated and their forces closed up to the rivers Oder and Neisse. Berlin was the final prize. General Dwight Eisenhower, the Allied supreme commander on the Western Front, agreed that it should be left to the Soviets. They attacked across the Oder on 16 April and remorselessly fought their way to the centre of the city. Hitler, who had taken up residence in a bunker complex near his chancellery, committed suicide on 30 April and Berlin surrendered two days later. This was followed on 8 May by Germany's unconditional surrender.

The war against Japan went on. In Burma, Rangoon was finally liberated at the beginning of May 1945. While US bombers based in the Marianas subjected Japan itself to intense attack, the Americans tackled the last two stepping stones, the islands of Iwo Jima and Okinawa. The Japanese continued to resist fiercely, increasingly employing suicide tactics. Iwo Jima was secured in mid-March 1945 after a month's fighting, but Okinawa took three months to subdue. While plans were being drawn up for the invasion of Japan itself, the atomic bomb had been produced (see Box). At the end of July the Allies gave

BELOW *Soviet troops in Berlin just after its fall. While the battle for the German capital caused considerable damage, even more had resulted from nearly five years of attacks by Allied bombers.*

The race for the bomb

THE CONCEPT OF THE NUCLEAR WEAPON had its origin in the discovery of radioactivity by Frenchman Henri Becquerel in 1896 while experimenting with uranium. Further investigation over the following decades resulted in the ability to split atoms and recognition that this process was capable of releasing vast amounts of energy. This was eventually established by two Germans, Otto Hahn and Fritz Strassmann, in 1938. On the eve of the outbreak of war, Albert Einstein warned President Roosevelt that Germany was intent on developing a nuclear weapon. The British were also working to the same end. The French were developing nuclear energy for peaceful purposes and recognized that a moderator was needed for the necessary chain reaction to work. Heavy water produced by a plant in Norway was identified and the French bought all existing stocks just before Norway fell. These were then brought to Britain. Lacking the resources to create a bomb on their own, the British proposed to the USA in June 1942 that their efforts be pooled and the so-called Manhattan Project was established. Two parallel concepts, based on uranium and plutonium respectively, were then pursued. The Germans, meanwhile, were drawing on Norwegian heavy water production. Norwegian special forces mounted a successful attack on the plant in February 1943, but this was not enough to prevent the resumption of production. US bombers attacked it that November, so the Germans decided to move all remaining stocks of heavy water and its associated equipment to Germany. However, Norwegian agents succeeded in sinking the ferry transporting these and Germany's dreams of developing a bomb were at an end. Then, on 16 July 1945 a nuclear device was successfully detonated at Alamogordo, New Mexico. Two bombs, one uranium-based and the other plutonium, known as Little Boy and Fat Boy from their respective shapes, were then taken by US cruiser to Tinian in the Marianas from where they were dropped over Japan by B-29 bombers.

Japan an ultimatum to surrender or face the consequences. It was known that the Japanese government was split and the fear was that the faction wanting to fight on until the end would maintain the upper hand. Consequently, atomic bombs were dropped on Hiroshima and then Nagasaki. On 9 August, the day the latter bomb was dropped, Soviet forces invaded Manchuria. It was enough. Emperor Hirohito insisted that peace must be made and the Japanese formally surrendered on 2 September. The war was finally at an end.

Legacies of the Second World War

The Second World War cost some 50 million lives, the majority of them civilians, including some six million Jews, victims of the Holocaust. Much of Europe lay in ruins, as did considerable areas of southeast Asia and the Far East. There were other changes to the world. The United States emerged from it as economically by far the most powerful nation, but the Soviet Union, in spite of the suffering it had endured, now had all of eastern Europe under its thrall. The war spawned a new international organization dedicated to world peace – the United Nations. The initial Japanese successes also encouraged the peoples of southeast Asia to increase their demands for independence from their now exhausted European overlords. Indeed, the war marked the beginning of the end for European colonial empires. Finally, the dropping of the atomic bombs signalled the prospect of a terrible new form of war.

'**EVERYTHING REACTIONARY** IS THE SAME;
IF YOU DON'T HIT IT, IT WON'T FALL.'
Mao Zedong, 1945

THE
CHINESE
CIVIL
WAR
1945–9

The war that brought Mao Zedong and the Communists to power in China was the culmination of almost 20 years of continuous conflict. While Chiang Kai-shek's Nationalists were actually at war with the Communists from 1927, the Japanese invasion of China a decade later caused both to turn against the common foe, and there would be an eight-year interlude before they once more locked horns.

In 1911 Sun Yat-Sen had overthrown the rule of the emperors of China, whose centuries-old feudal style had kept the country anchored to the past and vulnerable to economic pillage by foreign states. He did his best to modernize the country, but was unable to control the anarchy created by the warlords and their private armies. Sun Yat-Sen died in 1925 and was succeeded by his protégé Chiang Kai-shek, a professional army officer. At the time China was being assisted by the Soviet Union in its quest for unification. Indeed, Chiang Kai-shek himself had spent three months in Moscow studying the Soviet military and political systems. The Chinese Communist Party, which was sponsored by the USSR, was also closely allied to the Guomindang (Kuomintang), the Nationalist Party.

The Communist–Nationalist split

In 1926 Chiang Kai-shek launched a military expedition into northern China with two objectives in mind. He wanted to bring the warlords to heel and to remove the Western presence from the so-called treaty ports, where foreign nations were allowed to trade and exploit China's economy. Several warlords were vanquished and Chiang Kai-shek was now approaching Shanghai, where the garrisons of the foreign settlements had been hastily reinforced. Yet open splits between the Communists and Nationalists were appearing, especially over the former's strategy of fomenting urban and rural unrest, which ran counter to Chiang Kai-shek's desire for stability. He now realized that the country needed money to establish a strong central government and this could only come from foreigners and indigenous landowners, but the Communists were opposed to both. Consequently, in April 1927, he broke with the Communists and arrested some of their leaders. He also expelled his Soviet advisers. He secured Beiping (Beijing) in 1928 and the country appeared to be united under the Guomindang government. But the problem of the Communists remained, even though they had been driven from the cities.

The Communists had withdrawn to the Jing Gang Mountains in southern China. Beginning in 1930, Chiang Kai-shek mounted a series of drives to winkle them out. The third of these managed to force them to withdraw further south. In November 1933, this time with a German general as principal adviser, Chiang Kai-shek launched his fifth drive, using aircraft and much artillery, and he eventually succeeded in isolating the Communists

PREVIOUS PAGE *Troops of the People's Liberation Army, called the Red Army until 1946, prepare for the assault on Shanghai, May 1949. The Communist soldiers, carrying a mixture of Japanese, Soviet and US weapons, could be counted in their millions.*

from the support of the local communities. Consequently, in October 1934, the Communists, some 200,000 strong, began a withdrawal that became known as 'the Long March'. Throughout the next year, they marched westwards to Yunnan province and then north to the remote Shaanxi province, constantly harried by Chiang Kai-shek's forces. They crossed numerous mountain ranges and only a quarter of those who set out survived, though another 50,000 joined on the way. By the end of the march Mao Zedong, a founding member of the Chinese Communist Party, had become its overall leader.

Interlude: Japanese aggression

China, however, was facing an external threat from Japan. So engrossed had Chiang Kai-shek been in overcoming the Communists that he had paid little attention to the Japanese annexation of Manchuria, northeast of China proper, in 1931, and its transformation into the puppet state of Manchukuo. Eventually he was kidnapped by two of his generals, who forced him to make a truce with the Communists so that they could both fight the Japanese. This was timely since in July 1937, after Japanese and Chinese troops had exchanged fire at a bridge north of Beiping, open war erupted between the two countries. Within a short time the Japanese had captured Nanking, the Chinese capital at the time. The Guomindang government moved to Chungking (Chongqing) in the mountains above the Yangtze River gorges. By the end of 1938 the Japanese had secured most of China's ports and main railway communications, leaving Mao Zedong and his Communists in the northern hinterland and the Guomindang in the southwest. Mao waged guerrilla warfare against the Japanese, while

BELOW *Mao Zedong addressing Communist troops and Party workers, November 1944. At this stage his priority was to rid China of the Japanese but, unlike Chiang Kai-shek, he was receiving no material support from the Allies.*

Chiang Kai-shek relied on more conventional tactics, but mutual suspicion remained and there were a number of clashes between their forces during 1940–1.

When the United States introduced Lend-Lease in early 1941, it was Chiang Kai-shek who was the beneficiary, not Mao Zedong. Supplies flowed to him through Burma. When the Japanese overran it in early 1942 the supplies were flown across the mountains from India. American suspicion grew, however, that Chiang Kai-shek's priority was to rebuild his armed forces in order to renew his war against the Communists rather than fight the Japanese. In contrast, while Mao's guerrilla tactics did not make much impression on the Japanese, his efforts did gain increasing support from the Chinese people.

When the dropping of the atomic bombs on Japan finally brought the Second World War to an abrupt end, the Chinese were caught by surprise. According to the surrender terms, the Japanese forces in China were to surrender to the Guomindang and not the Communists. To this end, the Americans airlifted Chiang's troops to cities that were in Japanese hands. The 700,000 Japanese troops in Manchuria surrendered to the Soviets, who had overrun the region in the closing days of the war. Some of their arms were then passed to the Communists, who had quickly moved into Manchuria with a view to taking control before the Nationalist forces could arrive. But the Soviets were not able to give the Communists as much help as they wished, since they had signed a treaty with the Guomindang recognizing its right to govern Manchuria.

Resumption of the Civil War

While the US ambassador to China had arranged a meeting between Chiang Kai-shek and Mao Zedong just before the end of hostilities, the mutual mistrust remained and within a few weeks fighting had broken out between the two groups. As far as the Americans were concerned, it was essential that peace be restored. This was especially since China, as one of the major victor states, had been made a permanent member of the United Nations Security Council. Accordingly, at the end of September, US Marines were landed in eastern Hebei and Shandong provinces, with the aim of keeping the Nationalists and Communists apart. The force grew to over 50,000 men and it occupied Beiping and the coastal region of both provinces. The Nationalists took advantage of this. Prevented by the Soviets from landing troops on the Manchurian coast, they sent forces through Hebei and Shandong and attacked the Communists in Manchuria.

In mid-December 1945 General George C. Marshall, the wartime Chairman of the US Joint Chiefs of Staff, was sent out to China on a special mission. He was to encourage Chiang Kai-shek and Mao Zedong to form a government of national unity. If they agreed to do this, the USA would reward them with a large amount of financial aid to help make good the ravages of war. In the middle of the following month he succeeded in brokering a truce, though it did not apply to Manchuria. Marshall followed up this success by getting both sides to agree to the formation of a national army to

Mao Zedong's doctrine of warfare

MAO RECOGNIZED FROM VERY EARLY ON in his career as a committed communist that the overthrow of reactionary regimes could not take place without the support of the people. He also realized that to engage in conventional warfare at the outset was suicidal. He therefore conceived the tactic of *cadre* organization – small groups of dedicated party members, who would be established in remote rural areas, well away from the security forces. These would set up bases and seek to enlist the support of local people through education in communist ideals. They would then be trained in guerrilla warfare and deployed to harass local government forces with the aim of expanding the local area of Communist Party control. Other bases would be set up throughout the country in a system that has been likened to drops of ink on blotting paper. The security forces would become overstretched and demoralized and weaponry captured from them would enhance the firepower of the guerrilla groups. This would lead on to the second phase in which the revolutionary forces were powerful enough to resist destruction by the security forces. It was at this stage that he hoped that popular discontent with the government would be so strong that it would collapse. If this did not happen, the campaign would move on to a third phase: this involved the creation of a proper army capable of taking on government forces in open battle and defeating them. The key to all three phases was to seize the initiative and retain it.

consist of 50 Nationalist and 10 Communist divisions, but this proved to be stillborn. The Soviet forces began to withdraw from Manchuria on 1 March 1946, taking all the Japanese-installed industrial plant with them. The Communists immediately moved into a number of cities and also engaged Chiang Kai-shek's troops as they advanced from the southwest. Both sides were intent on controlling as much territory as possible before the peace negotiations chaired by Marshall came to fruition. The main focus became the city of Sipingjie, an important communications centre south of Changchun in Jilin province. The Communists decided to hold it and were put under siege by the Nationalists in April 1946. They managed to hold out for a month. The Nationalists then brought up reinforcements and, totally outnumbered, the Communists withdrew northwards.

At the beginning of June Marshall managed to establish a truce in Manchuria. This gave the Communists a valuable breathing space, but the truce broke down after just a few weeks and the Nationalists resumed their northward advance. Meanwhile Chiang Kai-shek had re-established his capital at Nanking, before shattering the ceasefire in July by launching a full-blown offensive in northern China. Angered by this, General Marshall ordered an embargo on US military assistance to both sides. This was then followed in September by the US Marines beginning their withdrawal from China. The main effect of the arms embargo was that the Nationalist offensive in Manchuria was halted to conserve supplies, leaving the Communists still in control of the northern part of the region. In China proper, however, Chiang's offensive was very successful, regaining a significant amount of territory. At its conclusion in early November, he told Marshall that he was ready to resume negotiations with the Communists, but they were no longer interested. As a consequence, in January 1947, Marshall asked to be recalled. China was now on its own.

As far as northern China was concerned, Chiang spent the remainder of 1947 concentrating on securing the provinces to the southwest of Beiping, which were the Communist heartland. In March the Nationalists drove Mao out of his capital of Yan'an. That autumn, however, the Communists launched a series of counter-offensives, and succeeded in cutting the Nationalists' lines of communication in northern China. In Manchuria, both sides mounted offensives, but neither made much progress.

By now China as a whole was suffering. The economic situation was becoming worse, with inflation rising sharply. It served to create disillusionment with the Guomindang government. This was aggravated by widespread corruption. The result was that Chiang Kai-shek was losing popular support. He introduced reforms, but it was too little too late. The initiative therefore passed into the hands of the Communists.

The Communists resumed an operation in Manchuria in 1948 that they had attempted the previous autumn, namely to cut Shenyang (Mukden), the main Nationalist base in the region, from northern China, by severing the so-called Liaosi Corridor. Such was its importance that in January 1948 Chiang Kai-shek flew up from Nanking to take personal charge of its defence. Eventually, in September, the Communists succeeded in cutting the corridor. Chiang again flew up and, accepting that Manchuria was now a lost cause, ordered his garrisons to withdraw. They were caught by the Communists near Shenyang at the end of October and annihilated. Enormous quantities of weaponry fell into the hands of the Communists and this provided a significant boost to their military strength.

The Communists were also on the offensive in northern China, recapturing Yan'an in April 1948. They then advanced eastwards, driving the Nationalist armies back towards the coast, as well as securing their hold over northwest China. On 8 July the Nationalists stood and fought at Kaifeng in Hunan province. They forced the Communists to disperse, but suffered some 80,000 casualties. Another major battle was fought at Jinan, the key communications centre on the Yellow River. The Nationalists again suffered heavily, and a significant number of them deserted to the Communists. Then, beginning in early November, came the two-month Battle of Suzhou in the extreme south of Shandong province. Two Communist armies attacked the National forces spread along the Lung-hai railway. In total some 1.2 million men took part and while one Nationalist army group did manage to escape, the other was completely destroyed.

Nationalists exiled to Taiwan

As a result of this disaster Chiang Kai-shek stepped down as president on 21 January 1949, with Vice-President Li Tsung-jen taking over. The next day, Beiping, which had been under siege, surrendered. Mao Zedong then moved his government from Yan'an and established Beiping as his capital, renaming it Beijing again. The following month the last US Marines left the treaty port of Tianjin (Tientsin), signifying the end of US involvement with China. Then, on 1 April, Li Tsung-jen sent a delegation to Beijing with a proposal that the Communists rule China north of the Yangtze and the Nationalists all of the land to the south. Mao Zedong rejected this out of hand, demanding a total Nationalist surrender. The war therefore went on, with the Communists now turning south and advancing across the Yangtze. The Nationalist government had already left Nanking and re-established itself in its previous seat of Chungking. Nanking itself fell to the Communists on 22 April, but two days earlier a British frigate, HMS *Amethyst*, which had been taking supplies to the British legation in Nanking, was engaged by Chinese batteries on the Yangtze. She was disabled and trapped for over three months before making a run for it and escaping to Hong Kong.

The Communist advance southwards was remorseless. Xuzhou (Hsuchow), Nanchang and Shanghai fell in rapid succession. Nationalist soldiers defected in increasing numbers. Guangzhou (Canton) passed into Communist hands on 15 October. Chiang Kai-shek came back into power, but there was nothing he could do to stop the rot. His government was forced to evacuate Chungking and moved to Chengdu, 200 miles to the northwest. On 7 December 1949, with the Communists now approaching his new seat of government, Chiang decided that there was no option but to evacuate the mainland and withdraw to the island of Formosa (Taiwan). He took with him some 600,000 troops and two million civilian refugees.

Two Chinas

Two Chinas now existed – Mao Zedong's People's Republic of China and Chiang Kai-shek's Republic of China. Few gave the latter much chance of survival, but the outbreak of the Korean War changed the situation. When Mao sent troops in to help his beleaguered North Korean ally, the United States vowed that it would give military help to Chiang Kai-shek for the defence of Taiwan. As it was, during the next two decades the People's Liberation Army repeatedly shelled the two Nationalist-held islands of Quemoy and Matsu, which were just off the mainland and regarded by Chiang as essential stepping stones for a return to it, but Beijing never attempted to invade Taiwan. The Americans also supported Taiwan's continued membership of the United Nations at the expense of the People's Republic. Not until 1971 was this finally overturned, with Beijing recognized as the true representative of the Chinese people. Taiwan was offered a separate UN membership, but declined to accept it.

In spite of the fact that Taiwan remains a thorn in the flesh of mainland China (though in recent years economic ties have become close), the Chinese Civil War did result in a unification of the mainland that had never existed before and laid the foundations for the major world power that it has become today. The outcome of the war and Mao Zedong's doctrine of revolutionary warfare (see Box), also served to inspire liberation movements throughout the world, especially in southeast Asia.

THE
COLD WAR
1948–89

"**THUS FAR THE CHIEF PURPOSE** OF OUR MILITARY
ESTABLISHMENT HAS BEEN TO WIN WARS. FROM NOW
ON ITS CHIEF PURPOSE MUST BE TO AVERT THEM."

Bernard Brodie, *The Absolute Weapon: Atomic Power and World Order*, 1946

The 45 years following the end of the Second World War were a period of upheaval. Regional conflicts, many involving struggles for independence from colonial masters or the overthrow of repressive regimes, abounded. For much of the time there was also the threat of a third world war, one very likely to be much more destructive than 1939–45 had been.

The main geographical focus of the Cold War was Germany. In 1945, the Allies agreed to partition the country into four zones of occupation. In the west were the British, French and Americans, while the Soviets held eastern Germany. Berlin, the former German capital, was in the Soviet zone, but all four powers were given a sector of the city to administer. As for the rest of Europe, it had been agreed that the USSR would exercise dominance over those countries that it had liberated, though in Yugoslavia this would be shared with the Western Allies. Democratic elections were also to take place in the liberated East European states. Joseph Stalin had also agreed that Greece should be in the Western sphere. He was true to his word in that when Greece was liberated in late 1944, the Greek Communists attempted a takeover. Civil war erupted and British forces had to intervene. There was no Soviet help for the communists and they were defeated.

In the West there was a general belief that the wartime victors could work together and restore a largely shattered Europe. Doubts soon began to surface among the Western Allies. The Soviets were unwilling to release details of Axis prisoners of war in their hands and were causing difficulties at routine meetings among the occupying powers. While the Western powers believed that it was important that the former enemy states should be encouraged to develop a degree of self-sufficiency, the Soviets appeared bent on removing all surviving industrial plant. More seriously, while it had been agreed that Germany would be treated as one country with freedom of movement between the zones of occupation, in June 1946 the Soviets forbade any further movement of Germans from their zone, though this did not apply to Berlin. Furthermore, while the Western Allies quickly reduced their occupation forces to mere constabularies, the Soviet forces in Eastern Europe remained at almost the same strength as at the end of the war. There were also indications that the Soviets were attempting to export communism. Civil war broke out once more in Greece and there was firm evidence that the communist faction was being given material support by Bulgaria and Albania, both of which had communist governments. There was also communist-inspired unrest in Turkey.

There were other warning signs. In March 1947, US President Harry Truman announced that the United States would provide economic and military assistance to any country threatened by another state. Greece and Turkey were the first to receive this help and the Truman Doctrine would remain in place for the next 20 years. Europe was clearly

OPPOSITE *The Berlin Wall, 1964. The East German border guards in the watchtowers had orders to shoot anyone attempting to escape across it. Officially 133 people lost their lives in this way, but the total may have been higher.*

struggling to recover, leaving it vulnerable to communism, so the Americans came up with another initiative. This was the Marshall Plan, named after General George C. Marshall, former Chairman of the Joint Chiefs of Staff and now Secretary of State. It offered a financial package to all European countries to help them get back on their feet and was eagerly accepted by those in Western Europe. By contrast, Stalin refused to allow Eastern European states to become involved and established his own scheme, Cominform. Indeed, when it looked as if Czechoslovakia might accept Marshall aid, the Soviets engineered a *coup d'état*, enabling a communist takeover. It meant that all of Eastern Europe now had communist governments, which were quick to ban other political parties.

The reaction of the West to the Czechoslovak coup took two forms. In Europe, Britain, France and the Low Countries signed the Brussels Treaty in March 1948. This was a political, economic and military alliance designed to last for 50 years. It was followed by the establishment of the Western European Defence Organization. In the United States, President Truman wanted the armed forces to be quadrupled in strength, but Congress, believing that sole ownership of the nuclear weapon meant that large ground forces were unnecessary, would only allow him a modest increase.

Berlin crisis

The first real test of the West's will came on 24 June 1948 when the Soviets sealed all ground links to West Berlin. Since the inhabitants were completely dependent on these for the essentials of life, the threat of starvation loomed. The Western Allies therefore mounted a massive air supply operation, which became known as the Berlin Airlift. The Soviets did not believe that the airlift could be sustained, but it was, and road and rail links were eventually reopened in early May 1949.

American complacency over nuclear weapons received a rude shock. On 29 August 1949 the Soviet Union carried out a successful atomic bomb test. That it had been able to develop the weapon so quickly was largely as a result of information passed by spies who were working in the US nuclear programme. Their motivation was partly ideological and partly because they believed that the world was more unstable with just one side possessing nuclear weapons. Three years later the USA successfully exploded the hydrogen bomb, many times more powerful than the A-Bomb, but the Soviets did the same less than a year later. A nuclear arms race quickly developed, as did a nuclear strategy. The West signalled that any attack on Western Europe would bring an immediate nuclear response, while Moscow warned that any nuclear attack would bring about an immediate response in kind. This became known as the doctrine of Mutually Assured Destruction (MAD).

The North Atlantic Treaty Organization (NATO) had been established in April 1949 to improve the protection of Western Europe, and it included the USA and Canada. An attack on one member state would be considered an attack on the alliance as a whole. The USSR was unsurprisingly hostile. NATO continued to believe in the concept of Germany as one country, but the Soviets had already formed a German government in their zone and in 1952, after this began to complain about the number of East Germans continuing to flee to the West, they began to fence it in, sowing minefields along its length. It became the Inner German Border and the symbol of the divided Germany.

Korean War, 1950–3

The Cold War did become hot at one point. In June 1950, communist North Korea invaded its southern neighbour. In line with the Truman Doctrine, the USA wanted to go to the support of South Korea. It obtained UN Security Council backing, since the USSR was boycotting the UN for its refusal to recognize the recently created People's Republic of China, and a multinational force was deployed under US command. In spite of Soviet technical support for the North Koreans, they were driven back and the multinational force invaded the North. Mao Zedong then sent in troops, which drove the UN forces back to the border with South Korea. The UN commander, General Douglas MacArthur, wanted to launch a nuclear strike against China, but President Truman was not prepared to risk another world war and removed him from command. Eventually an armistice was signed in 1953.

By this time the United States was gripped by an anti-communist hysteria, led by Senator Joseph McCarthy, who convinced many that communists had infiltrated every walk of life. Even Hollywood fell victim to this, with a number of stars, including the legendary Charlie Chaplin, being forced to leave the country. But 1953 did witness glimmers of hope for the West. In May there was widespread industrial unrest in East Germany that resulted in a number of fatalities. More significant was the death of Stalin in the same year, but his successor Nikita Khrushchev proved to be just as hardline. In 1954 he reaffirmed the German Democratic Republic (founded in 1949) to be a sovereign state. The West refused to recognize it as such and the following year established the Federal Republic of Germany, granting it instant membership of NATO. The immediate Soviet response to this was the creation of the Warsaw Pact.

The military blocs

Not all of the Soviet Union's satellite states were content to be dictated to by Moscow. In October 1956 Hungarians staged an uprising against their hardline government, replacing

timeline

1948
Berlin Airlift in response to blockade.

1949
NATO established; USSR carries out A-bomb test; GDR founded.

1950
Korean War begins.

1953
Korean War armistice; Stalin dies.

1956
Suez crisis; Hungarian revolt.

1961
Bay of Pigs invasion of Cuba fails; Berlin Wall erected.

1962
Cuban missile crisis.

1969
SALT begins in Helsinki.

1975
Helsinki Conference.

1979
Soviet troops invade Afghanistan.

1985
Gorbachev becomes Soviet leader.

1989
Berlin Wall falls; collapse of Eastern Bloc.

it with one that was more liberal. The Soviet reaction was swift. They sent tanks into Budapest and crushed the dissidents, installing a new hardline government. There was little that the West could do. Its attention had been distracted by the Suez crisis, which had caused a difference between Britain and France on one side and the USA on the other. In any event, taking military action over Hungary would very likely have led to all-out nuclear war. The Western Allies did try to condemn the USSR at the UN, but the Soviets merely used their veto, as they often did to frustrate the West. In the context of Suez, the Warsaw Pact was making its presence felt in the Middle East, supplying arms and military advice to a number of Arab countries, notably Egypt and Syria. It was also beginning to provide support for liberation movements in Africa, as the Chinese were doing in southeast Asia.

A propaganda war was also being waged, especially directed at the Third World. Radio Moscow and the Voice of America fought it out over the airwaves. Literature in the form of newspapers and magazines glorified communism and capitalism. Disinformation became a key tool. Another propaganda medium was the space race, with the USSR achieving a significant coup with its 1957 Sputnik launch and subsequent space successes. Espionage was intense on both sides and there were a number of high-profile spy trials. Particularly embarrassing for the Americans was that of Captain Gary Powers in 1960: he was shot down over Soviet territory in his U-2 spy plane and Moscow reaped maximum propaganda from the episode.

The end of the 1950s and the beginning of the next decade was an especially tense time. In January 1959, and after a six-year campaign, Fidel Castro overthrew the corrupt Batista regime in Cuba. His Marxist views gave immediate concern to the Americans, as Cuba was in their 'backyard'. Consequently, they gave support to an attempt by Cuban exiles to reclaim the island. The 1961 Bay of Pigs landing was a disaster, however, and put Castro firmly in the Moscow camp, so much so that he allowed the Soviets to establish a nuclear

BELOW *Soviet T-54 tanks on the streets of Budapest, November 1956. The Hungarian patriots had no anti-tank weapons, apart from homemade 'Molotov cocktail' petrol bombs, and it was inevitable that they would be crushed.*

rocket base on Cuba. In October 1962 the Americans identified what was happening and warned Moscow that they would sink the Soviet ships carrying the rockets to Cuba unless the installations were dismantled and withdrawn. It was a very tense time, but President John F. Kennedy and Khrushchev were able to defuse the situation. The Soviets agreed to withdraw from Cuba in return for the Americans removing nuclear weapons sites that they had recently established in Turkey. Castro, however, remained a hero in leftwing eyes and inspired Marxist movements throughout Latin America. The result of this was that the USA often found itself supporting repressive rightwing regimes or helping to overthrow potentially hostile governments and replacing them with those more to its liking. A more positive result of the Cuban missile crisis, however, was the setting up of a direct telephone link between the Kremlin and the White House so that future crises could be defused more quickly.

From the 1960s to détente

Worried by the constant flow of East Germans to the West via Berlin, the GDR government constructed a wall to separate East Berlin from the rest of the city in August 1961. Those attempting to escape over it were shot by the East German border guards. As a result, the Berlin Wall soon took over from the Inner German Border as the primary symbol of the Cold War. As the 1960s continued, the United States became increasingly embroiled in Vietnam. Under President Lyndon Johnson there were attempts to encourage a thaw in US–Soviet relations, but these received a setback in August 1968. That spring a more liberal government had taken over in Czechoslovakia. Civil rights were improved and censorship relaxed. This was not, however, to the liking of Soviet premier Leonid Brezhnev, who organized other Warsaw Pact members to send troops into Czechoslovakia. Unlike in 1956 there was no armed resistance and the Czech government was replaced by one more amenable to Moscow. A month later Brezhnev justified his actions by stating that the Soviet Union had the right to assist any Marxist-Leninist government to deal with counter-revolutionary forces. This became known as the Brezhnev Doctrine.

Under President Richard Nixon, America gradually disengaged from Vietnam. The country had lost its appetite for foreign interventions and the Truman Doctrine was at an end. Instead he embarked on a policy of détente with the Eastern Bloc. He was helped by the West German Chancellor Willy Brandt, who accepted the fact that, like it or not, Germany was two separate states and at the end of 1972 signed a treaty with the German Democratic Republic in which each recognized the other's sovereignty. Nixon, on the other hand, was primarily concerned with reducing the nuclear arms race. By the early 1970s, NATO had adopted a new strategy, known as Flexible Response. Rather than immediately respond with nuclear weapons if the Warsaw Pact carried out aggression against a NATO member, the response would be graduated, using conventional weapons first before resorting to tactical nuclear weapons. The Soviets were also considering an initial conventional strike. This was combined with the realization that both sides had a surplus of nuclear weapons, even when retaining a second strike capability was taken into account. The upshot was the beginning of the Strategic Arms Limitation Talks (SALT) in 1969. These resulted in a number of agreements being signed during 1972–4. The key agreements limited the number of strategic missile launchers that each side could possess and also imposed severe restrictions on the deployment of anti-ballistic missile systems on the grounds that an effective defence against nuclear attack would reduce the deterrence value of nuclear weapons. A further step towards reducing tension in Europe was the 1975 Helsinki Conference on Security and Cooperation, at which 35 nations agreed to recognize national borders as they existed, legitimizing the Soviet dominance of Eastern Europe. They also concurred over the free movement of people across state borders and agreed to an improvement in human rights. These, however, were largely ignored by the Soviet Union.

Although tensions in Europe were reduced, the Soviet Union was nonetheless looking to exert its influence elsewhere in the world. To this end it had created a large and very modern navy, whose ships were increasingly seen all over the world. In December 1979 it also demonstrated that the Brezhnev Doctrine did not just apply to Warsaw Pact states. There had been a Soviet-engineered Marxist coup in Afghanistan in 1978. The new government embarked on a modernization programme that proved unpopular and led to open rebellion. The Soviets therefore sent troops in to prop up the government. The United States, its confidence shaken by Vietnam, felt powerless to do anything, apart from boycotting the 1980 Moscow Olympics. There was also a realization that the Soviet Union had been modernizing its theatre nuclear weapons and now possessed a dangerous superiority in these.

Gorbachev and the end of the Cold War

The early 1980s saw changes, however. In 1981 there was considerable industrial unrest in Poland and martial law was introduced. In Afghanistan it became clear that the Soviet forces were becoming bogged down and it was increasingly being called the Soviet Union's Vietnam. By contrast, two new figures arrived on the scene in the West: US President Ronald Reagan and British Prime Minister Margaret Thatcher. They demonstrated a new resolve and began by deploying new theatre nuclear missiles to Europe. The 1982 Falklands campaign and the US intervention in Grenada in 1983 demonstrated that they were not afraid to use force, as did significant increases in US defence spending and high-profile large-scale military manoeuvres. Brezhnev died in 1982 and both his two successors died soon afterwards. This brought a much younger man, Mikhail Gorbachev, to the fore. He well appreciated the growing unrest in Eastern Europe, the strain of Afghanistan and the fact that the Soviet economy could no longer sustain the arms race. He opened a dialogue with Reagan and reached agreement on arms reductions. He also encouraged a new policy of *Glasnost* (openness) within the Soviet Union and made life much freer for Soviet citizens. Finally, in 1988 he began a withdrawal from Afghanistan.

Gorbachev's reforms worried the hardline leaders of some East European states. They believed that liberalization would weaken their iron grip. Others allowed matters to take their course. 1989 proved to be the pivotal year. In May the Hungarians opened their borders with the West and an increasing flood of East Germans used this route to reach West Germany. A general election in Poland that June saw the communists swept from power. Increasingly vociferous demonstrations in East Germany ousted its long-time leader Erich Honecker in mid-October. The successor communist administration lasted just three weeks. On 10 November crowds gathered on both sides of the Berlin Wall and began to tear it down. Within weeks every communist regime in Eastern Europe had been toppled.

The Cold War was at an end and a new dawn appeared to beckon. Germany was reunified, though it has not become the major economic power that many believed it would. Elsewhere a resurgence of nationalism caused a disintegration of states. The Soviet Union broke up. Czechoslovakia split into two, and Yugoslavia was dismembered. The United States was now the only superpower and saw itself as the global policeman, as evidenced by the 1991 Gulf War. Yet, new threats increasingly made the world a far more uncertain place than it was during the Cold War.

NATO's Central Region defence plans

THE NATO CENTRAL REGION was West Germany, which was considered the most likely target of a Warsaw Pact attack. The NATO planners accepted from the outset that the Soviets and their allies would enjoy numerical superiority in both manpower and weapons and that the aim would be to reach the English Channel in 10–14 days. To achieve this they would launch a high-speed mechanized offensive based on the echelon system that they had developed during the Second World War. The first echelon would carry out the breakthrough and advance as far and fast as possible until it had suffered 40 percent casualties. Then the second echelon would pass through and continue the advance. Nuclear weapons might well be used to clear the way ahead. Initially NATO planned a withdrawal to the Rhine, where it would aim to stand and fight. When the Federal Republic of Germany came into being, it demanded that the whole of its territory right up to the Inner German Border be defended and the concept of Forward Defence was born. Tactical nuclear weapons in the form of rockets, shells and mines were developed. While it was accepted that the likely immediate response to a Warsaw Pact attack would be a massive nuclear strike, tactical nuclear weapons would be used against Warsaw Pact forces by luring them into Nuclear Killing Zones. When the Flexible Response doctrine was introduced, an increasing emphasis was placed on conventional warfare. In particular, the development of anti-armour guided missiles and their employment in helicopters, as well as on the ground, helped to strengthen NATO's conventional defence. More fluid tactics, including the use of blocking positions, combined with counterstrokes launched into the flanks of an attack, were developed. These culminated in the US AirLand Battle concept, which took advantage of the introduction of precision-guided weapons to strike at the Soviet second echelon before it could deploy. The irony is that the lengthy training carried out by NATO forces in Europe actually came to fruition in the deserts of Kuwait and Iraq in 1991, and then in offensive rather than defensive operations.

VIETNAM
1946–75

'**THE CONVENTIONAL ARMY LOSES** IF IT DOES NOT WIN, THE GUERRILLA WINS IF HE DOES NOT LOSE.'

Henry Kissinger 'The Vietnam Negotiations' *Foreign Affairs* January 1969

The long agony of Vietnam dominated southeast Asian affairs for almost 30 years. It comprised two distinct phases – the war of liberation from colonial rule, followed by a war of ideology as oriental communism battled with a Western-backed regime that often appeared to be remote to the ordinary Vietnamese. The conflict illustrates only too clearly that massive superiority in firepower does not necessarily win wars.

French Indo-China had been established during the last half of the 19th century and consisted of five provinces: Tonkin, Annam, Laos, Cambodia and Cochin-China. The Japanese occupied the region from mid-1941. When Japan surrendered in 1945, the French were in no position to send troops in to reclaim it, so it was the British, in the form of an Indian division from Burma, who arrived to disarm the Japanese troops there. There had been a resistance movement in the region during the Second World War led by Nguyen Ai Quoc, who had helped to establish the French Communist Party while working as a waiter in Paris in 1920. In 1941 he established the Viet Minh organization, which was dedicated to achieving independence for Tonkin, Annam and Cochin-China under the name of Vietnam. He himself adopted the name Ho Chi Minh ('the enlightened one') and declared independence before the British arrived. The British themselves lacked the resources to bring the entire region under control and instead concentrated on the area around Saigon, then capital of Cochin-China.

Viet Minh war against the French

French forces began to arrive in October 1945 and by the end of the year they had secured southern Indo-China. They attempted to negotiate with Ho Chi Minh, offering limited independence and proposing that Bao Dai, who had been king of Annam, be appointed head of state. The Viet Minh rejected this and so in November 1945 French troops landed at Haiphong and entered Hanoi. The Viet Minh withdrew to the hinterland and the French set up garrisons throughout the north, but made little attempt to hunt down the Viet Minh.

Mao Zedong's victory over the Nationalists in China in 1949 changed the apparent live and let live situation in Indo-China. The Viet Minh now had an ally on their northern border. In January 1950 Ho Chi Minh therefore declared his government to be the only legitimate one in Vietnam and this was recognized by the People's Republic of China, the USSR and the Eastern Bloc as a whole. The French countered this by installing Bao Dai as emperor of Vietnam and his regime received recognition from the West. The United States also began to supply arms to the French in line with its policy of containing communism. The Viet Minh now began to attack and overrun the French garrisons in the north. French morale plummeted and civilians began to leave the country. Leading French

OPPOSITE *US Marines landing from Sikorsky S-58 transport helicopters for yet another search and destroy operation. The force has been guided in by smoke from a phosphorous landing marker, visible in the background.*

soldier Marshal Jean Marie de Lattre de Tassigny was then sent to Indo-China as high commissioner and commander-in-chief. He instituted a new strategy, constructing the de Lattre Line to protect Hanoi and the Red River delta and then using the remainder of his forces, including paratroops, to locate and engage the Viet Minh. This began to reap results, with the Viet Minh suffering a series of defeats. De Lattre now decided to deploy troops to the border with China in an effort to cut the Viet Minh supply lines, but in November 1951 he fell ill and had to return to France, where he died two months later.

Redeployment to the border tied down considerably more French troops than hitherto because of the need to secure the supply lines to these garrisons. More troops were therefore needed, but the war was becoming unpopular in France, especially on account of its cost, and the government refused to commit conscripts to it. As a consequence of this, the French forces became stretched, especially after the Viet Minh invaded Laos in spring 1953. Thanks largely to the Americans, the French did have superior firepower and believed that if they could tempt the Viet Minh to attack in strength they could inflict a decisive defeat on them. The French selected the village of Dien Bien Phu, which lay in northern Tonkin close to the border with Laos, as the bait. This threatened the Viet Minh supply lines into Laos and the inhospitable surrounding terrain would make it difficult for them to deploy heavy artillery.

French paratroops dropped on Dien Bien Phu in November 1953 and fortified it. The Viet Minh duly rose to the bait, but their ingenuity and determination enabled them to deploy artillery, including anti-aircraft guns, which made air resupply, on which the French were dependent, difficult. Subjected to frequent attacks, and impeded by the arrival of the monsoon season, which caused severe flooding of the trenches, the French were eventually forced to surrender in May 1954. Accepting that the war was for them unwinnable, they immediately opened negotiations with Ho Chi Minh. Agreement was reached in Geneva that July. The French would withdraw entirely from Indo-China, Cambodian and Laotian independence were recognized and Vietnam was divided. North of the 17th parallel was Ho Chi Minh's Democratic Republic of Vietnam while the Western-leaning Republic of Vietnam lay to the south. Emperor Bao Dai, who had been a mere figurehead, stepped down and went into exile.

One further stipulation of the Geneva Accords was that the two Vietnams should hold elections in July 1956 with a view to reunifying the country, but the South refused to take part, stating that those in North Vietnam would be rigged. It was encouraged in this by the fact that the Americans, continuing their containment policy, were providing South Vietnam with weaponry and military advisers to help build up its armed forces. Hanoi, however, was still determined that the whole of Vietnam should come under its rule. Viet Minh members who had remained underground in South Vietnam were ordered to prepare themselves for military action. Now known as the National Front for the Liberation of Vietnam, or 'Viet Cong', they began guerrilla activity in the rural areas of South Vietnam in 1957. To combat this the Saigon government introduced repressive measures, which made it unpopular. The Americans increased the number of their advisers and began to deploy support units, initially two helicopter companies, further to encourage the armed forces. In 1963 the South Vietnamese government was overthrown and a military junta took its place.

While the junta declared that it would act positively to defeat the Viet Cong, the truth was that by mid-1964 the latter controlled most of the rural areas, even levying their own taxes. The South Vietnamese armed forces were demoralized and largely reduced to static guards. This caused deep concern in Washington. Then, on 2 August 1964, a critical development took place. A US destroyer engaged in intelligence-gathering duties in the Gulf of Tonkin was fired on by North Vietnamese patrol boats. Fire was returned and some of these boats sank. Two nights later the destroyer was supposedly fired on again. The American response was to bomb North Vietnamese naval and oil installations. While President Lyndon Johnson told the American people that it was not his intention to widen the conflict, US involvement in Vietnam was now set to increase rapidly.

US involvement escalates

The Viet Cong now began to attack US installations in Vietnam. They also increased the tempo of their operations against the South Vietnamese and at one point, at the beginning of 1965, succeeded in temporarily cutting the country into two. Washington decided that the only option was an air offensive. On 8 February Operation Rolling Thunder was put into effect. Attacks on selected North Vietnamese targets were designed to weaken Hanoi's support for the Viet Cong and bring it to the conference table. It backfired almost immediately. Soviet premier Alexei Kosygin visited Hanoi on the second day of the bombing and Soviet surface-to-air missiles were soon being deployed. China, too, declared that it would also provide material support. In March US Marines landed in Vietnam, initially to protect US air bases. The poor performance of the South Vietnamese forces meant a change of policy, though. General William Westmoreland,

timeline

1945
Ho Chi Minh declares Vietnam independent; anti-colonial war ensues with France.

1954
French defeated at Dien Bien Phu; Vietnam divided.

1957
Viet Cong guerrilla activity begins in South.

1964
Gulf of Tonkin Incident provides premise for US escalation.

1965
Bombing of North Vietnam intensifies.

1967
Nguyen Van Thieu assumes power in Saigon; 500,000 US troops in South.

1968
Tet Offensive; My Lai massacre; Paris peace talks begin as worldwide opposition to war peaks; Nixon elected.

1969
Ho Chi Minh dies.

1970
Bombing of Cambodia disrupts Ho Chi Minh Trail.

1973
US withdraws troops following ceasefire.

1975
Saigon surrenders to North Vietnamese army.

commanding the US Military Assistance Command in Vietnam, told President Johnson that US troops must be allowed to take part in offensive operations with the Vietnamese and that he needed considerable reinforcements. The president authorized both in mid-1965. In the meantime, the bombing of North Vietnam continued and air attacks were also made on suspected Viet Cong bases in the south and the main supply line from North Vietnam, which ran through the Laotian and Cambodian jungles and was popularly known as the Ho Chi Minh Trail.

In early 1966 Ho Chi Minh and his military commander, Vo Nguyen Giap, hatched a new plan. They viewed Saigon as the key objective and intended to lure the bulk of the South Vietnamese and US forces to the central highlands in the north, then isolate South Vietnam's capital and assault it. They estimated that it would take two years to achieve and also accepted that the North Vietnamese army would have to be used to ensure the success of the plan.

During 1966 the US military strength in Vietnam rose to nearly 270,000 men. South Korea and Australia sent contingents, as did New Zealand and Thailand the following year. Since there had been no formal US declaration of war against North Vietnam, it was not considered apt to deploy the National Guard or reservists, apart from a few specialists, and the burden fell on young conscripts who served a one-year term in Vietnam. Since middle-class youths were often able to defer the draft on the grounds of embarking on further education, the brunt was borne by America's underprivileged. This, together with the bombing of Vietnam, generated a growing anti-war movement. True, the bombing of North Vietnam was halted for a time at the end of 1965, but Hanoi showed no interest in talks to resolve the situation and so it was resumed. Improved North Vietnamese air

Airmobile operations

THE HELICOPTER HAD BEEN USED to a very limited extent during the Second World War and in Korea. The French employed them on a wider scale in Algeria during the late 1950s, but it was in Vietnam that helicopters really came into their own. The helicopter's three main roles were and still are reconnaissance, the transportation of troops and equipment, and as a weapons platform. The Americans in Vietnam soon recognized the helicopter's ability to increase the flexibility of ground forces and developed the airmobile concept, which had been pioneered by the French. Search and destroy operations designed to locate and rid a particular area of Viet Cong and North Vietnamese army elements employed helicopters extensively. Once an area had been selected for such an operation, light observation helicopters would locate a suitable landing ground. The force would then be flown in using utility and heavy lift helicopters, while armed helicopters and the HueyCobra attack helicopter provided suppressive fire. A temporary fire base might well be set up, in which case artillery would also be flown in. When the force deployed, it would be supported by fixed and rotary wing aircraft. Command helicopters would often be used to control operations, while others evacuated casualties. Once the operation had been completed the force would be extricated, again by helicopter. Such airmobile operations continue to be employed today, especially in Iraq and Afghanistan.

defences meant the loss of an increasing number of US aircraft though, and the crews who fell into North Vietnamese hands provided useful propaganda.

US tactics on the ground during 1966–7 largely involved the establishment of fire bases from which frequent search and destroy missions were mounted. As troop levels rose – by the end of 1967 the US strength was nearly half a million – so these operations increased in scale. The principal means of transport became the helicopter (see Box) because of its ability to deploy troops quickly and provide an element of surprise. Success was measured in terms of 'body counts' and there is no doubt that both the Viet Cong and the increasing number of North Vietnamese army elements deployed via the Ho Chi Minh Trail suffered heavy casualties. On the other hand, the South Vietnamese government had undergone frequent changes as a result of internal coups and some stability was only established when General Nguyen Van Thieu came to power in 1967. He was more popular than his predecessors, especially because he was prepared to talk to Hanoi, and would remain in office for the next seven years. But the peasantry who made up the majority of South Vietnamese were largely indifferent. All they could do was to bow to the demands of whichever side was dominant in their local area at the time. The situation was not helped by the fact that the average US soldier knew little about the country in which he was fighting and tended to regard every Vietnamese as potentially hostile.

Tet Offensive

At the beginning of 1968 General Giap put the final phase of his plan into effect. On 21 January the North Vietnamese and the Viet Cong launched a major attack on the US air and fire base at Khe Sanh, 20 miles from the border with North Vietnam and also close to the Cambodian border. The garrison of 5000 US marines soon found themselves under siege. Fearing a repeat of the French disaster at Dien Bien Phu, General Westmoreland deployed relief forces, but they were unable to lift the siege. But Khe Sanh was merely a diversion. On 30 January, in the midst of Tet – the Vietnamese New Year on which ceasefires had been observed in previous years – the communists mounted simultaneous assaults on no fewer than five major cities and 100 district and provincial capitals in South Vietnam. The attackers themselves had infiltrated the rural areas during the previous few months. While most of the attacks were quickly repulsed, the fighting in both the northern city of Hue and Saigon itself was fierce and protracted. Not until the end of February did it end. By then considerable physical damage had been done to the two cities, especially Hue. The communists, however, had taken some 50,000 casualties and the American high command declared it a major victory.

Back in America the reaction was very different, however. The country had become used to following the war nightly on their television sets and generally believed that it was being won. The Tet Offensive therefore came as a rude awakening, especially television coverage of fighting in the grounds of the US embassy in Saigon. There was a feeling that the authorities had not been telling the whole truth. There was also an awareness that US deaths in Vietnam were rising – 10,000 in 1967 and 14,500 during 1968. The result was that the anti-war movement increased in strength, and not just in the USA. Furthermore, Khe Sanh was still under siege and would remain so until mid-April, when the communists withdrew in the face of a relief force of 30,000 Americans and South Vietnamese.

US public opinion turns against the war

President Johnson began to appreciate that the war could not be won. It now became a question of how the United States could withdraw with dignity. Consequently, he halted the bombing of the North and invited the North Vietnamese to talks. At the same time he declared that he would not stand for re-election. Heartened by the growing anti-war movement, Ho Chi Minh agreed and talks began in Paris in May 1968. These, however, were merely exploratory and the fighting went on. Just before the US presidential election that November, Lyndon Johnson declared a cessation of all warlike activity against North Vietnam to keep Hanoi at the negotiating table. When Richard Nixon, the new White House incumbent, came into office, he did so on a platform of peace with honour. He aimed to hand the war over to the South Vietnamese in a process called Vietnamization, while maintaining military pressure on North Vietnam. Nixon's election did prompt formal peace talks to begin in Paris, but the North Vietnamese were also keen to keep up the military pressure to give themselves a stronger bargaining position. As a result the fighting remained intense throughout 1969.

On 3 September 1969 Ho Chi Minh died, bequeathing a message to his people to fight on until Vietnam had been reunited. The following March, Prince Sihanouk, Cambodia's leftwing ruler, was deposed by a pro-Western general who gave permission for US forces to cross into his country to disrupt the Ho Chi Minh Trail. Although they withdrew after two months, fears that President Nixon was widening the war further fuelled the anti-war movement. Vietnamization was proceeding, however, and it was South Vietnamese forces that spearheaded further incursions into Laos and Cambodia in early 1971. They also took over control of South Vietnam's most northerly province. In March 1972 the North Vietnamese took advantage of this to attack across the border, capturing the provincial capital of Quang Tri. Nixon's response was a renewed bombing of North Vietnam and the mining of ports. At the end of June the South Vietnamese launched a counter-offensive supported by US air power and eventually succeeded in recapturing Quang Tri. By this time all American involvement in ground operations had ceased.

Meanwhile the Paris negotiations had continued, but little progress had been made. US Secretary of State Henry Kissinger now had secret discussions with the North Vietnamese envoy and announced at the end of October 1972 that a breakthrough was imminent. President Nixon therefore halted the bombing campaign, but the negotiations stalled once more, so it was resumed. Hanoi then stated that it was willing to continue

ABOVE *Saigon, 30 April 1975. A North Vietnamese T-55 tank, with the national flag flying from its radio aerial, enters the presidential palace grounds.*

talking and the bombing was halted once again. On 23 January 1973 a ceasefire was finally announced. The United States agreed to withdraw its remaining forces in return for the repatriation of US prisoners of war held by North Vietnam. Ceasefires followed in Laos and eventually in Cambodia.

Fall of Saigon

Talks between Saigon and Hanoi continued on the future of Vietnam itself, but soon became deadlocked and were broken off in April 1974. In South Vietnam, however, disillusion with the government was growing and US aid had been drastically reduced. Taking advantage of this the North Vietnamese launched a sudden invasion in March 1975. They swept aside all before them and entered Saigon on 30 April. For American television viewers the final scenes of US involvement were chaotic scenes of panic-stricken refugees attempting to escape via helicopter from the grounds of the US embassy.

Ho Chi Minh's dream of a communist-ruled Vietnam had finally been achieved. The experience, however, scarred a generation of Americans. US foreign policy became much more cautious and it would be a decade before American confidence returned. The Vietnam War also resulted in the end of US conscription and was a proving ground for the precision-guided weapons that characterize conventional warfare today. Finally, the media now had the means to influence policy as never before.

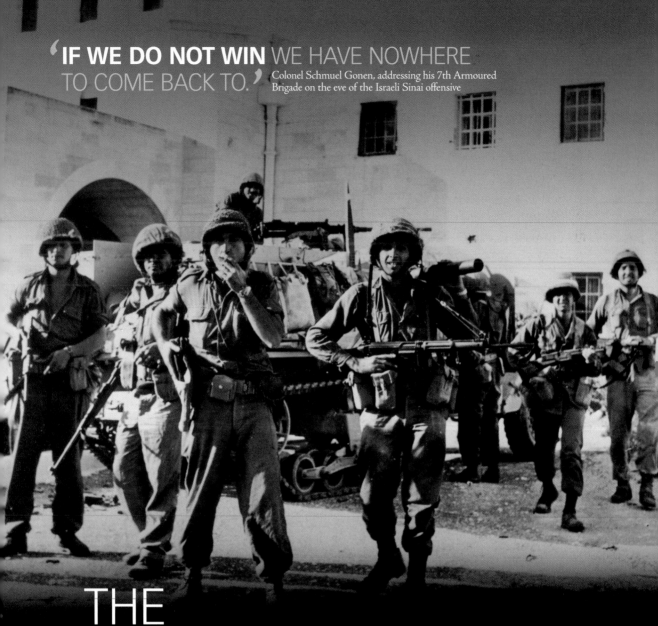

'**IF WE DO NOT WIN** WE HAVE NOWHERE TO COME BACK TO.' Colonel Schmuel Gonen, addressing his 7th Armoured Brigade on the eve of the Israeli Sinai offensive

THE
SIX-DAY
WAR
1967

In the years since 1945, the Middle East has remained one of the world's hot spots. The main cause of this has been the friction between Israel and its Arab neighbours. Indeed, the state of Israel itself was established amid bloodshed and the conflict continues to this day.

Palestine was the traditional home of the Jewish people, but they had lost their hold over it in the first few centuries AD. A yearning to return to the homeland developed during the late 19th century with the creation of the Zionist movement. During the First World War, in which Palestine was wrested from the Turks, the British declared that they would view the creation of a Jewish homeland with favour. At the end of the war they were given the mandate of Palestine and allowed an increasing number of Jewish immigrants to settle there. Their policy was one of the Jews co-existing with the indigenous Arabs, but the Zionist movement wanted an independent Jewish state. Arab resentment at the Jewish influx grew and erupted in revolt in 1936, with only the onset of the Second World War bringing it to an end.

Creation of the modern Israeli state

While many of the Palestinian Jews served in the British forces during 1939–45, the more extreme elements formed two armed groups prepared to use force against the British to realize their dream of an independent Israel, and these began to attack British targets. Once the war with Germany was at an end, their attacks intensified. The British retaliated by imposing severe restrictions on Jewish immigration, at a time when many victims of Nazism were desperate to go to Palestine to mend their broken lives. The result was illegal immigration, which the British did their best to stop, earning few friends internationally. With the violence unabated, between Arab and Jew as well as against the occupying power, the British turned to the United Nations in early 1947. The eventual UN solution was the creation of independent Arab and Jewish states in Palestine, with Jerusalem to be placed under UN administration. This pleased no one, apart from the Jews, and violence between them and the Arabs increased. The British mandate was to end in mid-May 1948, and they agreed to withdraw from Palestine by August 1948.

No sooner had the mandate ended than the Jews proclaimed the state of Israel. The Arab League sent 30,000 troops into the part of Palestine allocated to the Arabs and attacked Israel. The UN stepped in and arranged a truce, while the British completed their withdrawal by the end of June. The truce was then broken, but another longer one was arranged. This enabled the Israelis to gain arms from abroad and when the fighting broke out again in October 1948 the Israelis launched counter-offensives on all fronts, gaining all the territory allocated to the Palestinian Arabs. Armistices with Egypt,

OPPOSITE *Troops of the Israeli Jerusalem Brigade outside Government House, Jerusalem, which had been the UN headquarters and was captured from the Jordanians on the first day of the war.*

Jordan, Syria and Lebanon were signed during the early months of 1949, with Jerusalem being divided between Israel and Jordan. The UN was to supervise these agreements. The Arab countries refused, however, to recognize the state of Israel and there was also a major refugee problem. Of the nearly 900,000 Palestinian Arabs, some 80 percent chose not to remain in Israel, settling in either the Gaza Strip or in the Nablus–Hebron district of Jordan west of the river Jordan, an area that became known as the West Bank.

The Arab world against Israel

The next few years witnessed frequent raids across Israel's borders, mainly from the Gaza Strip by Palestinian refugees. In Egypt a military junta seized power in 1952. This turned increasingly towards the Soviet Union and its satellites, culminating in 1955 with a deal to purchase arms from Czechoslovakia. The Egyptians under Gamal Abdel Nasser also formed a military command with Syria, with Jordan joining later. Although being supplied with arms by the USA and France, Israel felt increasingly hemmed in. Then, in July 1956, Nasser nationalized the Suez Canal, which was owned by an Anglo-French company. The British and French resolved to take the Canal back by force. The French colluded with Israel, which at the end of October 1956 launched a surprise attack on Sinai and quickly overran it. British and French forces then landed at Port Said, the northern end of the Canal. This brought international condemnation and, with the USA declining to support the action, the British and French were forced to bow to United Nations pressure. The Anglo-French forces were replaced by UN troops, Israel withdrew from Sinai, and UN troops deployed to the Gaza Strip and Sharm el Sheikh at the southern tip of the peninsula.

The UN presence in Sinai did reduce the cross-border violence across the Israeli–Egyptian border, but not elsewhere. This became more formalized when, at an Arab summit conference in Cairo in 1964, it was agreed to establish the Palestine Liberation Organization (PLO) and give it active support. The Arab nations also resolved to divert the river Jordan, which supplied two thirds of Israel's water. They began to undertake work on this and the Israelis attempted to disrupt it with artillery fire and air strikes, especially across the Syrian border. The PLO was convinced from the outset that the only way it could regain its homeland was through another war and believed that the best way of provoking Israel into initiating another conflict was through terrorist action. When Egypt and Syria signed a fresh alliance in November 1966, the noose appeared to be tightening once more around Israel's neck.

Preparations for war

The border clashes between Israel and Syria intensified and in May 1967 the Soviet Union stepped in. The Soviets informed Nasser that the Israelis were preparing to attack Syria. This was not true, but it was enough to make the Egyptian leader act to help his ally. Thanks to Warsaw Pact help he had been able completely to re-equip his forces after the 1956 war and now planned to deploy 100,000 men and 1000 tanks to Sinai. He realized,

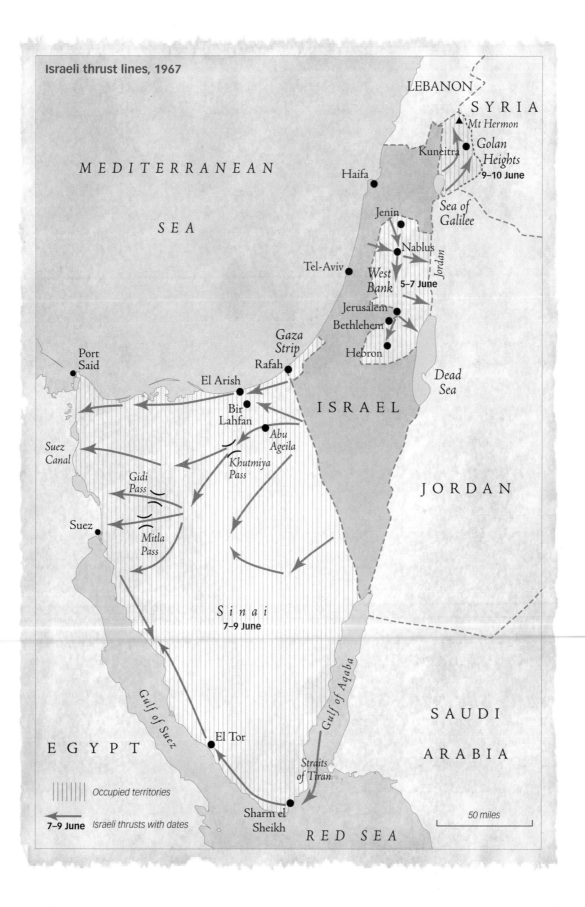

Israeli thrust lines, 1967

LEBANON

SYRIA

Mt Hermon

Kuneitra

Golan
Heights
9–10 June

Haifa

Sea of
Galilee

MEDITERRANEAN

SEA

Jenin

Nablus

Tel-Aviv

West
Bank

5–7 June

Jordan

Jerusalem

Bethlehem

Hebron

Dead
Sea

Gaza
Strip

Rafah

ISRAEL

Port
Said

El Arish

Bir
Lahfan

*Abu
Ageila*

JORDAN

Suez
Canal

*Khutmiya
Pass*

Gidi
Pass

Mitla
Pass

Suez

S i n a i
7–9 June

EGYPT

Gulf of Suez

El Tor

Gulf of Aqaba

SAUDI

ARABIA

*Straits
of Tiran*

50 miles

Sharm el
Sheikh

RED SEA

||||| Occupied territories

7–9 June Israeli thrusts with dates

though, that he could not take military action while UN troops were still present. So, on 16 May, Nasser demanded their withdrawal. UN Secretary-General U Thant asked the Israelis whether they would be prepared to have the UN troops on their side of the Egyptian border. They refused. Jordan and Iraq had just joined the Arab alliance and the Egyptian Sinai deployment made war seem ever more likely. The situation further escalated on 22 May when Nasser closed the Straits of Tiran at the mouth of the Gulf of Aqaba. Military contributions from other Arab states arrived in Egypt and Nasser publicly declared that he aimed to destroy Israel. The Israelis turned to the West for material support in getting the Straits of Tiran reopened, but it was not prepared to risk war with the Soviet Union. This left the Israelis with just one option.

The Israeli government was convinced that if it sat on its hands the Arab forces facing it would merely increase their numerical superiority. Consequently, the only course of action was to mount a pre-emptive attack. For this to be successful it was essential that air supremacy be gained at the outset and this could best be done by catching the Arab aircraft on the ground. The Israeli Air Force was not strong enough to attack the Egyptian, Syrian and Jordanian airfields simultaneously. They therefore decided to attack the Egyptians first and leave the others for later in the day. To achieve surprise the Israeli aircraft would fly out over the sea and approach from the north. The time of attack was to be 7.45 a.m., since the Egyptian senior officers would generally be travelling to work at that time. It was also known that the Egyptians flew dawn patrols, but that these would have landed by the time the attack took place.

Six days in June

On 5 June the Israeli Air Force struck. Flying low to evade the Egyptian radar, the Israeli aircraft attacked ten Egyptian airfields, taking the defences completely by surprise. Indeed, the Egyptians initially believed that it was the Americans who were attacking. Flying in waves, they machine-gunned the aircraft on the ground and used special bombs to crater the runways. By 10.30 a.m. the Israeli aircraft were back on the ground, being rearmed and refuelled. At midday the Syrians and Jordanians made retaliatory attacks on an Israeli airfield and oil refineries. The Israeli aircraft then took to the air again and struck the airfields of these two countries, together with one in Iraq. They then returned to the Egyptian airfields. By the end of the day they had achieved air superiority, destroying 240 Egyptian aircraft alone. Just 20 Israeli aircraft were shot down, mainly by ground fire.

The Israeli ground plan was initially to remain on the defensive in the north and east while they attacked into Sinai. Here the Egyptian defences appeared at first sight formidable. Based on the Soviet model, they consisted of well-prepared infantry strong-points, which also included dug-in tanks. These positions were mutually supporting and behind them lay two armoured divisions. Faced with this the Israelis accepted that they would have to mount a break-in operation. They chose to do this in two places. One would be in the Rafah area of the Gaza Strip and the other would be directed towards Abu Ageila. The Rafah attack was mounted by Colonel Shmuel Gonen's 7th Armoured Brigade. To assist him, a parachute brigade, supported by a tank battalion, was to swing round well to the south of Rafah, turn north, advance through sand dunes that the Egyptians believed to be impassable, and assault the artillery supporting the Rafah defences. Gonen had a tough time breaking through, but the paratroops' attack on the gun lines unlocked the door and he was soon advancing on El Arish, reaching it during the night.

The other break-in was to be carried out by General Ariel Sharon's armoured division. The defences were even stronger in this area and there was no possibility of any form of outflanking move. Sharon therefore delayed his attack until nightfall on 5 June and employed a paratroop battalion mounted in helicopters to attack the Egyptian gun line as well as a concentrated artillery bombardment. It was a confused and complicated battle, but by 6 a.m. the following morning Sharon had broken through. It would take a further 24 hours of mopping up, but the road to Abu Ageila was now open.

On the other fronts, the Syrian reaction was muted. They restricted themselves to artillery fire and a couple of half-hearted small probes, which were easily beaten back. On the Jordanian front the situation was more complicated. Israel had expected the Jordanians to stay out of the conflict and indeed that was the wish of King Hussein. However, on the morning of 5 June, Nasser had telephoned the king and told him that his forces had destroyed numerous Israeli aircraft and that he was sending tanks to link up with the Jordanians. Hussein therefore gave orders to attack. His artillery opened fire on targets inside Israel and his troops began to attack south of Jerusalem in order to link up with the Egyptian armour that was supposed to be advancing towards Jordan. The Israeli reaction was to counter-attack. They began to assault into the Old City in Jerusalem, while in the north the orders were to capture Nablus and Jenin and advance to the river Jordan.

On the second day of the war in Sinai, a new Israeli thrust developed. This was launched between those towards El Arish and Abu Ageila and was designed to prevent the Egyptians moving reinforcements laterally across their front. Moving through sand dunes that were generally considered to be impassable, this force covered 35 miles in some nine hours and reached Bir Lahfan, 15 miles south of El Arish, and then successfully engaged Egyptian armoured and mechanized brigades. The main task now was to secure the Khutmiya, Gidi and Mitla passes, which barred the routes leading from Sinai to the Suez Canal. The Egyptian forces in Sinai would then be cut off. The Israelis achieved this by the evening of the third day, 7 June. It was then a question of destroying the retreating Egyptian columns as they tried to force their way through the passes. During this day three Israeli motor torpedo boats captured Sharm el Sheikh and paratroops were dropped at El Tor further up the Gulf of Suez.

On the Jordan front, the Israelis had encircled Jerusalem, but on 6 June they met stubborn opposition while attempting to gain control of the Old City. Jenin was also

captured after a hard fight. Next day the Israelis succeeded in clearing most of the West
Bank. They secured the Old City, from which the Jordanian garrison had withdrawn,
and Bethlehem and Hebron. In the north, the Jordanians mounted a number of counter-
attacks, but could not prevent the Israelis from capturing Nablus just before darkness fell.

The UN had been attempting since the first day of the war to impose a ceasefire, but
without success. On the evening of 7 June they finally had a breakthrough, when both
Israel and Jordan agreed to stop fighting. Neither Egypt nor Syria, although the latter had
so far done little, was yet prepared to do the same. The battle in Sinai therefore continued.
The pressure on the Israeli forces holding the passes became intense as the Egyptians tried
desperately to force a way through. It was at its greatest in the Mitla Pass. The brigade
holding it had to be relieved because of exhaustion and being out of ammunition and the
Israeli Air Force had to mount continuous bomb, rocket and napalm attacks. At midday on
8 June the Israelis also began to close in on the Suez Canal. The Egyptians fought fiercely,
and mounted a number of skilful ambushes, but they could not prevent the inevitable and
by the early hours of 9 June the Israelis had reached the Canal. With the whole of Sinai
now in its hands Israel agreed to a UN ceasefire, with Egypt following suit the next day.

This left just Syria. A UN ceasefire was imposed on this front on 8 June, but artillery
exchanges that night broke it. The Israelis therefore decided to attack. The front itself was
dominated by the Golan Heights, which extended the entire 45 miles of the Israeli–Syrian
border and enabled the Syrians to bring down fire on the settlements in northernmost
Israel. Israeli defence minister General Moshe Dayan had been hesitant over attacking for
fear that the Soviets might become involved, but pressure from the northern settlements
made him order an offensive on 9 June. The attack in the extreme north was a bitter fight
against a complex of Syrian strongpoints. Barbed wire was everywhere. The only way to take
out the Syrian positions was from the rear, which made the battle even more complicated.
Casualties were heavy on both sides, but by evening the Israelis had managed to establish
themselves on top of the heights. Another assault was made along the road running from
the border east to Kuneitra. Using forces released from the Jordan front, the Israelis also
assaulted just south of the Sea of Galilee. On 10 June the northern and centre thrusts
combined to advance to Kuneitra itself, while the southern force cleared the remainder of
the Golan Heights. By mid-morning the Syrians had finally crumbled and the Israelis
entered Kuneitra without a fight. Elsewhere a small heliborne force established itself on the
lower peak of Mt Hermon, the most dominant feature of the northern Golan. The Syrians
had had enough and accepted a UN ceasefire, which took effect on the evening of 10 June.

Legacy of occupation

In the space of just six days the Israelis had defeated three Arab nations and seized territory
equivalent to at least twice the size of their own country. Most significant of all was that
they had now acquired some naturally defensive borders – the Suez Canal in the south, the

river Jordan in the east and the Golan Heights in the north. But there were also 1.5 million Palestinian Arabs in the Gaza Strip and West Bank. The international reaction to this was encapsulated in UN Resolution 242 of November 1967. It stated that no country should seize and occupy territory through force of arms and that all states in the Middle East were to recognize each other's independence and sovereignty. As for the Palestinians, many had now sought refuge in Jordan and Lebanon, and Resolution 242 called for a 'just settlement' of the refugee problem. Israel refused to surrender the occupied territory and this caused the PLO to widen the scope of its operations. These took the shape of what became known as international terrorism, with aircraft hijackings and attacks on Israeli targets abroad. In 1973 Egypt and Syria tried to regain Sinai and the Golan Heights by force, in what became known as the Yom Kippur War. The Camp David Agreement of 1978, which was brokered by the United States, did see Israel and Egypt make peace, with Israel completing a withdrawal from Sinai, apart from the Gaza Strip, by May 1982. Yet Israel has remained intransigent over handing back the Golan Heights and the West Bank. True, the Gaza Strip and the West Bank have been granted Palestinian self-rule, but the security measures imposed by Israel and encroachments by Jewish settlers have done little to reduce discontent. This in turn has encouraged the formation of groups more radical than the PLO that embrace Islamic fundamentalism and continue to refuse to recognize Israel's right to exist. The violence therefore continues and the hopes of a lasting solution to the Palestinian problem remain distant, while the fundamentalists also believe that Western support for Israel, especially from the USA, represents a vehement hostility to Islam.

The Palestinian Liberation Organization post-1967

AFTER THE SIX-DAY WAR, the PLO became very much the Palestinian government-in-exile. It set up its headquarters in Jordan under the leadership of Yasser Arafat. From there it conducted its campaign of terror against Israel and its interests abroad, but not for long. King Hussein began to fear that the PLO was aiming to remove him. In 1970, after the PLO had hijacked four airliners and destroyed three of them on Jordanian soil, Hussein sent in his army to disarm the organization. There was a fight and the PLO moved to Lebanon. Yet, although branded a terrorist organization, in 1974 the UN General Assembly recognized it as representing the Palestinian people and gave it observer status at the UN. The Arab states also insisted that it be present at any peace talks. Its attacks across the Lebanese border reached such a pitch that in June 1982 the Israelis invaded. When a ceasefire was finally negotiated that August, the PLO had to leave its heavy weapons behind and was dispersed among other Arab countries, the leadership settling in Tunis. The PLO has long comprised different factions: Arafat's Fatah, the Syrian-backed Popular Front for the Liberation of Palestine (PFLP), and other groups opposed to Arafat. Even so, he launched a successful *intifada* (uprising) in the Gaza Strip in 1987, and it was this that eventually led to Palestinian self-rule. The following year he renounced terrorism and the USA then formally recognized the PLO. Self-rule initially meant that Fatah was in charge, but a new radical grouping, Hamas, began to make its presence felt and continued to carry out terrorist attacks. Eventually, in 2006, after Israel had removed its settlements in the Gaza Strip, Hamas overthrew Fatah and it withdrew to the West Bank.

'**AL-QAEDA IS TO TERROR** WHAT THE MAFIA IS TO CRIME.' President George W. Bush, 20 September 2001

THE
WAR
ON
TERROR
2001–?

The events of 11 September 2001, commonly known as '9/11', shocked the world. Three out of the four hijacked airliners struck their targets and the iconic twin towers of the New York World Trade Center were totally destroyed, with some 3000 people losing their lives. It was a truly audacious plan and the work of a highly sophisticated terrorist organization. Yet, although the attacks appeared at the time to be a bolt from the blue, the warning signs had been in place for some time.

The literal translation of *al-Qaeda*, the name of the network behind the attacks, is 'the base'. Its origins lie in the war waged by the *mujaheddin* ('strugglers') against the Soviet occupation forces and their local Afghan Marxist allies during the 1980s, a conflict that they proclaimed as a *jihad* or 'holy war'. A number of foreign Islamists joined the mujaheddin in their fight. Among them was Osama bin Laden, who came from a wealthy Saudi family. Using his own family's money as well as contributions from the Saudi government and other rich Arabs, he established an organization that recruited and processed the foreign fighters. He later formed his own band of warriors and it was this that became known as al-Qaeda. Bin Laden returned to his homeland in 1990, shortly before the Iraqi invasion of Kuwait. When this happened he offered his own fighters as a contribution to the defence of Saudi Arabia, but this was turned down. The fact that the Saudi government turned to the Americans instead rankled, not only because it meant that the forces of the 'unbelievers' would be based on Saudi soil, but also because bin Laden believed that it was the Americans who were propping up the hated state of Israel.

Origins of the Taleban and al-Qaeda

Osama bin Laden turned against the Saudi establishment for allowing the Americans into the country and moved to Sudan in 1992. From there he began to expand his operations. He gave support to the fundamentalists in their bloody war against the Algerian government, which broke out after elections held at the end of 1991 indicated that the fundamentalists were likely to gain power. Bin Laden gave encouragement to terrorist opposition to President Hosni Muburak of Egypt. He provided help to the mujaheddin fighting in Bosnia and Chechnya. He also turned back to Afghanistan, where the Marxist government had managed to survive until 1992; three years after the Soviets had left the country. It then dissolved into civil war and anarchy as various warlords fought with former mujaheddin for power. Eventually a fundamentalist movement surfaced in the south of the country. Calling themselves the *Taleban* (religious students), many had indeed been educated in madrassas (religious schools) in Pakistan, and were filled with religious zeal. Their discipline was in stark contrast to some of the

OPPOSITE *New York, 11 September 2001. United Airlines Flight 175 about to crash into the South Tower of the World Trade Center, some 17 minutes after the North Tower was struck by American Airlines Flight 11.*

militias, and many Afghans supported them in a desire to rid the country of anarchy. By 1996 they had secured the whole country, apart from a small region in the far north, and established the Islamic Emirate of Afghanistan. It was ruled under the strictest *sharia* law and in bin Laden's eyes it was a model of what an Islamist state should be, so he established his base there, as well as terrorist training camps.

Al-Qaeda operatives were also active elsewhere. In late December 1992 they detonated bombs at two hotels in Aden, Yemen, in the mistaken belief that American soldiers en route to Somalia were staying there. The following year one Ramzi Yousef attempted to blow up the World Trade Center in New York. Six people were killed, but its twin towers stood firm on that occasion. Yousef was, however, probably unconnected to al-Qaeda, although he did receive training in Afghanistan. Then, on 13 November 1995, a van blew up near a Saudi National Guard base in Riyadh, the Saudi capital, where a US training cadre was operating. The Saudi authorities arrested four men, who stated that Osama bin Laden had inspired them through his speeches. It was not, however, until the following year that he issued a formal declaration of war against the USA and its allies for their occupation of Islamic lands. This was followed in June 1996 by the detonation of a fuel tanker bomb beside a complex housing US Air Force personnel at Khobar in Saudi Arabia in which 19 US airmen and one Saudi were killed.

However, it was not until 1998 that the United States really began to take notice of Osama bin Laden and al-Qaeda. On 7 August car bombs were simultaneously detonated outside the US embassies in Dar es Salaam, Tanzania, and Nairobi, Kenya. Almost all of the more than 200 fatalities were local Kenyans and Tanzanians, but both embassies were badly damaged. This time the Americans struck back. President Bill Clinton ordered cruise missile strikes on suspected al-Qaeda bases in Afghanistan and Sudan. Unfortunately, the latter target proved to be a pharmaceutical plant with no connection to any terrorist activity. Then, in October 2000, two al-Qaeda operatives carried out a suicide attack using a speedboat packed with explosives against the guided missile destroyer USS *Cole* off the Yemeni coast. The ship suffered damage and 17 sailors lost their lives. Bin Laden, however, already had preparations in train for a far more spectacular attack.

During the months leading up to 9/11 a number of Arabs, mainly Saudis, had attempted to enter the United States. Some had been refused entry, but others had got through, among them some individuals who then attended a flight-training school. It was later noted that some had appeared to show little interest in take off and landing techniques and were merely concerned with learning how to handle an airliner in flight. Other intelligence was also available and it is possible that the tragedy could have been averted if this had been pooled and properly collated. Unfortunately America's two main intelligence-gathering agencies, the CIA and FBI, were not communicating with one another, and both had had their budgets severely cut during the previous decade. As it was, in the immediate aftermath of the attacks there was a global tide of sympathy for the United States. Most significant was that the member states of NATO invoked Article 5 of the North Atlantic Charter, which stated that an attack on one member was an attack against the alliance as a whole. This encouraged President George W. Bush to issue an ultimatum to the Taleban regime on 20 September 2001. He demanded that the Taleban surrender Osama bin Laden or face the consequences. The Taleban dismissed Bush's demand and preparations for an invasion of Afghanistan were duly set in train. The USA quickly organized co-operation with the Northern Alliance, the anti-Taleban forces in the far north of the country. President Pervez Musharraf of Pakistan also agreed to assist, even

ABOVE *Osama bin Laden's face stares out from a placard carried during an anti-Western rally. The Pepsi advertisement shows that many Islamic countries are able to accept a degree of foreign culture.*

though the leaders of his Inter-Services Intelligence (ISI) agency, which had traditionally supported the Taleban, were opposed. In return the USA lifted sanctions imposed after Pakistan's 1998 nuclear test and restructured loans that it had made to the country.

Operation Enduring Freedom

Operation Enduring Freedom was launched against the Taleban on 7 October 2001, with aerial bombing and cruise missile attacks, the latter from ships stationed in the Indian Ocean. In terms of the ground assault the key was seen to be the Northern Alliance. US and British special forces groups were inserted within its fighters, while CIA operatives strove to generate opposition to the Taleban in the south and east of the country. Then, with massive US air support, the Northern Alliance began its advance south. The Taleban was forced to abandon Kabul and by the end of November they had been ousted from 27 of the country's 30 provinces. It was noticeable though that the main resistance came from foreign Arab fighters. Kandahar fell on 7 December, after some protracted negotiations for its surrender, and the focus then switched to the White Mountains in the southeast, where some 1200 foreign fighters were holed up in the Tora Bora and Khost areas. The mainly-US forces tackled these, capturing over 500, but many managed to escape south into the Pakistani tribal areas. Osama bin Laden and Mullah Omar, the Taleban leader, were probably among them. This was almost the end, but not quite. In March 2002 there was a further battle in the northeast of the country against some 1500 Taleban and al-Qaeda fighters. By now further NATO forces were beginning to deploy and the priority was reconstruction of the country.

Fighters captured in Afghanistan were flown to a special prison camp constructed at Guantanamo Bay, the US military base on Cuba. They would later be joined by suspected terrorists from many parts of the world, some secretly transported by air under 'extraordinary rendition'. With the Americans apparently making little effort to charge the Guantanamo Bay inmates formally and bring them to trial, there was increasing international unease that the USA was abandoning the principles of democratic justice.

Enduring Freedom was applied to other countries troubled by fundamentalist terrorism. In January 2002 US Special Forces were deployed to the Philippines to give advice and support to the authorities in their battle with two fundamentalist groups – *Abu Sayyef*, a separatist group operating in the southern islands, and *Jemaah Islamiyah*, whose tentacles spread throughout southeast Asia. The following month the USA agreed to send military advisers to the former Soviet republic of Georgia, where the Pankisi Gorge region in the north of the country had fallen into mujaheddin hands. Also, in October 2002, elements of the US Fifth Fleet and Allied warships began to carry out anti-terrorist operations off the Horn of Africa. As if to emphasize that it was now a global war being fought by fundamentalist terrorism, *Jemaah Islamiyah* suicide bombers attacked two popular nightspots on the Indonesian island of Bali on 12 October 2002. The death toll was 202, many of them tourists, including a large number of Australians.

Iraq and Weapons of Mass Destruction

If the world was once again shocked by this further loss of innocent lives, the US government had another problem on its hands. The 1991 Gulf War had been fought to liberate Kuwait from Saddam Hussein's grasp. It had UN approval, but this did not extend to toppling the Iraqi leader and there were many, especially in the USA, who felt that the Coalition forces should have advanced into Iraq and finished the job. Apart from Saddam Hussein's dismal human rights record, there were also growing fears that he was resurrecting his chemical and biological weapons programme, which had been closed

Cyber intelligence

ONE OF THE MOST NOTEWORTHY ASPECTS of the War on Terror is the use of cyberspace by the terrorist. This has provided intelligence agencies with fresh challenges. In pre-digital days communications between terrorist cells were usually by means of written messages delivered through the conventional mail, or by courier or oral messages passed in face-to-face meetings or over the telephone. These could be intercepted, usually through surveillance operations or by tapping in the case of old analogue telephone systems, which required dedicated lines between two telephones. Digital communications, on the other hand, enable large numbers of data streams to occupy the same telecommunication link. This means that while it is relatively easy to intercept electronic mail, its volume is so huge that it requires considerable skill to identify suspect items amid the vast quantities of innocent traffic that are generated daily around the world. Encryption of data is also very much faster. One critical weakness that computer communications do have, however, is the fact that it is very difficult to wipe a hard drive clean of all data.

down as a result of the Gulf War, and that he might pass some of these on to terrorists. UN inspection teams were sent into the country, but found no evidence of Weapons of Mass Destruction (WMD). But President Bush also had other reasons for invading Iraq. Deposing Saddam would remove a threat to the Middle East and, he hoped, provide the basis for increased liberalism and democracy in the region. This, in turn, would defuse the conflict between Israel and the Palestinians, and thus remove one of al-Qaeda's main pretexts for its war against the West. Many nations, however, did not agree. Led by France and Germany, and backed by Russia and most of the Arab states, they argued that, given the massive US military superiority, this might set a dangerous precedent for future pre-emptive military action and that invasion was bound to inflame Arab sensitivities. Even so, UN Security Council Resolution 1441, which demanded that Iraq destroy and cease manufacture of WMDs, was approved unanimously.

President Bush believed that this gave him authority to take military action, even though evidence of Iraq's WMDs had still not been found. Britain, Australia and others supported him, but the opposition to it remained, even in those countries that were backing him. Accordingly, on 20 March 2003, after issuing an ultimatum to Saddam demanding that he step down from power, the United States, with its allies, launched a massive aerial attack on Iraq. Turkey refused to allow US forces to invade Iraq from the north and so the ground attack came from the south only. Even so, the advance was rapid and by the end of April it was all over. Little thought, however, had been given to what should happen next. As it was, the Iraqi armed forces were immediately disbanded and the apparatus of the state dismantled. This left a total vacuum and anarchy in the form of widespread looting was the initial result, but very soon more sinister forces came into play. The Sunnis and Shias formed militias, the latter backed by Iran. Al-Qaeda, too, was quick to take advantage of the situation. It began to send in foreign fighters. Very quickly the violence became widespread and the Coalition occupation forces were too thin on the ground to control it. Apart from an increasing number of vehicle bombs and suicide attacks, there were numerous attacks on the country's infrastructure, notably the oil pipeline running to the main port of Basra. Reconstruction efforts were severely hampered by both this and the worsening security situation. The UN had sent a special representative to assist with reconstruction, but in August 2003 he was killed by a truck bomb exploding outside his office in Baghdad and the UN staff were withdrawn. As for al-Qaeda, it soon became apparent that its main intention was not only to attack the occupation forces, but also to cause civil war between Sunni and Shi'ite so as to make the country entirely ungovernable.

Prospects for Afghanistan and Iraq

Those who had warned against invading Iraq on the grounds that it would encourage further terrorism were proved right. Muslims throughout the world were angered by it. Fundamentalist mullahs preached damnation of the West and encouraged young men to go to Pakistan where they could obtain terrorist training in the virtually lawless tribal territories of the north. Al-Qaeda cells were established in many countries and soon made themselves felt. On the morning of 11 March 2004 bombs exploded on four commuter trains in the Spanish capital Madrid, killing 191 people and injuring more than 1000. The government initially blamed Basque separatists and paid for this mistake when it was roundly defeated in the general election that followed shortly afterwards. One of the first actions by the new Socialist government was to withdraw its troops from Iraq. Fundamentalists also began a bombing campaign in Saudi Arabia. On 7 July 2005, the day after the city won the competition to host the 2012 Olympics, four suicide bombers attacked the London transport system, killing 52 people. Four more bombers attempted another attack two weeks later, but their bombs failed to detonate and all were apprehended. There were numerous other attacks elsewhere in the world and many plots for further atrocities were identified before they could be put into effect.

In 2004 Hamid Karzai became president of Afghanistan and established a government, but found it difficult to exert control over the whole of the country. A resurgent Taleban began to make its presence felt in the south of the country, which led to some fierce fighting with NATO troops, who were now responsible for helping the Afghan authorities with security. This has served to slow reconstruction down drastically. There is also the problem of the poppy fields, the source of much of the world's heroin. To destroy them would remove the growers' livelihoods and throw them into the arms of the Taleban, but as yet alternative sources of income barely exist.

Iraq, too, has an established government, but again reconstruction is taking place far too slowly. The security situation has improved to an extent, in that at least the rate of violent deaths has decreased. There are two reasons for this. First, many Iraqis have come to resent the al-Qaeda-inspired foreign fighter. Second, in spring 2007, the Americans sent in significant extra numbers of troops in what was called 'the surge'. This has enabled robust action to be taken in areas which the security forces were previously hesitant to enter. Much, though, still needs to be done to create a stable country.

Prospects for the War on Terror

The War on Terror is unique in world history for a number of reasons. Never have terrorists of the same beliefs operated across so much of the world simultaneously. The now widespread threat of the suicide bomber is a phenomenon that is completely new to many security agencies. For America, in particular, 9/11 caused a sea change on how it views its own security in the face of external threats. Finally, there are many non-Islamic countries that have indigenous Muslim minorities and there is no doubt that the War on Terror has introduced tensions within these nations that did not previously exist. As for how the conflict will end, no one knows for certain. What many are agreed upon is that the War on Terror is likely to continue for some considerable time, in terms of both homeland security and the provision of military assistance to other states engaged in the fight.

INDEX

*Page numbers in italics denote
illustrations or maps*